Cognitive Development and Individual Variability

Cognitive Development and Individual Variability

Special Issue Editors

Anik De Ribaupierre
Thierry Lecerf

MDPI • Basel • Beijing • Wuhan • Barcelona • Belgrade

MDPI

Special Issue Editors
Anik De Ribaupierre   Thierry Lecerf
University of Geneva   University of Geneva
Switzerland   Switzerland

Editorial Office
MDPI
St. Alban-Anlage 66
4052 Basel, Switzerland

This is a reprint of articles from the Special Issue published online in the open access journal *Journal of Intelligence* (ISSN 2079-3200) in 2018 (available at: https://www.mdpi.com/journal/jintelligence/special_issues/cognitive_development)

For citation purposes, cite each article independently as indicated on the article page online and as indicated below:

LastName, A.A.; LastName, B.B.; LastName, C.C. Article Title. *Journal Name* **Year**, *Article Number*, Page Range.

ISBN 978-3-03921-052-7 (Pbk)
ISBN 978-3-03921-053-4 (PDF)

Contents

About the Special Issue Editors

Anik De Ribaupierre, (Professor), Honorary Professor in Developmental and Differential Psychology at the University of Geneva, Anik de Ribaupierre conducted her undergraduate and graduate studies in Geneva, and obtained her PhD from the University of Toronto. She then spent most of her academic career in Geneva. Trained initially as a Piagetian, she joined the neo-Piagetian movement initiated by Pascual-Leone. The majority of de Ribaupierre's numerous studies focus on cognitive development and individual variability, first in children, and then later across the lifespan from childhood to old age. In the last twenty years, her lifespan studies have focused on topics such as working memory, inhibition, and executive functions. Her most recent work consists of a large multivariate study on children, young adults, and older adults on within-task intraindividual variability ("inconsistency") in a number of working memory and processing speed tasks; this cross-sectional study was extended into a longitudinal study on older adults, some of the results of which are described in the present book.

Thierry Lecerf, (Dr.), Senior Lecturer in Clinical Differential Psychology at the University of Geneva, Thierry Lecerf conducted his undergraduate and graduate studies at Grenoble (France), and obtained his PhD from the University of Geneva. He has focused on cognitive psychology (working memory), cognitive development, and individual variability (inter- and intraindividual) for some years. Lecerf's most recent work concerns the Wechsler intelligence scales for adults and children, which has mainly focused on the factorial structure of these scales in cross-sectional and longitudinal studies.

Journal of
Intelligence

MDPI

Editorial

On the Importance of Intraindividual Variability in Cognitive Development

Anik de Ribaupierre * and Thierry Lecerf

Faculty of Psychology and Education Sciences, University of Geneva, 40 Boulevard du Pont d'Arve,
CH-1205 Geneva, Switzerland; Thierry.Lecerf@unige.ch
* Correspondence: Anik.DeRibaupierre@unige.ch

Received: 16 March 2018; Accepted: 19 March 2018; Published: 22 March 2018

Developmental cognitive psychology (as well as cognitive psychology in general) has a long-standing tradition to ignore all variations other than age, as if individual variations were only measurement error or noise. Even though Cattell [1,2] has drawn attention long ago to the necessity for psychology to consider at least three sources of variation in data collection: variables or situations, individuals, and occasions (the "Data Box"), the emphasis has essentially been placed on the influence of variables to the detriment of the individuals. In a very different perspective, Piaget focused on the "epistemic subject", that is the theoretical core (rather than a mean subject, based on statistics) without any interest for individual differences [3]. A generalist focus was legitimate because of his epistemological interest for the development of knowledge rather than for the development of children [4,5]. This epistemological stance has not been retained by most theories suggested in developmental psychology in the last fifty years. Yet the focus has remained on general (usually statistical means), universal trends. Although between-individuals differences (interindividual variability) are often acknowledged, they have usually been relinquished to applied psychology if not considered as mere noise or measurement error. Moreover, little interest has been granted to within-individual variations (intraindividual variability) until recently. Psychology might actually be the last discipline to believe, at least implicitly, in some sort of universals as concerns the individuals. This is not the place to develop the role of diversity in other sciences, but let us just evoke physics with concepts such as complexity, dynamical systems or chaos, and catastrophe theory (for application to developmental psychology, see [6,7]), or biology with its interest for the variability of the living species (e.g., [8]).

The proposition to grant fundamental importance to individual variations in developmental and lifespan psychology is not new (see Wohlwill [9] for a precursor). Nesselroade [10] has warned against the danger of ignoring intraindividual variability (see also [11,12]). Molenaar [13–15] has very elegantly demonstrated, relying on simulations of factor analyses, that the ergodicity hypothesis does not hold for psychology. Phrased simply and applied to psychology, the hypothesis of ergodicity implies that the individual is similar to the group. However, Molenaar's work shows that observations relative to interindividual differences (factor analyses) cannot be applied to an individual to draw the same conclusion about intraindividual variability. Note that this equivalence is an assumption implicitly held by most studies in psychology when the mean performance or the developmental trend of a group is considered to apply to all individuals composing that group. Recently, a renewed interest has emerged for variability, particularly in lifespan developmental psychology, and there are a number of empirical studies integrating individual variability (see examples below; see also [16]). Yet, the bulk of studies remains cross-sectional and centered on group means and univariate data (that is, data collected task-by-task). The present special issue aims at providing a broad picture (although of course not exhaustive) of how individual, in particular intraindividual, variability is presently addressed both theoretically and empirically, by gathering a number of authors who have contributed for quite some time to this increased interest in variability.

Several types of variability should be distinguished. Interindividual variability (also labeled diversity, see [17]) concerns differences between persons in a given group in at least one task; it should not be confused with age differences even though a number of experimental psychologists tend to classify age differences within interindividual differences [18]. Diversity is the type of individual variability that is most frequently acknowledged, although a focus on individuals remains rare; it generally suffices to report that individual differences are large or/and significant. Intraindividual variability (designated as IIV in the remainder of this text) concerns variations that occur within individuals, such as short-term fluctuations (labeled inconsistency) either within-task trial-to-trial variability, or in frequent repetitions of the same task within a relatively short period of time (measurement bursts), or across tasks (dispersion or heterogeneity), or across longer time periods (intraindividual change).

All papers in the present issue address one or/and the other type of intraindividual variability, while (a) presenting empirical data to demonstrate its importance; and (b) showing how IIV brings specific information relative to a centration on a central tendency. Together, the papers cover the entire lifespan, by presenting data on children (at least from school age upwards) and young and older adults. Most papers concern healthy individuals, and one also concerns non-healthy older adults.

In the first paper, Jacques Lautrey proposes a multiprocess framework; it opens the possibility to uncover and analyze the existence of different developmental pathways susceptible to account for phenomena that are usually considered as controversial results. He takes the example of the development of numerical cognition in young children as analyzed in a large number of empirical studies from the scientific literature in the field. Jacques Lautrey's model is based on four fundamental concepts: (1) reconstruction by which primitive cognitive functions are transformed; (2) plurality, that is, the suggestion that many processes are simultaneously available to fulfill the same function, but not necessarily by using the same information; (3) interaction, notably between several of these processes; and (4) substitution, borrowed from Reuchlin's [19] suggestion that various processes can function vicariously, that is, they would be available (unless damaged) in all individuals but might differ in their probability of activation depending on the individual and/or the situation.

The proposition that several processes co-exist within individuals as proposed by Lautrey is not new. However, the assumption of the simultaneous activation of several processes in a given task, and more importantly of their mutual interrelationships, is the signature of a multidimensional model, the term dimension being here understood as in factorial analyses. It can be contrasted with a unidimensional model, such as Piaget's theory, but also of many other, more specific developmental theories, in which development in one task is considered to be subtended by a single process, identical for all individuals. The consequence of a unidimensional perspective is that children are all construed to develop along an identical path, and only differ by the speed of their development. In contrast, several developmental paths for different children may be envisaged within a multidimensional framework. Although most contemporary theories do no longer look for general mechanisms and hypothesize the existence of multiple, often very specific processes, it is still the case that they rarely address the question of whether development relies on different processes for different individuals. Moreover, the interrelationships between several processes are rarely considered. Interaction and substitution are conceived in Lautrey's model as sources of within-individual variability and are therefore susceptible to account for interindividual differences in IIV. Also, all these processes and their interactions are inscribed within a dynamic systems perspective. Lautrey's thorough analyses of studies dealing with the quantification of sets of discrete objects help in overcoming some contradictory findings in the abundant literature on that topic. Moreover, he also argues that another famous and controversial distinction in cognitive psychology, namely propositional or symbolic processing, on the one hand, and analogical processing, on the other hand, can yield both intra- and interindividual differences. A given task is not necessarily propositionally (or analogically) processed once and for all. Processing could be propositional for some children and analogical for others; it could also be analogical at one moment of development and propositional at another (see also [20–22]). Lautrey's paper constitutes a very good introductory chapter to this special issue, because he defines concepts that can be applied to most empirical papers to follow, even though their respective authors do not necessarily or explicitly refer to the same processes as Lautrey.

In the second paper, Galeano-Weber, Dirk, and Schmiedek address IIV in (school age) children. They report part of an intensive microlongitudinal study included within a larger project; precision in a spatial working-memory task, with different memory loads, was assessed three times a day over a period of four weeks. Adopting such a complete and complex design allows for a number of novel theoretical and methodological contributions. First, the authors introduce a sophisticated procedure to study IIV in accuracy. Usually, inconsistency is measured in terms of Response Times (RTs) because RTs allow for computing an individual standard deviation across trials. Studies in which inconsistency in accuracy has been examined are rather rare because accuracy is often scored in binary terms (success/failure), which does not allow for devising a quantitative index of IIV. In contrast, in Galeano-Weber and collaborators' paper, accuracy is assessed in terms of spatial recall precision (i.e., the distance between the participant's reported and the true target location). Second, the authors refine the construct of IIV by distinguishing several temporal levels: (a) IIV across items (i.e., single responses within trials for the different elements to be stored in working memory); (b) IIV across trials, a trial consisting of two or three items, depending on the memory load; (c) IIV across occasions (three administrations by day); and (d) across days. Third, the authors used mixed models, which makes it possible to compare IIV at these different levels. As could be expected, considerable IIV was observed at all temporal scales. Yet, and very interestingly, only item-to-item variability correlated with a change in memory load. Moreover, this type of IIV was related to age (older children showing somewhat less variability), fluid intelligence, and school achievement. Such findings demonstrate the interest to further decompose IIV while also showing that using only an average performance is not sufficient (although of course simpler) to understand performance at the level of an individual.

Third, Perret and Dauvier also examine IIV in school age children by using response times in the Raven's Progressive Matrices task; RTs are used here as a sort of proxy for strategies. It is indeed often not easy to study strategies, particularly with children, even though numerous studies have insisted on the importance (and necessity) of strategies in this well-known task. It has been shown in several studies (including the Perret and Dauvier one) that global RTs across the task (mean RT for instance) does not relate to performance, probably because it is too global. The authors' hypothesis was that modulation of times as a function of item difficulty (i.e., responding more slowly in a difficult item) would be more appropriate. They devised an intraindividual index of modulation by computing individual correlations between an RT for an item and that item difficulty; hence, a high positive correlation for a given child reflects more time spent on a difficult item. Results indicated that the modulation index correlated not only with age but also with performance. RT modulation also functioned as a mediator for the relation between age and performance. Pushing further the analysis by using a generalized additive model, the authors found that the relation between RT and item difficulty was linear only for children presenting an efficient performance; RTs in less-efficient children increased between easy and intermediate items, but did not increase for the most difficult items, perhaps reflecting some kind of discouragement. Results were similar when a Rasch model was used to estimate the child's ability instead of raw performance. The authors conclude that the modulation of study time is a key strategic factor for understanding developmental and individual differences. We wonder whether modulation is a strategy as such or whether it simply indicates that children use a more complex strategy. In any case, this study demonstrates very nicely (a) the need to go beyond a global index of time, such as the mean; and (b) that the profile of different children (efficient and less-efficient) differs qualitatively.

In the fourth paper, Hofman, Jansen, de Mooij, Stevenson, and van der Maas also present a study conducted with school age children. This study is truly striking by the size and length of the project within which it is inscribed. Inspired by an idiographic approach requiring a study at the level of the individual [14], the authors have developed several educational projects in which a novel method for monitoring and measuring computer adaptive testing (CAT) is used. These projects involved thousands of children in schools (or at home) on a daily or weekly basis. The authors have adopted a subtle measuring system making it possible to compromise between the number and difficulty of items in principle required by adaptive testing, on the one hand, and the discouragement that the task generated on the basis of these principles could generate in children, on the other hand. Interestingly, the scoring rule adopted is based on an adaptation of the Elo system used for the ranking of chess players, and combines speed and accuracy. The data presented in this paper come from a subset of addition and multiplication data obtained on children playing on a daily basis for 15 weeks, and the analysis focuses on intraindividual analyses (other analyses on interindividual differences have been presented in other papers). Results show a large variability across items despite their similarity in content. In a first set of analyses (learning analytics), the authors present the interest to (a) distinguish whether the child learns the item (switches between incorrect and correct responses); (b) describe the learning pattern; and (c) analyze the stability (and variability) of responses across time. We refrain here from reporting the number of players studied and the number of their responses! They are truly overwhelming. To summarize in a simplistic manner, the results indicate that irregularities in learning (e.g., switches to correct responses combined with frequent relapse to lower ability) were the rule rather than a smooth, improving learning pattern. In a second set of analyses, the authors address the question of the unidimensionality versus the multidimensionality of items, and show that additive items are not incompatible with a hypothesis of unidimensionality (all items addressing the same construct). In contrast, for multiplicative items, two types of items should be distinguished, which do not correlate with each other. Remember that all problems are relatively simple items played over 3 months on which basis one could think that they would be relatively similar. In sum, this paper demonstrates the usefulness of adopting an approach centered on the individual. Given its degree of methodological sophistication and the size of the data collected, it might lead to some feeling of helplessness in the reader (including us): Who can adopt such an approach in developmental studies? Probably few research groups, thus collaboration between different research groups might offer an alternative solution.

In the fifth paper, Joly-Burra, van der Linden, and Ghisletta deal with older adults. Their approach is novel in three aspects, in addition to stressing the importance of intraindividual variability. First, they assess prospective memory and inhibition within the same task, a Go/No Go task in two versions, focusing on intraindividual variability. Inhibition was indexed by the number of commission errors in the Go/No go task (incorrectly pressing the target key in a NoGo trial); prospective memory was measured by the number of omission errors. Second, they distinguish two types of IIV in RTs: amplitude of fluctuations measured by an intraindividual standard deviation (as is usually done in assessment of IIV), and time dependency based on time-series (asking whether RT at a given time is influenced by previous RTs). The latter type of IIV can be considered as assessing temporal dynamic effects. Third, they use a dynamic structural equations modeling to measure the joint effects of these two types of IIV (amplitude-based and time-dependent) together with the mean level. Results show that both higher latencies (mean RTs) and amplitude-based IIV were associated with inhibition failures, whereas time-dependent IIV predicted inhibition only at the beginning of the task. Then, inhibition was associated with prospective memory. There was, however, no association between either type of IIV and prospective memory performance. Of interest is the fact that the two types of IIV differed from one another in their correlational patterns; the authors suggest that the amplitude of fluctuations might be detrimental whereas time-dependent IIV could reflect the use of exploratory strategies to attain a better level; this second type of IIV would thus be functional.

The sixth article, by Halliday, Stawski, Cerino, DeCarlo, Grewal, and MacDonald, also presents data collected in older adults, and contains a clinical facet. They examine intraindividual variability across tasks rather than across trials; that is, they examine dispersion across a number of cognitive measures, comparing three groups: healthy older adults, an amnestic MCI group, and a small sample of carefully screened Alzheimer patients. A further objective was to relate dispersion with lifestyle activities (physical, social, and cognitive). The focus on dispersion is interesting, as this type of IIV has been much less investigated in older adults than inconsistency. Results showed that dispersion was already relatively large in healthy controls as other studies have also shown [23]. Yet, dispersion was significantly larger in Alzheimer patients than in both healthy controls and MCI patients. Using discriminant analyses, the authors also observed that dispersion was a significant predictor in examining the risk of being classified as Alzheimer (but not the risk of MCI) relative to healthy controls. A more engaged lifestyle was associated with a reduced likelihood of being classified as Alzheimer or MCI. When studying the joint effect of dispersion and of lifestyle, the authors noted that dispersion remained predictive of Alzheimer, whereas lifestyle remained predictive of MCI. As the authors note, an analysis in which the lifestyle activities would be further decomposed would be interesting. Furthermore, it would be crucial to assess whether inconsistency and dispersion correlate or are independent from one another; such a comparison does not seem possible here: Most tasks (currently used in neuropsychological assessments) provide only global scores and most probably do not contain enough trials to compute trial-by-trial variability. The larger project within which the present study was included might hopefully contain a few tasks in which inconsistency can be computed and then compared with dispersion.

The seventh paper, by Fagot, Mella, Borella, Ghisletta, Lecerf, and de Ribaupierre, reports abundant data documenting age differences in inconsistency (across trials IIV) over the lifespan (primary school age children to older adults) in several tasks. It is important to note that the tasks were identical for all participants, making it possible to compare age trends. A further objective was to contrast inconsistency measures in latencies in processing speed tasks, on the one hand, and in accuracies in working memory (WM) tasks, on the other hand. There are indeed some controversial results in the literature: A number of authors did not observe age differences in inconsistency in accuracy scores. Computing inconsistency in relatively complex tasks in which accuracy scores are used is often not possible because accuracy is usually scored in binary terms (success/failure), as also noted in the Galeano Weber et al.'s paper. An intraindividual standard deviation cannot then be computed unless using response times again, or simply percentage of success across blocks of trials; the latter solution is in turn not informative in an adaptive task because it only indicates whether the task is adapted to the participant's level of performance. In the present study, WM tasks were adaptive; this made it possible to administer a large enough number of trials of the same complexity to compute a standard deviation on the number of correct responses across trials whether the response was fully correct or not. Beyond the existence of a large IIV in all tasks (this should not come as a surprise by now for the reader), clear differences between age groups were observed. For all RT tasks, children were the most variable, then the older adults, and the least variable were young adults. There were a few further age differences, depending on the task: younger children (9–10 year-olds) were more inconsistent than older ones (11–12 year-olds), and young-old adults (between 60 and 70 years of age) showed less inconsistency on some tasks than older-old adults (over 70 years of age). In contrast, in the WM tasks, the differences between age groups were not significant in most comparisons; moreover, the descriptive statistics showed a tendency for the young adults to be more inconsistent. This difference between the two types of tasks could of course be linked to the type of scores: A high value in an RT task is associated with being slower (poorer performance), whereas a high value in the WM tasks is associated with a better performance. As a result, higher IIV might directly reflect the mean level. Yet, intraindividual standard deviations were all computed on values residualized for the participant's mean; therefore, they should be relatively independent from the performance level. There seems to be a more profound difference between the two types of tasks, leading the authors to suggest that inconsistency might be dysfunctional in the RT tasks as is often argued, but functional or adaptive in the WM tasks because it would index changes in strategies.

Finally, the paper by Mella, Fagot, Renaud, Kliegel, and de Ribaupierre is issued from the same project as the previous one, but reports on a longitudinal facet that was conducted on the older adults only over a period of approximately 7–8 years. It centers on the individual patterns of change observed in the first and the last (fourth) wave of assessment. The objective of the authors was to focus on the individual using an idiographic approach. Some longitudinal studies mention the existence of (significant) interindividual differences in trajectories, but almost no study defines change at the level of the individual. The reason why there are so few studies focusing on intraindividual change is probably because the reliability of such change is not assured. For instance, in an RT task, it is of course insufficient to observe a 20-millisecond difference (or any other higher value) in the mean response over several years for considering that there is a significant change. A frequent solution consists in relying on a standard error of measurement (SEM); yet SEM is defined at the group level and not at the individual level. As a result, a single individual might be considered to have changed when included in a given sample, but not if he was included in another group. The authors propose two novel methods to assess change within individuals, both made possible because a relatively large number of trials was used in all tasks: estimate a bootstrap-based confidence interval and individual analyses of variance. The former method was used to determine for each pair of assessments—the paper reports on waves 1 and 4—whether the individual significantly declined, improved, or remained stable. The latter method made it possible to assess the degree of heterogeneity of change across the tasks. Only the RT tasks of the project could be used, because the WM tasks did not contain enough identical trials (10 by condition and complexity level) to obtain estimates in the bootstrap-based approach. Results showed, task-by-task, that all three patterns of change (stability, increase, decrease) were obtained in almost all individuals. This demonstrates clearly that any longitudinal group curve does not reflect the participants that compose it and illustrates Molenaar's claim that a hypothesis of ergodicity cannot be adopted in developmental psychology. Trajectories differed widely among individuals. Decline was more frequent when considering all the tasks and over 8 years but still far from being the rule. For instance, there were only 3 individuals out of 92 who showed decline in the nine conditions analyzed. Moreover, the analyses of variance demonstrated a large heterogeneity of change, meaning that for a given individual, change may differ (quantitatively or qualitatively) considerably from task to task. The data offer an empirical demonstration of the necessity to focus on the individual, and a strong support for Nesselroade's [10,24] repeated claim that intraindividual variability should be examined seriously, and for Molenaar's manifesto on the necessity for psychology to adopt an idiographic approach [14,25].

In sum, the present special issue offers a wide array of approaches to the study of intraindividual variability. Not only does it present trial-to-trial fluctuations (inconsistency), the type of IIV most commonly reported in the literature (although certainly not yet sufficiently represented), across-tasks variability (dispersion), and across-years variability (longitudinal, intraindividual change), but it also offers novel openings to IIV, such as time-dependency (Joly-Burra et al.'s paper) and variability at different time scales (Galeano-Weber et al.'s paper). Together, the papers demonstrate that variability is observed at all age periods of the life span. We consider that the present papers represent very well this domain of research in full expansion—or so do we hope—and want to thank all our colleagues to have played the game.

All the researchers working on IIV have one day or another encountered some doubt or even opposition as to the novelty or usefulness of such an approach. The field of developmental psychology still consists in its majority of cross-sectional studies, using often a single task with a few small groups, and of statistical analyses centered on group analyses. Anecdotic but very illustrative, we read recently the following statement in a review: *"The findings make a compelling case that intraindividual variability exists but not such a strong case that it matters. Said another way, measuring such variability often increases the testing burden on participants and researchers alike, sometimes substantially. What deep theoretical insights are likely to justify the extra effort? Many readers may conclude something like, 'Yeah, interesting, but not worth the time, effort, and cost".* We hope that, together, all the papers presented in this special issue will convince our readers not only to consider IIV as an existing reality and to contribute to its study, but also that it matters theoretically. They show that IIV contributes other information relative to the mean, sometimes complementary, sometimes very different. Perhaps, the sophisticated statistical models and/or the abundance of data in certain studies may induce some discouragement in the reader: *"my group and I will just not be able to conduct such research"*. If a better understanding of the meaning of such variability does indeed require large data sets and new methods, the field is still in need of more data to offer some counterpart to the decades of research spent in restricting research on means and (small) groups. Also, it is time that groups of labs be formed and collectively contribute to this novel way of collecting data.

Conflicts of Interest: The authors declare no conflict of interest.

References

1. Cattell, R.B. The three basic factor-analytic research designs—Their interrelations and derivatives. *Psychol. Bull.* **1952**, *49*, 499–520. [CrossRef] [PubMed]
2. Cattell, R.B. The data Box. Its ordering of total resources in terms of possible relational systems. In *Handbook of Multivariate Experimental Psychology*; Nesselroade, J.R., Cattell, R.B., Eds.; Plenum Press: New York, NY, USA, 1988; pp. 69–130.
3. Piaget, J. The theory of stages in cognitive development. In *Measurement and Piaget*; Green, D.R., Ford, M.P., Flamer, G.B., Eds.; McGraw Hill: New York, NY, USA, 1971; pp. 1–11.
4. De Ribaupierre, A. Why Should Cognitive Developmental Psychology Remember that Individuals Are Different? *Res. Hum. Dev.* **2015**, *12*, 237–245. [CrossRef]
5. De Ribaupierre, A. Piaget's Theory of Cognitive Development. In *International Encyclopedia of the Social & Behavioral Sciences*, 2nd ed.; Wright, J.D., Ed.; in Chief; Elsevier: Oxford, UK, 2015; Volume 18, pp. 120–124.
6. Van der Maas, H.L.J.; Molenaar, P.C.M. A catastrophe theoretical approach to stagewise cognitive development. *Psychol. Rev.* **1992**, *99*, 395–417. [CrossRef] [PubMed]
7. Van Geert, P. *Dynamic Systems of Development*; Harvester: New York, NY, USA, 1994.
8. Atlan, H. *La Fin Du "Tout Génétique"? Vers De Nouveaux Paradigmes En Biologie*; INRA Editions: Paris, France, 1999.
9. Wohlwill, J. *The Study of Behavioral Development*; Academic Press: New York, NY, USA, 1973.
10. Nesselroade, J.R. The warp and woof of the developmental fabric. In *Views of Development, the Environment, and Aesthetics: The Legacy of Joachim F. Wohlwill*; Downs, R.M., Liben, L.S., Palermo, D.S., Eds.; Lawrence Erlbaum: Hillsdale, MI, USA, 1991; pp. 213–240.
11. Nesselroade, J.R.; Molenaar, P.C.M. Emphasizing intraindividual variability in the study of development over the lifespan. Concepts and issues. In *The Handbook of Lifespan Development*; Lerner, R.M., Lamb, M.E., Freund, A.M., Eds.; John Wiley: Hoboken, NJ, USA, 2010; pp. 30–54.
12. Nesselroade, J.R.; Molenaar, P.C.M. Some Behavioral Science Measurement Concerns and Proposals. *Multivar. Behav. Res.* **2016**, *51*, 396–412. [CrossRef] [PubMed]
13. Molenaar, P.C.M. Variabilité interindividuelle et intra-individuelle dans le développement cognitif. In *Invariants Et Variabilités Dans Les Sciences Cognitives*; Lautrey, J., Mazoyer, B., Van Geert, P., Eds.; Editions de la Maison des sciences de l'homme: Paris, France, 2002; pp. 355–369.
14. Molenaar, P.C.M. A Manifesto on Psychology as Idiographic Science: Bringing the Person Back Into Scientific Psychology, This Time Forever. *Measurement* **2004**, *2*, 201–218. [CrossRef]
15. Molenaar, P.C.M. The future of analysis of intraindividual variation. In *Handbook of Intraindividual Variability Across the Lifespan*; Diehl, M., Hooker, K., Sliwinski, M.J., Eds.; Routledge: New York, NY, USA, 2015; pp. 343–356.
16. Diehl, M.; Hooker, K.; Sliwinski, M.J. *Handbook of Intraindividual Variability Across the Lifespan*; Routledge: New York, NY, USA, 2015; p. 371.
17. Hultsch, D.F.; MacDonald, S.W.S. Intraindividual variability in performance as a theoretical window into cognitive aging. In *New Frontiers in Cognitive Aging*; Dixon, R.A., Bäckman, L., Nilsson, L.G., Eds.; Oxford University Press: Oxford, UK, 2004; pp. 65–88.
18. Baddeley, A. *Working Memory*; Oxford University Press: Oxford, UK, 1986.
19. Reuchlin, M. Processus vicariants et différences individuelles. *J. Psychol.* **1978**, *2*, 133–145.
20. Lautrey, J.; De Ribaupierre, A.; Rieben, L. Operational development and individual differences. In *Learning and Instruction. European Research in an International Context*; De Corte, E., Lodewijks, H., Parmentier, R., Span, P., Eds.; Pergamon Press: Oxford, UK, 1987; pp. 19–30.

21. Rieben, L.; De Ribaupierre, A.; Lautrey, J. Structural invariants and individual modes of processing: On the necessity of a minimally structuralist approach of development for education. *Arch. Psychol.* **1990**, *58*, 29–53.
22. De Ribaupierre, A. Structural and individual differences: On the difficulty of dissociating developmental and differential processes. In *The New Structuralism in Cognitive Development: Theory and Research on Individual Pathways*; Case, R., Edelstein, W., Eds.; Karger: Basel, Switzerland, 1993; pp. 11–32.
23. Mella, N.; Fagot, D.; De Ribaupierre, A. Dispersion in cognitive functioning: Age differences over the lifespan. *J. Clin. Exp. Neuropsychol.* **2016**, *38*, 111–126. [CrossRef] [PubMed]
24. Nesselroade, J.R. Intraindividual Variability and Short-Term Change. *Gerontology* **2004**, *50*, 44–47. [CrossRef] [PubMed]
25. Molenaar, P.C.M. On the necessity to use person-specific data analysis approaches in psychology. *Eur. J. Dev. Psychol.* **2013**, *10*, 29–39. [CrossRef]

Journal of
Intelligence

MDPI

Article

Cognitive Development Is a Reconstruction Process that May Follow Different Pathways: The Case of Number

Jacques Lautrey

Institut de Psychologie, Paris Descartes University, 71 Avenue Edouard Vaillant,
92774 Boulogne-Billancourt, France; jacques.lautrey@wanadoo.fr

Received: 21 December 2017; Accepted: 26 February 2018; Published: 8 March 2018

Abstract: Some cognitive functions shared by humans and certain animals were acquired early in the course of phylogeny and, in humans, are operational in their primitive form shortly after birth. This is the case for the quantification of discrete objects. The further phylogenetic evolution of the human brain allows such functions to be reconstructed in a much more sophisticated way during child development. Certain functional characteristics of the brain (plasticity, multiple cognitive processes involved in the same response, interactions, and substitution relationships between those processes) provide degrees of freedom that open up the possibility of different pathways of reconstruction. The within- and between-individual variability of these developmental pathways offers an original window on the dynamics of development. Here, I will illustrate this theoretical approach to cognitive development—which can be called "reconstructivist" and "pluralistic"—using children's construction of number as an example.

Keywords: cognitive development; number; numerical cognition; individual differences; variability

---

1. Introduction

The objective of every science is to uncover the invariants that underlie the variability of observable phenomena occurring in its domain. Each science nevertheless makes epistemological choices that are specific to it. In doing so, it makes a distinction among the various forms of variability to which it is confronted, between those it deems relevant to its object of study and those it sees as bothersome. The latter, which it decides to ignore or control in one way or another, by averaging for example, are often the ones that cannot be interpreted in the framework of current theoretical paradigms [1].

The major theoretical paradigms that dominated developmental psychology in the past—Piagetian constructivism starting in the 1950s, and neo-nativism starting in the 1960s—did not lend themselves to explaining variability phenomena. In positing that deep cognitive structures are neither general nor constructed but domain-specific and innate, Chomsky's theory differs fundamentally from Piaget's, granted, but resembles it in its quest for universality. Both the constructivist approach and the nativist approach were aimed at uncovering the deep cognitive structures that characterize the human species and are invariant across eras, individuals, and cultures. In the end, it was the structuralist approach that led, in both cases, to the search for what is common to all individuals, and that considered between- and within-individual variabilities to be irrelevant to this object of study.

If more recent theories of cognitive development are more interested in variability, it is probably because they are inspired by theoretical paradigms in which fluctuations, within- and between-individual variabilities are not seen as bothersome background noise that can be ignored when extracting the general laws of cognitive development but, on the contrary, as an essential ingredient of evolution and change. This is the case of theories inspired by dynamic systems modeling [2–4], connectionist modeling [5,6], and theories that make use of the conceptual framework of Darwin's theory of evolution, to model developmental changes [7]. This is also the case of theories that seek to integrate the contributions of the factorial approach to intelligence, based on individual differences, and the developmental approach to cognition [8–10].

The pluralistic approach to the relationships between cognitive development and variabilities proposed in this article is part of this trend. It proposes a conceptual framework capable of integrating both the general and the variable into cognitive development.

2. Conceptual Framework

The main concepts underlying this approach are reconstruction, plurality, interaction, and substitution. Each of these concepts is explicated below and will be illustrated in a concrete way using the example of the development of numerical quantification in children.

2.1. The Notion of Reconstruction

Cognitive development is not seen as a product of innate structures, nor as a de novo construction process, but as a process by way of which primitive functions are reconstructed. The neo-nativist trend gave rise to studies on the cognitive abilities of infants and contributed to a complete renewal of knowledge in this field. Many studies using methods suited to the capacities of infants showed that certain behaviors regarded by Piaget as indicators of the acquisition of new structures had been observed much earlier in development. It was sometimes concluded that early infant abilities evidenced in this way are underlain by the same cognitive structures as those found in older children, and hence, that these structures are innate. My own hypothesis about the resemblance between infants' abilities and those of older children is that it does not originate in the fact that they have the same underlying cognitive structure, but in the fact that they perform the same function at both ages. The major cognitive functions that enable living beings to adapt to their environment—for example, categorizing, quantifying, orienting oneself in space, and communicating—were selected in the course of phylogenesis and were gradually integrated into the genetic heritage of certain animal species, including the human species. In this primitive form, they are operational soon after birth. But the cognitive structures in which they are rooted are different in nature from those that will be reconstructed during development. In humans, the further phylogenetic evolution of the brain endowed the species with other capacities, such as symbolic representation and cognitive control. One can assume that in situations where the primitive function is elicited, the underlying neural structure acts as an attractor around which will aggregate groups of neurons that are likely to perform the function in a more reliable and efficient way using other means.

2.2. The Notion of Plurality

As the reconstruction process takes place, a system is constituted that aggregates all cognitive processes capable of performing a given function. In the end, it is a plurality of processes that get activated to fulfill one and the same function, but not all of these processes will necessarily treat the same information. Some will be more suited to treating certain situations; some will be preferred by certain individuals. As we shall see below, processing plurality gives degrees of freedom to cognitive functioning and provides several possible pathways toward the reconstruction of the function [11–13].

2.3. The Notion of Interaction

If the different processes activated to fulfill a given function interact, then—insofar as they do not all process the same information—each one can transmit to each of the others, either directly or via a common interface, information that is not available to the other processes. When this occurs, the conditions are satisfied for the joint generation of a system in which the functioning of each process affects the functioning of each of the others. Models of such dynamic systems have shown that a system with these characteristics can be a source of self-organization. In the approach to development based on dynamic-system modeling [2,4,14], this kind of self-organization is seen as one of the potential sources of developmental change. Several types of interaction are possible (e.g., complementarity, competition, mutual support). The type considered here is an interaction of mutual support or reciprocal causality that is particularly conducive to initiating an improving self-organization process. For an example, see van der Maas et al. [15], who simulated the self-development of a system with five initially unrelated but mutually supportive components. There are, of course, other sources of development, such as the myelination of neural structures, but interactions between processes capable of carrying out a given function can be another source of change.

2.4. The Notion of Substitution[1]

Whenever several cognitive processes are capable of fulfilling the same function, a certain amount of redundancy is generated in the system they form, and this offers some functional degrees of freedom. Consequently, if one of the processes in the system is damaged, another can compensate for its absence—either partially or fully—by performing the shared function. In this case, we speak of compensatory relationships between processes. Substitution possibilities may also exist when none of the co-functional processes are damaged but have different probabilities of activation, depending on the individual and the situation. Reuchlin [16] proposed a probabilistic model of substitution relationships between cognitive processes. It postulates the existence of an activation-probability hierarchy that ranks the processes that perform the same function. The hierarchy is not necessarily the same for all individuals confronted with the same situation. This is a source of *between-individual variability* in the nature of the cognitive processes activated to accomplish the task. Symmetrically, the hierarchy may not be the same, for a given individual, in different situations or at different moments in time. It will depend on the degree of situational affordance of each process. This is a source of *within-individual variability*. Substitution relationships between processes give plasticity to the cognitive system and contribute to its reliability. They also help account for—and this is our key point of interest here—between- and within-individual variations in a general model of development [12,13].

The conceptual framework presented above is theoretical and largely hypothetical. In what follows, I will try to demonstrate its validity using the quantification of sets of discrete objects as an example to illustrate and concretize the conceptual framework proposed.

3. Initial State of Numerical Cognition Development

Two non-verbal, non-symbolic systems via which infants quantify sets of discrete objects have been brought to the fore. The first, called the "Approximate Number System" (ANS), provides an approximate, noisy estimate of the numerosity of large sets of objects. The second, called the "Parallel Individuation System" (PIS), gives an exact quantification of small sets of no more than three or four objects. Only the main characteristics of these two systems will be presented here. More detailed descriptions can be found elsewhere [17,18].

3.1. The Approximate Number System (ANS)

The function of the ANS system of numerical information processing is to provide an approximate estimate of the numerosity of a set of perceived objects. In the experiments designed to study its properties, the stimuli are sets of points or objects. The number of items in the set is varied while controlling the continuous variables likely to co-vary with that number (total area occupied, total perimeter, density). The task consists of discriminating or comparing the number of points or objects presented. With infants, the experimental paradigm used is habituation [19]. With older children or adults, the task usually consists of having the participant point to the greater of the two numerosities

---

[1]   In his model, Reuchlin [16] used the French word *"vicariance"* to refer to this type of relationship between processes. For lack of an exact equivalent in English, I use the expression "substitution" to translate this term.

presented. In this case, the experimenter ensures that the display time is too short to allow the participant to count [20]. With primates, this same task is presented using conditioning methods [21].

In all cases, whether with humans (infants or adults) or apes, the participants prove capable of approximately estimating the number of items to discriminate or compare, provided the difference in number is large enough. The larger the to-be-distinguished numerosities, the noisier the estimates and hence, the farther away from each other the numerosities must be to be perceived. The ratio between this distance and the set size nevertheless remains constant. More specifically, the approximate estimation of numerosity obeys Weber's law: the estimates are a logarithmic function of the real numerosity. This logarithmic function is considered to be the signature of the ANS, and Weber's fraction[2] tells us about the acuity of the ANS, i.e., the smallest difference in numerosity that an individual is capable of detecting.

The acuity of the ANS increases with the child's age, rapidly at first and then more slowly. In six-month-old infants, a reaction to novelty does not occur unless the ratio between the two numerosities to be discriminated is about 1:2 (on average). For example, an infant habituated to the numerosity of sets of eight points exhibits a novelty reaction during the test phase only for numerosities of at least 16 points. This ratio is about 2:3 at nine months (8 can thus be discriminated from 12) and continues to decrease exponentially until it stabilizes at about 7:8 in adulthood. Note, however, that at any given age, stable individual differences in ANS acuity exist, even at the early age of 6 months [22]. Among 14-year-olds, for example, the dispersion of this ratio ranges from 2:3 to 9:10 [20]. The search for correlations between ANS acuity and mathematical ability—a question we will address below—is based on these individual differences.

In sum, the behavioral signature of the ANS in numerosity quantification tasks is the same in humans and some animals. This numerical information processing system also activates homologous brain regions in man and primates. It is operational soon after birth in humans (at three months in [23]). These three characteristics suggest that the ANS was integrated into the genetic heritage of our species relatively early in the course of its phylogenesis and can therefore be seen as the initial state in the development of the numerical quantification function of human beings [24].

3.2. The Parallel Individuation System (PIS)

When the number of objects is less than or equal to three, quantification behavior differs from that described above for larger numerosities. Discrimination accuracy no longer depends on the ratio of the two perceived quantities; it is the same for 1 vs. 3, 1 vs. 2, and 2 vs. 3. At a more general level, neither accuracy nor response time depends on the ratio of the two quantities compared. This time, we are dealing with a form of exact representation of small quantities. The system relies on parallel processing in which each object perceived is individualized and represented in short-term memory (STM) by its own symbol, a kind of place holder. The STM representation incorporates the characteristics (shape, area, etc.) that enable the perceiver to track each object through time and space. Unlike with ANS, these continuous variables cannot be dissociated from the number in this system. It is sometimes called the Object Tracking System [18] and sometimes the Parallel Individuation System [25].

The information contained in the PIS-based representation of objects is not itself numerical, but number is implicitly taken into account in the term-by-term comparison between the objects perceived and their symbols already stored in short-term memory. Accordingly, the infants in Wynn's study [26] showed surprise when one of the objects was secretly added to or taken away from the set initially presented. For up to three objects, this system thus gives an exact representation of quantity and furnishes a non-numerical equivalent of adding or subtracting one object.

---

[2] Weber's fraction w, which is constant across a range of numerosities, is the difference between the two closest discriminable numerosities, normalized by their size. The same information is given by the coefficient of variation (standard deviation/mean).

The cortical network supporting the PIS is different from that of the ANS. This time, rather than the inferior intraparietal sulcus, it is the occipital-temporal sites that are activated [27]. Like ANS, PIS is operational shortly after birth and develops rapidly. The number of objects an infant can simultaneously take into account goes from one at about one month, to two or three at about 12 months [18]. PIS is also present in the repertoire of primates [28] and like ANS, gives rise to substantial individual differences [29].

The above findings suggest that the quantification of small numerosities (from 1 to 3) is based on a system different from the ANS, but one that, like ANS, became part of the genetic heritage of humanity relatively early in phylogenesis. Some authors call the ANS and PIS "core systems", defined as domain-specific representational systems that constrain the cultural acquisition of new representations [17,30].

These core systems are very different from what will later become the cognitive structures underlying the concept of number, so these structures are neither innate nor constructed de novo by a general process of equilibration[3]. The resemblance between the quantification behavior of infants and older children lies in the function common to the two kinds of cognitive structures implicated in these behaviors. The development of numerical cognition in children, then, should be regarded as a process that reconstructs the primitive function of discrete-object quantification. The reconstruction process relies on its evolutionary precursors (ANS and PIS), on cognitive abilities that have emerged more recently in the phylogenesis of the human species, and on the knowledge that these abilities have allowed us to construct and transmit. It follows from all this that the reconstruction of the quantification of discrete objects is in fact grounded in a plurality of cognitive processes that treat different kinds of information about number.

4. Plurality of Processes Supporting Reconstruction

For Piaget, the construction of numbers in children relied on logical operations, or more specifically, on the synthesis of the operations needed to understand its two great properties: seriation operations, which enable the child to grasp the order relations that structure the sequence of numbers, and class inclusion operations, which enable the child to understand inclusion relationships between sets whose cardinals correspond to consecutive numbers [32]. Later studies painted a much more complicated picture by providing evidence of several other processes that play a substantial role in the construction process. Below is a brief description of what appear to be the most important processes. They can be divided into two main categories on the basis of whether they can be called "analogical"[4] or "symbolic". The former quantify on the basis of an analogical relationship between the size of a set of objects and the representation of that size. The latter rely on arbitrary symbols (number words or Arabic numerals) to represent numbers.

4.1. Analogical Processing

Two of these processing systems, the ANS and the PIS, were presented above. The analogical nature of ANS lies in the (logarithmic) relation between numerosity and its representation; for PIS, it lies in the correspondence between the number of objects perceived and the number of place holders representing that number in short-term memory. Three other analogical ways of quantifying sets of discrete objects are briefly described below.

---

[3] In Piaget's theory, Equilibration is a general process of cognitive functioning which, whatever the knowledge domain, regulates: (1) the equilibrium between the *assimilation* of objects into the action schemes of the subject and the *accommodation* of these schemes to the objects; (2) the equilibrium in *reciprocal assimilation and accommodation* between schemes; (3) at the higher level, equilibrium between the *differentiation* of schemes and their *integration* in a more general structure [31].

[4] In the literature, these processes are in fact usually called non-symbolic or non-verbal, which emphasizes what they are *not* and advantageously avoids having to make a statement about what they *are*. In my mind, they are analogical, but this is clearly a point of discussion.

4.1.1. One-to-One Correspondence

Before using any numerical symbols, children can judge the equality or inequality of two collections of objects by setting up a one-to-one correspondence between the items in one collection and those in the other. Here, the analogy resides in the spatial correspondence of the collections being compared. This is one of the procedures that Piaget and Szeminska [32] used to test for the conservation of numbers by getting the child to agree on the numerical equality of two rows of tokens before changing one of them. Piaget did not, however, grant this procedure an important role in the construction of numbers precisely because, before the age of six or seven, the equality it permits is not conserved when the spatial spread of the two collections is changed. Yet when children become capable, at the age of about two or three years, of mapping the elements of two collections, they are abstracting an identity relation that paves the way to the notion of exact equality.[5] This was demonstrated in Mix, Moore, and Holcomb's experiment [34], where three-year-old children's ability to judge numerical equivalency (assessed by showing them two cards and asking them to choose which one had the same number of objects as the target card) improved considerably when the children were first given toys designed to stimulate a one-to-one mapping activity (e.g., objects made up of two parts that fit together).

4.1.2. Early Finger Counting

Another way to use one-to-one correspondence to determine how many elements there are in a set is to put up as many fingers as there are elements in the set; this is a peculiar procedure, however, in that it can be regarded as an instance of embodied cognition because the fingers are part of the body [35]. The finger-based representation of the number of objects also rests on an analogy, i.e., it uses as many fingers as there are objects. It implicitly involves several properties of numbers, which is an aid to understanding them later on. The order relation is intrinsic to the sequence of fingers held up [36,37], and so is the successor function:[6] the same unit—a finger—separates each element from its successor.

There are good reasons, then, to contend that the representation of numbers with fingers contributes to the development of numerical cognition. This was shown in an experiment in which four-year-old children who had not yet learned the concept of cardinality had to state the number of objects displayed on cards ("What's on this card?" task). In one of the experimental conditions, the children had to reply with a number word; in the other, they had to put up the corresponding number of fingers. The results indicated that response accuracy (measured by how close the response was to the correct answer) was greater in the gestural modality, whether the number was small (1 to 4) or large (5 to 10). Moreover, in cases where both response modalities were used at the same time by the child, if the two responses did not match, the finger response was the more accurate one. As the authors stated, "These results show that children convey numerical information in gesture that they cannot convey in speech and raise the possibility that number gestures play a functional role in children's development of number concepts" ([38] p. 14).

4.1.3. The Sequence of Number Words

Between the ages of two and three, children learn from people in their surroundings to recite the list of the first few number words. At this stage, the list is merely an unbreakable string of sounds, recited by heart [39]. The words that compose the sound string start becoming separate entities when the child learns to imitate the procedure consisting of saying each word while pointing to a different

---

[5] This is not yet a relation of numerical equality because if, say, the identity is modified by replacing an item in one of the two collections by an item that is not identical to it, the relation of numerical equality is disrupted in the child's eyes [33].

[6] The successor function is a rule establishing the existence of a minimal quantity—one—that corresponds to the minimal distance between two consecutive numbers.

object. At this point, even if the number words are individualized, they do not yet have the properties of numerical symbols. However, the order in which they are uttered, which is intrinsic to the numerical sequence recited in the past, is analogous to the order relation that structures numbers, and as such can promote its acquisition and comprehension.

4.2. Symbolic Processing

Symbolic processing relies on arbitrary symbols (e.g., number words, Arabic numerals) to represent exact numbers of objects. It enables us to directly perform mental quantification operations on these symbols. Unlike the analogical type of processing considered above, it is not based on any kind of resemblance between the symbol and the quantity it represents. The advantage of this route is that the relationships between the symbols are only those defined by the formal rules governing the numerical system. The disadvantage is that it is difficult for children to mentally represent the exact quantity that corresponds, by convention, to each symbol and makes it meaningful.

4.2.1. Subitizing

Subitizing is the rapid apprehension, without counting, of small numbers of objects, from 1 to 3 and sometimes 4. It is very similar to the parallel individuation process presented above and is probably an extension of it [40]. The essential difference is that this kind of rapid apprehension of number is accompanied by verbalization of the corresponding number word (the cardinal of the collection), which requires minimal access to language. This explains why subitizing is rarely observed in children under two. It supplies no information about the ordinal properties of numbers but constitutes an initial form of mapping between a number word and the cardinal of the perceived set.

4.2.2. Counting

Counting is a complex process whose role was underestimated by Piaget but reevaluated by Greco [41]. We are indebted to Gelman and Gallistel [42] for having brought back into the foreground the role of counting in the genesis of the notion of number. These authors identified five principles that must be obeyed to count correctly. The most important ones are one-to-one correspondence, stable order, and cardinality. The principle of one-to-one correspondence states that the items to be counted must be mapped, via a one-to-one correspondence, to the set of number tags used to count (e.g., the set of number words). The stable order principle states that the number tags have a fixed order. The cardinality principle states that the last number used in a count represents the cardinality of the items counted. In the spirit of the neo-nativist era of the seventies, Gelman and Gallistel assumed that these principles were rooted in an innate cognitive structure specific to number. Later research, however, did not confirm their innateness. Rather, they are acquired gradually in the course of early childhood and hardly ever show up in counting behavior before the age of four years [39,43].

The principle of cardinality is assessed using the "Give me N" task (Wynn, [43,44]). The experimenter places the child in front of a set of objects and asks the child to give him/her N objects. Cardinality is considered to be acquired when the child starts to count and, upon arriving at the number N (and only at that moment), gives the experimenter the set of objects just counted. Understanding that the cardinal of a collection also and necessarily includes all the cardinals of smaller collections is a much more advanced stage that no doubt requires mastery of logical operations such as class inclusion, to which Piaget granted a unique role. Children who master the principle of cardinality have begun to understand that each of the number words in the sequence they know refers to an exact quantity that is specific to it.

The various processes reviewed above, both analogical and symbolic, have a shared function, that of quantification, but they perform it by processing different information. Plurality of processing opens up the possibility of interactions, a potential source of development [45].

5. Interaction

How are these different processes related to each other in the course of development? Are they independent or interdependent? If they are interdependent, are the relationships between them symmetrical or asymmetrical? If they interact, what types of interactions are involved, conflicting ones or mutually supportive ones?

These questions will be addressed below for the two processing systems reviewed here, the analogical system of approximate number representation or ANS, and the symbolic system of exact representation. Both are subject to developmental change over time: ANS acuity increases with age and so do numerical skills. Both give rise to large individual differences, that is, ANS-acuity differences and performance differences in initial numerical skills (e.g., number list, counting, cardinality, small-number operations). Within the past few years, many experiments have looked at these individual differences, generally using correlation methods, to determine how the two systems are related. I will begin with an overview of the results of studies demonstrating the impact of the ANS on the symbolic system. Then I will present the results of studies showing the opposite impact.

5.1. Does ANS Have an Effect on the Development of the Symbolic System?

It is not possible here to describe all of the studies on how the ANS affects numerical-skill development, but the reader will find reviews of this question in Mussolin et al. [46] and in two meta-analyses (Fazio et al. [47]; Chen and Li, [48]). The conclusions of these studies are convergent, so to summarize the results, I will rely solely on the Chen and Li [48] meta-analysis (which is the most comprehensive).

The cross-sectional studies meta-analyzed dealt with 31 studies involving 36 independent samples. Many factors differed across experiments, including the age of the participants, the covariables controlled, the tasks used to assess ANS acuity, the indexes calculated to establish its signature, and the tasks employed to assess mathematical abilities. A positive correlation was found in 35 of the 36 samples and was significant in 20 of them. The mean correlation, 0.24, was not very high but significant. None of the factors just mentioned had a significant impact on the magnitude of the correlation.

The existence in the cross-sectional studies of a correlation between ANS and numerical skills does not, however, tell us anything about the direction of the relationship between the two variables. Longitudinal studies conducted to find out whether individual differences in ANS acuity at time t predict performance differences in numerical skills at time $t + 1$ are better suited to determining the direction of the relationship. Eight longitudinal studies involving 11 samples were included in the Chen and Li [48] meta-analysis. Once the covariables measuring more general cognitive abilities were controlled, the mean correlation between ANS acuity and numerical-skill performance was 0.25, which is similar in magnitude to that found in the cross-sectional research.

The structural analysis of the relationships between the variables provides further information. Chu et al. [49] showed that among the children they examined at the age of four and then again at the end of the school year, ANS acuity at four years predicted numerical skills at the end of the year. However, this relationship was fully mediated by the relationship between performance differences on the cardinality task and differences in numerical skill level. Insofar as the ANS precedes cardinality, this result suggests that differences in ANS acuity are the source of differences in the acquisition of cardinality, which, in turn, contribute to differences in numerical skills.

Other convincing data on the direction of the relationship between the ANS and symbolic arithmetic can be found in training experiments. Hyde et al. [50] gave first graders two training sessions on non-symbolic numerical approximation (approximate addition of sets of points or approximate comparison of numbers). The results showed that in both cases, the children's performance on a test of exact symbolic arithmetic was significantly better than that of the children in the control groups. Similar results were found by Obersteiner et al. [51]. Park and Brannon [52], who studied adult participants, also showed that training in approximate addition and subtraction of sets of points raised both ANS acuity and performance on a test of exact addition and subtraction.

It thus seems reasonable to conclude that the system of approximate number representation affects the development of the symbolic system of exact representation.

5.2. Does Learning the Symbolic System Have an Effect on ANS Acuity?

The correlation found in the cross-sectional studies analyzed above could also be due to an effect of numerical-skill acquisition on ANS acuity, but it does not demonstrate this effect.

Here again, longitudinal studies offer less ambiguous information. In Chen and Li's [48] meta-analysis, four longitudinal studies (with five samples) tested the relationship in this direction. The mean correlation was 0.23, which is comparable to the value found in the longitudinal studies where the relationship was tested in the other direction. Here again also, an analysis of the structure of the relationships at play can supply more precise information. Mussolin et al. [53] assessed numerical skills and ANS acuity in children at the age of 4 years and then again seven months later. Using the cross-correlation method, they showed that numerical skills at 4 years predicted ANS acuity at the end of the school year, but not the opposite.

Other convincing data on the relationship in this direction can be found in experiments analyzing the effects of numerical-system learning on ANS acuity. Opfer and Siegler [54] studied the developmental time course of the function linking the representation of the magnitude of numbers to their real magnitude. Children of different grades in school were asked to position numbers from different numerical intervals (0 to 10, 10 to 100, 100 to 1000, etc.) on a continuous line bounded on both ends. Their results showed that the logarithmic function became a linear function as school grade increased, but only interval by interval. For example, for the interval 0–100, the function was logarithmic for the preschoolers and linear for the second graders, but for these same second graders, the function was still logarithmic for the interval 0–1000, and so on. Hence, learning the rule of succession—whereby each number leads to the next by iteration of one unit and all intervals between two consecutive numbers are equal—is not transferred in an immediate way to the approximate representation of all numbers. It is more likely that the experience acquired through manipulation of the numbers in the interval being learned in each school grade transforms the ANS-based representation of approximate magnitudes.

Cross-cultural studies shed another type of light on this issue. Piazza et al. [55] studied the approximate estimation of numerosities in a native Amazon population, the Mundurucù. The language of these people has a very limited lexicon of number words and they have no symbolic way whatsoever to process discrete quantities. They can, however, compare the numerosities of two sets, or estimate their approximate sum. The authors compared adults who had gone to school to those who had not, on a task involving the approximate estimation of numerosities. The results showed that for all participants, schooled or not, the function that linked the discrimination capacity to the size of the compared numerosities looked very much like the logarithmic function already found in industrialized nations. However, Weber's ratio was significantly lower—indicating greater acuity—among the Mundurucù who had been taught arithmetic, and acuity grew as the number of years of schooling rose.

It thus seems reasonable, here also, to conclude that learning the symbolic system affects the developmental time course of the ANS, in particular by improving its acuity and changing the shape (from logarithmic to linear) of the function that links approximate representations of magnitude to their real magnitudes.

If each process that performs the quantification function has an impact on the unfolding of each of the others, then the relationship between them is one of mutual support, and together they form a dynamic system capable of self-organization [15]. Furthermore, whenever several processes fulfill the same function, they can also be related by substitution, i.e., substitution of one for another, depending on the situation and the individual.

6. Substitution and Variabilities

In situations that call upon the quantification function, it is hypothesized that the various processes capable of fulfilling that function are competing with each other. Depending on the type of information they process, their activation probabilities—or their respective weights if they are activated in parallel—are likely to vary as a function of the situation and the individual. The resulting possibilities for substitution are assumed to be one of the sources of within- and between-individual variability. This section gives three examples of variability that can be explained in terms of substitution (when all co-functional processes are available) or compensation (when one of those processes is impaired). The first example is drawn from the typical development of numerical cognition, the second from atypical development, and the third from arithmetic problem solving.

6.1. An Example of Substitution Relationships in Typical Development

Acquiring the principle of cardinality is decisive in the acquisition of the numerical system. It is at this time, between the ages of three and a half and four and a half that children begin to understand that each of the numerical symbols they know (number words, digits) represents an exact quantity, one that is specific to it. To grasp this, children must map these symbols to the analogical representations of quantity they have at their disposal. By the time they are two and a half, on average, children know that number words refer to quantities, but while they know and can learn to recite these words, they do not know the correspondence between the words and the quantities. First, they learn the meaning of "1", but it will take them several months to learn the meaning of "2", and then several additional months to learn the meaning of "3". The discovery of the meaning of numbers larger than 3 or 4 marks the transition to another stage and is based on a different process. This new capacity is a testimony to the fact that the child has discovered the principles of counting, in particular that of cardinality, and has become capable of generalizing those principles to larger numbers. The transition occurs between the ages of three and four, on average, and the criterion is the child's ability, on the "Give me N" task, to give the exact quantity corresponding to the number requested by the experimenter, for a number greater than four.

6.1.1. Two Hypotheses about the Route to Cardinality

There is an ongoing debate about the pathway taken by children to arrive at the principle of cardinality. For some authors (e.g., Le Corre, Carey, [25]; Carey et al. [56]), the transition rests on the "parallel individuation system" (PIS), the only one capable of enabling the child to map the number words from "one" to "three" or "four" to the exact quantities to which they correspond. For others (Dehaene [24]; Feigenson et al. [17]; Piazza [18]; Wynn [44]), the mapping can be achieved via the approximate number system (ANS).

The ANS-to-Word Pathway

Authors who advocate the role of the ANS in the acquisition of cardinality believe that this approximate representation system is sufficient to account for the increasingly precise matching between magnitudes and numerical symbols. They hypothesize that children begin mapping the first few number words because they are the most frequent in the language. Moreover, the quantities corresponding to these numbers are related to each other in ways that make them discriminable by three-year-olds. At this age, children are capable of discriminating ratios of 3:4, so they must also be able to discriminate 1 from 2, 2 from 3, and all the more so 1 from 3, since the ratios of these comparisons (1:2, 2:3, and 1:3) are easier than 3:4. Moving up from these small numbers to the following ones can be achieved by realizing that going from one number to the next involves adding one object.

J. Intell. **2018**, *6*, 15

The PIS-to-Word Pathway

Carey and her colleagues of course agree that numerical symbols are mapped to approximate representations of their magnitude, but they do not agree that this is what leads to cardinality [25,56]. Their hypothesis is that this type of mapping can only take place once the principle of cardinality has been acquired. One of the reasons for their reluctance is that cardinality is based on an exact correspondence between the quantity and the symbol that represents it, yet mapping via the ANS only supplies approximate representations. On the other hand, as we have seen above, PIS gives the exact representation outright for the numbers from 1 to 3 or 4. The parallel individuation of the elements of a small set nevertheless only furnishes fleeting representations in short-term memory, whereas representations of the magnitudes of number words must be permanently stored in long-term memory. To account for the fact that the mapping done in short-term memory is transferred to long-term memory, Carey and colleagues hypothesize that the representation of a set is enriched by knowledge of other sets of the same size (e.g., "me" for 1, "Mommy and Daddy" for 2, "Mommy, Daddy, and me" for 3. This process is called the "enriched parallel individuation system". It is assumed to enable mapping of each of the first three or four numbers to an exact representation of the quantities associated with them. When going from the exact representation of the number 1 to that of the number 2, and likewise for 2 to 3, the child has the opportunity, here also, to grasp that going from a given number word to the next involves adding 1. Cardinality, discovered on small numbers, thanks to PIS, would then be generalized to become the cardinality principle that counting obeys.

6.1.2. Experiments Aimed at Choosing between These Two Hypotheses

Experiments devised to decide which is the better hypothesis about the route to cardinality have given rise to contradictory results. The contradictions result from unexpected within- and between-individual variations in the execution of tasks where a number must be matched to a quantity of objects, or a quantity of objects must be matched to a number. This section begins by summarizing the findings, and then looks at how the model of substitution might help resolve the contradictions.

The first experiment aimed at choosing the better hypothesis was conducted by Le Corre and Carey [25]. It was designed around two main ideas. The first was that if the pathway to cardinality rests on ANS, we should find its signature. The second was that approximate ANS-based mapping most certainly exists for large numbers, but it should only be found after the principle of cardinality has been acquired.

In this study, Le Corre and Carey tested children whose mean age was 3.11 on two tasks, one ("Give me N") designed to detect their knowledge of the cardinality of numbers, the other ("Fast Cards") designed to see whether the signature of the ANS would be found in the children's matching behavior. In "Give me N", those who responded correctly only for N = 1 were labelled 1-knowers, and so on up to 4-knowers. Those who responded correctly only for these small numbers (1 to 4) were put in a group called "subset-knowers". Those who responded correctly for larger numbers, at least up to 5 or 6, were put in a group called "cardinality-principle knowers" (CP-knowers). In "Fast Cards", the children had to say the number word corresponding to the number of elements (circles) on the card shown by the experimenter. The number of circles varied between 1 and 10, but only the responses given for the larger numbers (5 to 10) were analyzed. To prevent the children from counting the circles, each card was shown for only one second.

As hypothesized, the ANS signature (logarithmic function) in the "Fast Cards" task was found only among the CP-knowers. According to the authors, the fact that the signature of the ANS was not found among the subset-knowers but only among the CP-knowers shows that the pathway toward cardinality does not rely on the ANS. It was only after the principle of cardinality had been acquired that mapping of large numbers to an approximate representation of their magnitude was observed.

In a more recent experiment, Wagner and Johnson [57] also studied the matching of number words to the magnitudes of sets of objects, by children whose mean age was 4.1 on the "Give me N" task. But unlike Le Corre and Carey, they did not stop task execution after the last correct response but went up to the number 10 for all children. The results showed that the mean number of objects given by the child increased with the magnitude of the difference between the number requested by the experimenter and the knower level of his/her last correct answer. The standard deviation also increased and the coefficient of variation (standard deviation divided by the mean) was constant, which is the signature of the ANS. The authors concluded that ANS plays a role in the representation of the magnitude of number words for children who have not yet acquired the principle of cardinality. This is the opposite of what Le Corre and Carey found. It should be noted, however, that the tasks used were not the same. "Fast Cards" consists of presenting a set of items and asking the child to say the number word that corresponds to it, whereas "Give me N" consists of saying a number word and asking the child to give the corresponding number of items. The direction of the required mapping is thus quantity to number word in the former case, and number word to quantity in the latter. Note also that the two tasks were not performed by the same children.

In an attempt to shed light on the contradictory results of the above studies, Odic et al. [58] had children (mean age 3.6) perform both mapping tasks: mapping in the quantity-to-word direction ("Fast Cards") and mapping in the word-to-quantity direction (an adapted version of the "Give me N" task). The results of the "Fast Cards" experiment replicated Le Corre and Carey's findings: in the quantity-to-word direction, the function linking the magnitude of the set of points to the magnitude of the number word produced had a positive slope only for some of the CP-knowers. The results of the adapted version of the "Give me N" task, in which the mapping was in the word-to-quantity direction, replicated Wagner and Johnson's results: the slope of the function linking the number of items to the number word requested by the experimenter was positive and significantly different from zero; this was true not only for the CP-knowers but also for the 2-knowers and the 3-knowers. These results allowed the authors to conclude that "before children have become CP-knowers, they are able to map from a discrete number word representation, e.g., 10, to a region on the continuous ANS mental number line" (p. 118).

Since the same children did both matching tasks here, there was within-individual variation in performance according to the mapping direction: quantity-to-word or word-to-quantity. The authors interpreted this within-individual variation as being due to a difference in difficulty comparable to that found in language development between production tasks (here production of a number word in the quantity-to-word direction) and comprehension tasks (here comprehension of a number word in the word -to-quantity direction), production being more difficult than comprehension.

However, in another experiment where both tasks were given to the same children, there was also within-individual variation in mapping success, but it went in the opposite direction (Gunderson et al. [59], experiment 2). In that experiment indeed, the children's responses exhibited the ANS signature in the quantity-to-word direction ("Fast Dots Task") but not in the "word-to-quantity" direction ("Give me N" Task). If the observed within-individual variations between these two tasks were only differences in difficulty, we would need to explain why the task that was the easiest for the children in Odic et al. experiment was the most difficult for the participants of Gunderson et al. experiment.

We are thus faced with a case of *within-individual* variation that went in the opposite direction for different children. This *between-individual* variation was probably due to the way in which the subjects in Gunderson et al. experiment 2 were selected. The authors chose older subset-knowers than in their experiment 1 in order to observe the behavior of subset-knowers whose ANS development was more advanced. To find children who were older that those in experiment 1, but still had not acquired the cardinality principle, they recruited participants (mean age 4.2, range 3.11–5.5) from nursery schools in a neighborhood with a lower sociocultural level than in their experiment 1.

6.1.3. A Possible Interpretation of the Observed Variabilities

The children just mentioned were all subset-knowers, that is to say, children able to match at least some small numbers (from 1 to 4) to the exact quantities that correspond to them, which is the signature of the PIS. Nevertheless, contrary to what Carey and Le Corre thought they were, at the same time, able-under certain conditions–to form an approximate representation of the magnitude corresponding to numbers greater than 4, which is the signature of the ANS. Therefore, in these children who have not yet acquired the principle of cardinality, both of these quantification processes are available for matching the number words to a representation of their magnitude.

As a consequence, subset-knowers have the opportunity to substitute the ANS for the PIS in the course of a mapping task when the latter becomes ineffective, but this possibility seems to depend on two conditions: the characteristics of the subjects and the direction of the mapping. Concerning the characteristics of the subjects, the age difference between those included in Gunderson et al. experiment and those included in Odic et al. experiment is confounded with a difference in sociocultural level. Children with a low sociocultural level are known, on average, to be less successful in the verbal domain than in the spatial domain and vice versa for those with a high sociocultural level. Concerning the direction of the mapping, the spatial configuration of the set of objects is the prime in the quantity-to-word direction, whereas the number word is the prime in the word-to-quantity direction. Therefore, the within- and between-individual variations observed in the results of the mapping tasks examined above could be due to the fact that the ability to substitute the ANS for the PIS when the number of objects goes up depends on the situation (here, the direction of the mapping), the characteristics of the individual (here his/her skill level in the verbal and spatial domains), and the potential interaction between the two.

Insofar as these experiments were not designed to test for substitution relationships, their interpretation can only be hypothetical. But these hypotheses could be tested by having children carry out tasks that assess verbal and spatial aptitudes independently.

6.2. An Example of Compensation in Atypical Development

Whenever a deficiency, whether genetic or accidental, is such that one of the co-functioning processes is absent from the child's repertoire or is inefficient, the existence of substitution relationships enables another process to take its place, either partially or totally. The word *compensation* is more suitable in this case than the word substitution, because a substitution relationship is reciprocal. We find compensation relationships in certain kinds of atypical development.

Children with Williams Syndrome, for example, have a unique developmental profile in which verbal abilities are less impaired, relatively speaking, than spatial abilities. Their acquisition of arithmetic is delayed. Ansari et al. [60] wondered whether these children could acquire numerical skills via the same route as typically developing children. They focused in particular on the acquisition of the principle of cardinality.

They studied two groups of children matched on spatial abilities: a group of typically developing children, mean age 3.5, and a group of Williams Syndrome children, mean age 7.6. Both groups had taken verbal aptitude tests. The cardinality principle was in the process of being acquired in each group, with comparable mean performance levels and dispersions. The most interesting finding is that for the typically developing group, individual differences in the scores on the cardinality task "Give me N" were linked to individual differences in spatial aptitude, whereas in the Williams group, the cardinality scores were linked to differences in verbal aptitude. This suggests that the two groups follow different pathways to arrive at the principle of cardinality.

Van Herwegen et al. [61] later study sheds an interesting light on this issue. These authors had a group of nine Williams children (mean age 2.11) perform a task involving the approximate estimation of large numerosities, and a task involving the exact discrimination of small numerosities. The children were capable of exactly discriminating the small numerosities but were unable to discriminate the large numerosities. This result suggests that the ANS, known to be operational shortly after birth in typically developing children, has not yet been acquired by Williams children who are nearly three years old. Insofar as the mental number line of the ANS has spatial properties [62], it could very well be that the ANS deficit of these children is linked to their spatial impairment. The PIS, where words are mapped with exact quantities, may not be affected as much because these children's language abilities are less altered than their spatial ones. The pathway taken by Ansari et al.'s children with Williams Syndrome, who, in spite of their impairment, were able to construct the notion of cardinality, is thus likely to be a route that relies on their relatively well-spared abilities, namely, the PIS and language.

Why, then, are Williams children so far behind in learning the principle of cardinality, knowing that the PIS is available in their repertoire? Undoubtedly, it is because this system can only partially compensate for ANS deficits. If this is indeed the case, then the above finding points in the same direction as those analyzed in the preceding section. It shows—a contrario—that typical development relies on both systems, including in the phase preceding the acquisition of cardinality.

Deaf individuals who lack a conventional language (spoken or signed) exhibit the opposite deficit. These individuals, called homesigners, devise their own gestures to communicate. Their gestures are not used as a tally system, and homesigners do not have the equivalent of a counting list or a counting routine. When they communicate about the magnitude of sets of objects, they are accurate for sets from 1 to 3. For sets from 4 to 20, they are approximately, but not exactly, correct. They understand that each set has an exact numerical value, but they do not have an errorless way of arriving at a gestural representation of that value. Their responses are centered on the target value, with a small dispersion around it [63]. These facts confirm the specific role of the PIS in the exact representation of the numbers from 1 to 3. They also show that acquisition of the cardinality principle is not a necessary condition for the development of the ANS. The system of approximate representation can partly compensate for impairment in conventional (spoken or signed) language, but it is also clear that both systems are necessary for optimal efficiency of the quantification function.

6.3. An Example of Substitution in Arithmetic Problem Solving

Within- and between-individual variations corresponding to pathway differences in long-term numerical development also exist in short-term arithmetic problem solving, in the form of variations in strategies. Siegler proposed a selectionist model of the developmental course of strategies, inspired by the conceptual framework of Darwin's theory of evolution, in particular its concepts of variation and selection [7]. This theoretical framework was applied to the development of arithmetic knowledge in a microgenetic study where the solving strategies applied to small-number addition problems were analyzed in five-year-old children, [64]. No fewer than eight different strategies were identified. This analysis revealed not only the existence of strong between-individual variability—indicating that the dominant strategy was not the same for all children—but also of strong within-individual variability. No matter what their dominant strategy was, all of the children also used other strategies at one time or another. Their choice sometimes depended upon the characteristics of the problem (for example, the size of the addenda or to the order in which they were stated), and sometimes on the point in time (when the same problem had to be solved again). This within-individual variability plays an important role in development. In Siegler's selectionist approach, it is considered a necessary condition for the selection process via which the most efficient and least costly strategy for this particular subject is gradually adopted for this particular category of problems, at this particular point in time. Its role is also important in the development of new strategies by the way of which elements are taken from strategies whose within-individual variability has enabled exploration.

There are both similarities and dissimilarities between Siegler's conceptual framework and that of the reconstructivist approach I am proposing here. The similarities lie in the emphasis put on the plurality of processes and on the relationships of substitution (between strategies or between processes) used to account for variability. The dissimilarities lie in the time scale of the processes observed and in the developmental mechanism brought to bear. Concerning the time scale, the strategies take effect in the short term of problem-solving (seconds or minutes) whereas reconstruction occurs in the long term (months or years). Concerning the developmental mechanism of change, Siegler's theory favors the variation-selection pair, inspired by the theory of evolution, while the approach I am proposing here, inspired by dynamic-system theories, favors mutual support as a source of self-organization.

From my point of view, Siegler's theory is effective at explaining the changes that takes place among a set of strategies—or components of strategies—already existing in the child's repertoire, but is less convincing to explain the emergence of truly new strategies.

7. Discussion

The concept of numbers is not constructed solely by the coordination of logical operations, as Piaget thought [32]. Nor does it result from the actualization of an innate cognitive structure that harbors the principles of counting, as Gelman and Gallistel thought [42]. These two theories, one constructivist, the other nativist, made major contributions to furthering our knowledge of the genesis of numbers in children, but later work has pointed out their limitations. The cognitive processes underlying numerical development are in fact more numerous and more diverse. Some rely on an analogical representation of quantity, others on a symbolic representation. Some make use of language, others do not. Some are best suited to representing small quantities, others to representing large numerosities. Some supply an approximate representation of quantity, others an exact representation. Although these diverse cognitive processes treat different information, they perform a common function (hence the term "co-functional")—namely, the quantification of sets of discrete objects.

Two of them, the ANS and the PIS, have a status of their own due to their anteriority on the phylogenetic and ontogenetic levels. We know very little about the exact role played by each of these core systems in the orchestration of the processes that take effect later in the development of numerical cognition. We can nevertheless assume that in situations that call upon the quantification function, all processes that have affordances in these situations are activated. At the beginning of child development, this only concerns the core systems, but as soon as other processes become operational, a growing number of co-functional processes are activated in quantification situations. During this phase—and by virtue of their anteriority—the neural structures that have been supporting the function's primitive form would attract those that are co-activated at the same time by quantification tasks. The system gradually formed in this manner is not built through the coordination of isolated, initially unrelated schemes, as Piaget thought. Rather, it is formed by the integration of new cognitive capacities that serve a preexisting function, around which they themselves are structured at the same time as they are transforming and reconstructing the function.

Two phases must be distinguished in this reconstruction process: invention and learning. During the initial invention phase, human beings gradually discovered new possibilities for quantification, ones that were more precise and more efficient, opened up by the evolution of the brain in their species. Some examples of inventions, for instance, are when a human being got the idea to have a stone, a finger, a notch, or a stick correspond to each member of his herd, or imagined assigning a name or a gesture to an exact quantity, etc. This phase of the reconstruction process took thousands of years and continues today. It gave rise to the number-based culture in which the children whose development we are now studying are immersed. The second form of reconstruction is not void of inventions—which for children are rediscoveries—but relies much more heavily on learning, and for this reason, takes only a few years. In a cultural environment where numerical information is an integral part of daily life, situations confronting children with quantification problems activate the available primitive quantification systems, granted, but they also activate all cognitive processes that can help in understanding the language, gestures, signs, etc. used in those situations by people in their surroundings. The co-activation of all processes that are co-functional but treat different information about quantity has implications not only from the developmental standpoint but also from the point of view of variability.

From the developmental standpoint, any process can affect the unfolding of any of the other co-functional processes, since each one treats information that the others cannot access directly on their own. If this is the case, the interactions between them can take on the form of relations of mutual support, and they form a dynamic system capable of self-organization. This is a source of development that differs from those rooted in the maturation of the nervous system and in learning. The findings on the reciprocal impact of the approximate number system and the symbolic system are compatible with the mutual-support hypothesis. It would be interesting to find out whether this type of interaction can be generalized to all cognitive processes that perform the quantification function.

From the standpoint of variability, a system containing a plurality of co-functional processes also opens up the possibility of substitution relationships. Reuchlin's [16] model of substitution can account for the contradictions between the results of experiments designed to show that only one of two co-functional processing systems, here ANS or PIS, is at play in the child's pathway toward cardinality. Substitution relationships can give rise to two sorts of variability in behavior. Firstly, we have within-individual variability, which is situation-dependent and stems from the fact that a given co-functional process does not necessarily have the same affordance for all situations (note in passing that situation-dependent alternation between the various processes promotes their interaction). Secondly, we have between-individual variability, which stems from the fact that in a given situation, not all individuals necessarily select the same process among those available in their repertoire, to perform the function in question. These different forms of variability are manifestations of the plasticity engendered by the existence of multiple co-functional processes. Variability, here, is not seen as a peculiarity that must be neutralized in order to gain access to the general laws of cognitive functioning and development, but as a consequence of those laws. It follows that studying the different forms of variability opens up an original window on the study of the general laws of cognitive functioning and development.

The reconstructivist approach illustrated here using the example of quantification could be generalized to other major cognitive functions that have also been integrated–into primitive forms–in the genetic heritage of the human species. Categorization, for example, also has primitive forms that are operational shortly after birth [65]. In addition, there are a number of co-functional processes involved in the developmental reconstruction of this function that occur in a more reliable, more efficient, and more controlled form. At the most general level, we find both similarity-based and theory-based processes. At a more specific level, several co-functional processes are available: taxonomic categorization (both birds and crocodiles are animals), thematic categorization (birds live in nests), "slot-filler" categorization (both oatmeal and bacon are breakfast foods) [66]. It would therefore be interesting to see if, in this domain as well, these co-functional processes exhibit mutual support relationships able to trigger self-organization of the categorization system, as well as substitution relationships able to explain the within- and between-individual variabilities observed in categorization tasks.

To look for development through the window of variability, one must adopt a different methodological approach from that most frequently used in developmental research. Rather than examining each co-functional process separately, one needs to study the dynamics of the system they form. This requires an idiographic [67] and longitudinal study of any within-individual variation in the developmental level attained by each child in each co-functional process. This would allow us to study the stability of each child's within-individual variation profile over time, and also to study between-individual variations in these within-child variations.

To my knowledge, studies that have taken this approach to numerical cognition are rare. One such study was transversal only. Dowker [68] evaluated the developmental level of four-year-olds in some of the skills involved in the construction of number, including counting, cardinality principle, order irrelevance principle, repeated addition of 1, and repeated subtraction of 1. A significant but moderate link was found between the performance on these different components, none of which seemed to be a prerequisite for the others. For example, 22% of those who mastered counting had not mastered cardinality and 41% of those who were poor counters had mastered cardinality. Another such study was longitudinal [69]. In this case, the authors made three assessments (at ages 4, 5, and 6) of the developmental level reached in three kinds of skills (non-symbolic, mapping, and symbolic). A confirmatory factor analysis of the data showed that the three types of skills were saturated by three distinct factors at ages four and five, but by a single common factor at age six. This means that there were between-individual differences in the direction of the within-individual variations on these different skills at ages four and five, but not at age six. In other words, the pathway differences observed at four and five years disappeared at six years. However, in this kind of factorial approach, the individual level is lost [70] and we do not know if the children contributing to each of the three factors were the same at ages four and five. There is one other study that gives us an idea of the degrees of freedom that substitution possibilities leave in the developmental pathway, and also of the variety of methods that can be used to highlight this phenomenon [36]. In this case study, the author described the developmental pathway of a child who learned to count by putting his fingers in a one-to-one correspondence with the objects to be counted and using the finger collection thus constituted as a representation of number. It was not until some time later that the child acquired number words by matching them to the analog representation of quantity that constituted the collections of fingers.

The pathway differences that the reconstructivist approach would uncover would be doubly interesting. Theoretically, these differences will tell us about the degrees of freedom that exist along the developmental pathway leading to the reconstruction of a given cognitive function. Practically, better knowledge of the various possible pathways could help with devising learning methods suited to each route.

Conflicts of Interest: The author declares no conflict of interest.

References

1. Lautrey, J.; Mazoyer, B.; van Geert, P. (Eds.) *Invariants et Variabilités dans les Sciences Cognitives*; Presses de la Maison des Sciences Humaines: Paris, France, 2002.
2. Thelen, E.; Smith, L.B. *A Dynamic Systems Approach to the Development of Cognition and Action*; MIT Press: Cambridge, MA, USA, 1994.
3. Van Geert, P.L.C.; van Dijk, M. Focus on variability: New tools to study intra-individual variability in developmental data. *Infant Behav. Dev.* **2002**, *25*, 370–374. [CrossRef]
4. Van Geert, P. Dynamic modeling of cognitive development: Time, situatedness and variability. In *Cognitive Developmental Change: Theories, Models and Measurement*; Demetriou, A., Raftopoulos, A., Eds.; Cambridge University Press: New York, NY, USA, 2004; pp. 354–378.
5. Bates, E.; Johnson, M.H.; Karmiloff-Smith, A.; Parisi, D.; Plunkett, K. *Rethinking Innateness: A Connectionist Perspective on Development*; MIT Press: Cambridge, MA, USA, 1996.
6. Rinaldi, N.; Karmiloff, A. Intelligence as a developing function: A neuroconstructivist approach. *J. Intell.* **2017**, *5*, 18. [CrossRef]
7. Siegler, R.S. *Emerging Minds*; Oxford University Press: New York, NY, USA, 1996.
8. Lautrey, J.; de Ribaupierre, A.; Rieben, L. Intra-individual variability in the development of concrete operations: Relations between logical and infralogical operations. *Genet. Soc. Gen. Psychol. Monogr.* **1985**, *111*, 167–192.
9. Lautrey, J. Is there a general factor of cognitive development? In *The General Factor of Intelligence: How General Is It?* Sternberg, R.J., Grigorenko, E., Eds.; Lawrence Erlbaum: Hillsdale, NJ, USA, 2002; pp. 117–148.
10. Demetriou, A.; Spanoudis, G.; Kazi, S.; Mouyi, A.; Žebec, M.S.; Kazali, E.; Golino, H.; Bakracevic, K.; Shayer, M. Developmental differenciation and binding of mental processes with g through the life-span. *J. Intell.* **2017**, *5*, 23. [CrossRef]
11. Lautrey, J. Esquisse d'un modèle pluraliste du développement cognitif. In *Cognition: L'universel et L'individuel*; Reuchlin, M., Lautrey, J., Marendaz, C., Ohlmann, T., Eds.; Presses Universitaires de France: Paris, France, 1990; pp. 185–216.
12. Lautrey, J. Structure and variability: A plea for a pluralistic approach to cognitive development. In *The New Structuralism in Cognitive Development: Theory and Research in Cognitive Development*; Case, R., Edelstein, W., Eds.; Karger: Basel, Switzerland, 1993; pp. 101–114.
13. Lautrey, J. A pluralistic approach to cognitive differentiation and development. In *Models of Intelligence: International Perspectives*; Sternberg, R.J., Lautrey, J., Lubart, T., Eds.; American Psychology Press: Washington, DC, USA, 2003; pp. 117–131.

14. van der Maas, H.L.; Molenaar, P.C. Stagewise cognitive development: An application of catastroph theory. *Psychol. Rev.* **1992**, *99*, 395–417. [CrossRef] [PubMed]

15. Van der Maas, H.L.J.; Dolan, C.V.; Grasman, R.P.P.; Wicherts, J.M.; Huizenga, H.M.; Raijmakers, M.E.J. A dynamical model of general intelligence: The positive manifold of intelligence by mutualism. *Psychol. Rev.* **2006**, *113*, 842–861. [CrossRef] [PubMed]

16. Reuchlin, M. Processus vicariants et différences individuelles. *J. Psychol.* **1978**, n°2, 133–145.

17. Feigenson, L.; Dehaene, S.; Spelke, E. Core systems of number. *Trends Cogn. Sci.* **2004**, *8*, 307–314. [CrossRef] [PubMed]

18. Piazza, M. Neurocognitive start-up tools for symbolic number representations. *Trends Cogn. Sci.* **2010**, *14*, 542–551. [CrossRef] [PubMed]

19. Xu, F.; Spelke, E.S. Large number discrimination in 6-month old infants. *Cognition* **2000**, *74*, B1–B11. [CrossRef]

20. Halberda, J.; Mazzocco, M.M.M.; Feigenson, L. Individual differences in non-verbal acuity correlate with maths achievement. *Nature* **2008**, *455*, 665–668. [CrossRef] [PubMed]

21. Nieder, A. Coding for abstract quantity by number neurons of the primate brain. *J. Comp. Physiol. A* **2013**, *199*, 1–16. [CrossRef] [PubMed]

22. Libertus, M.E.; Brannon, E.M. Stable individual differences in number discrimination in infancy. *Dev. Sci.* **2010**, *13*, 900–906. [CrossRef] [PubMed]

23. Izard, V.; Dehaene-Lambertz, G.; Dehaene, S. Distinct cerebral pathways for object identity and number in human infants. *PLoS Biol.* **2008**, *6*, e11. [CrossRef] [PubMed]

24. Dehaene, S. *The Number Sense: How the Mind Creates Mathematics*; Oxford University Press: New York, NY, USA, 2011.

25. Le Corre, M.; Carey, S. One, two, three, four, nothing more: An investigation of the conceptual sources of the verbal counting principles. *Cognition* **2007**, *106*, 395–438. [CrossRef] [PubMed]

26. Wynn, K. Addition and subtraction by human infants. *Nature* **1992**, *358*, 749–750. [CrossRef] [PubMed]

27. Hyde, D.C.; Spelke, E. Neural signatures of number processing in human infants: Evidence for two core systems underlying numerical cognition. *Dev. Sci.* **2010**, *14*, 360–371. [CrossRef] [PubMed]

28. Hauser, M.D.; Carey, S. Spontaneous representation of small numbers of objects by rhesus macaques: Examination of content and format. *Cogn. Psychol.* **2003**, *47*, 367–401. [CrossRef]

29. Vogel, E.K.; Machizawa, M.G. Neural activity predicts individual differences in visual working memory capacity. *Nature* **2004**, *428*, 748–751. [CrossRef] [PubMed]

30. Spelke, E.; Kinzler, K. Core knowledge. *Dev. Sci.* **2007**, *10*, 89–96. [CrossRef] [PubMed]

31. Piaget, J. *The Development of Thought*; Basil Blackwell: Oxford, UK, 1978.

32. Piaget, J.; Szeminska, A. *La Genèse du Nombre Chez L'enfant*; Delachaux et Niestlé: Neuchâtel, Switzerland, 1941.

33. Izard, V.; Streri, A.; Spelke, E.S. Toward exact number: Young children use one-to-one correspondence to measure set identity but not numerical equality. *Cogn. Psychol.* **2014**, *72*, 27–53. [CrossRef] [PubMed]

34. Mix, K.S.; Moore, J.A.; Holcomb, E. One to one play promotes numerical equivalence concepts. *J. Cogn. Dev.* **2011**, *12*, 463–480. [CrossRef]

35. Bender, A.; Beller, J. Nature and culture of finger counting: Diversity and representational effects of an embodied cognitive tool. *Cognition* **2012**, *124*, 156–182. [CrossRef] [PubMed]

36. Brissiaud, R. A tool for number construction: Finger symbol sets. In *Pathways to Number: Children's Developing Numerical Abilities*; Bideaud, J., Meljac, C., Fischer, J.-P., Eds.; Lawrence Erlbaum: Hillsdale, NJ, USA, 1992; pp. 41–65.

37. Roesch, S.; Moeller, K. Considering digits in a current model of numerical development. *Front. Hum. Neurosci.* **2015**, *8*, 1062. [CrossRef] [PubMed]

38. Gunderson, E.A.; Spaepen, E.; Gibson, D.; Goldin-Meadow, S.; Levine, S. Gesture as a window onto children's number knowledge. *Cognition* **2015**, *144*, 14–28. [CrossRef] [PubMed]

39. Fuson, K.-C. *Children's Counting and Concepts of Number*; Springer: New York, NY, USA, 1988.

40. Piazza, M.; Fumarola, A.; Chinello, A.; Melcher, D. Subitizing reflects visuo-spatial object individuation capacity. *Cognition* **2011**, *121*, 147–153. [CrossRef] [PubMed]

41. Gréco, P. Quantité et quotité: Nouvelles recherches sur la correspondance terme à terme et la conservation des ensembles. In *Structures Numériques Elémentaires*; Gréco, P., Morf, A., Eds.; Presses Universitaires de France: Paris, France, 1962; pp. 1–70.

42. Gelman, R.; Gallistel, C.R. *The Child Understanding of Number*; Harvard University Press: Cambridge, MA, USA, 1978.
43. Wynn, K. Children's understanding of counting. *Cognition* **1990**, *36*, 155–193. [CrossRef]
44. Wynn, K. Children's acquisition of number words and the counting system. *Cogn. Psychol.* **1992**, *24*, 220–251. [CrossRef]
45. Lautrey, J. Approche pluraliste du développement: L'exemple de la construction du nombre. *Enfance* **2014**, 313–333. [CrossRef]
46. Mussolin, C.; Nys, J.; Leybaert, J.; Content, A. How approximate and exact number skills are related to each other across development: A review. *Dev. Rev.* **2016**, *39*, 1–15. [CrossRef]
47. Fazio, L.K.; Bailey, D.H.; Thompson, C.A.; Siegler, R.S. Relations of different types of numerical magnitude representations to each other and to mathematics achievement. *J. Exp. Child Psychol.* **2014**, *123*, 53–72. [CrossRef] [PubMed]
48. Chen, Q.; Li, J. Association between individual differences in non-symbolic number acuity and math performance: A meta-analysis. *Acta Psychol.* **2014**, *148*, 163–172. [CrossRef] [PubMed]
49. Chu, F.W.; van Marle, K.; Geary, D.C. Early numerical foundations of young children's mathematical development. *J. Exp. Child Psychol.* **2015**, *132*, 205–212. [CrossRef] [PubMed]
50. Hyde, D.C.; Khanum, S.; Spelke, E.S. Brief non-symbolic approximate number practice enhances subsequent exact symbolic arithmetic in children. *Cognition* **2014**, *131*, 92–107. [CrossRef] [PubMed]
51. Obersteiner, A.; Reiss, K.; Ufer, S. How training on exact or approximate mental representations of number can enhance first grade students basic number processing and arithmetic skills. *Learn. Instr.* **2013**, *23*, 125–135. [CrossRef]
52. Park, J.; Brannon, E.M. Training the approximate number system improves math proficiency. *Psychol. Sci.* **2013**, *24*, 2013–2019. [CrossRef] [PubMed]
53. Mussolin, C.; Nys, J.; Content, A.; Leybaert, J. Symbolic number abilities predict later approximate number acuity in preschool children. *PLoS ONE* **2014**, *9*, e91839. [CrossRef] [PubMed]
54. Opfer, J.; Siegler, R.S. Development of quantitative thinking. In *The Oxford Handbook of Thinking and Reasoning*; Holyoak, K.J., Morrison, R.G., Eds.; Oxford University Press: New York, NY, USA, 2012; pp. 585–605.
55. Piazza, M.; Pica, P.; Izard, V.; Spelke, E.; Dehaene, S. Education enhances the acuity of the nonverbal approximate number system. *Psychol. Sci.* **2013**, *24*, 1037–1043. [CrossRef] [PubMed]
56. Carey, S.; Shusterman, A.; Haward, P.; Distefano, R. Do analog number representations underlie the meanings of young children verbal numerals? *Cognition* **2017**, *468*, 243–255. [CrossRef] [PubMed]
57. Wagner, J.B.; Johnson, S.C. An association between understanding cardinality and analog magnitude representations in preschoolers. *Cognition* **2011**, *119*, 10–22. [CrossRef] [PubMed]
58. Odic, D.; Le Corre, M.; Halberda, J. Children's mappings between number words and the approximate number system. *Cognition* **2015**, *138*, 102–121. [CrossRef] [PubMed]
59. Gunderson, E.A.; Spaepen, E.; Levine, S.C. Approximate number word knowledge before the cardinal principle. *J. Exp. Child Psychol.* **2015**, *130*, 35–55. [CrossRef] [PubMed]
60. Ansari, D.; Donlan, C.; Thomas, M.S.C.; Ewing, S.A.; Peen, T.; Karmiloff-Smith, A. What makes counting count? Verbal and visuo-spatial contributions to typical and atypical number development. *J. Exp. Child Dev.* **2003**, *85*, 50–62. [CrossRef]
61. Van Herwegen, J.; Ansari, D.; Xu, F.; Karmiloff-Smith, A. Small and large number processing in infants and toddlers with Williams syndrome. *Dev. Sci.* **2008**, *11*, 637–643. [CrossRef] [PubMed]
62. Dehaene, S.; Bossini, S.; Giraux, P. The mental representation of parity and number magnitude. *J. Exp. Psychol. Gen.* **1993**, *122*, 371–396. [CrossRef]
63. Spaepen, E.; Coppola, M.; Spelke, E.S.; Carey, S.E.; Goldin-Meadow, S. Number without a language model. *Proc. Natl. Acad. Sci. USA* **2011**, *108*, 3163–3168. [CrossRef] [PubMed]
64. Siegler, R.S.; Jenkins, E. *How Children Discover New Strategies*; Erlbaum: Hillsdale, NJ, USA, 1989.
65. Mandler, J. How to build a baby: II. Conceptual primitives. *Psychol. Rev.* **1992**, *99*, 587–604. [CrossRef] [PubMed]
66. Gelman, S.; Meyer, M. Child categorization. *WIREs Cogn. Sci.* **2011**, *2*, 95–105. [CrossRef] [PubMed]
67. Molenaar, P.C.M. A manifesto on psychology as idiographic science: Bringing the person back into scientific psychology—This time forever. *Measurement* **2004**, *2*, 201–218. [CrossRef]

68. Dowker, A. Individual differences in numerical abilities in preschoolers. *Dev. Sci.* **2008**, *11*, 650–654. [CrossRef] [PubMed]
69. Kolkman, M.E.; Kroesbergen, E.H.; Leseman, P.P.M. Early numerical development and the role of non-symbolic and symbolic skills. *Learn. Instr.* **2013**, *25*, 95–103. [CrossRef]
70. Nesselroade, J.R.; Gerstorf, D.; Hardy, S.A.; Ram, N. Idiographic filters for psychological constructs. *Measurement* **2007**, *5*, 217–235.

Journal of
Intelligence

MDPI

Article

Variability in the Precision of Children's Spatial Working Memory

Elena M. Galeano Weber [1,2,*], Judith Dirk [1,2] and Florian Schmiedek [1,2]

1   German Institute for International Educational Research (DIPF), Frankfurt am Main,
    Frankfurt 60486, Germany; schmiedek@dipf.de (J.D.); dirk@dipf.de (F.S.)
2   Individual Development and Adaptive Education (IDeA) Center, Frankfurt 60486, Germany
*   Correspondence: elena.galeano-weber@dipf.de or galeanoweber@gmail.com; Tel.: +49-(0)69-24708-806

Received: 16 November 2017; Accepted: 9 February 2018; Published: 28 February 2018

Abstract: Cognitive modeling studies in adults have established that visual working memory (WM) capacity depends on the representational precision, as well as its variability from moment to moment. By contrast, visuospatial WM performance in children has been typically indexed by response accuracy—a binary measure that provides less information about precision with which items are stored. Here, we aimed at identifying whether and how children's WM performance depends on the spatial precision and its variability over time in real-world contexts. Using smartphones, 110 Grade 3 and Grade 4 students performed a spatial WM updating task three times a day in school and at home for four weeks. Measures of spatial precision (i.e., Euclidean distance between presented and reported location) were used for hierarchical modeling to estimate variability of spatial precision across different time scales. Results demonstrated considerable within-person variability in spatial precision across items within trials, from trial to trial and from occasion to occasion within days and from day to day. In particular, item-to-item variability was systematically increased with memory load and lowered with higher grade. Further, children with higher precision variability across items scored lower in measures of fluid intelligence. These findings emphasize the important role of transient changes in spatial precision for the development of WM.

Keywords: working memory updating; spatial precision; intra-individual variability; cognitive development; micro-longitudinal design; ambulatory assessment; hierarchical modeling

---

1. Introduction

Working memory (WM) refers to the temporal storage and manipulation of sensory information online [1]. It is considered to be a core cognitive process that is severely limited in capacity [2–5]. WM for visuospatial information supports mental arithmetic [6–8], spatial thinking [9,10] and fluid intelligence [11–13]. Such higher cognitive functions are implicated to be essential for learning and development [14] but the specific factors that contribute to visual WM limitations in children are still not clear. Here, we aimed at identifying a cognitive component, spatial precision, that contributes to developmental changes and limitations in children's visuospatial WM updating performance in natural everyday life contexts.

1.1. Models of Visual Working Memory Capacity

Visual WM capacity can be measured by varying the number of objects that have to be remembered [2,3]. Fixed capacity or 'slot' models of visual WM suggest a limit of three to four storage slots, one of each object held in WM [2]. It has been criticized that slot models do not account for the presence of internal noise in memory which increases with increasing load [3,4]. Thus, WM may not store a limited number of discrete representations but rather consists of a flexible resource:

the more of this resource is allocated to an item, the less noise is present in its representation and the more reliable is the recall of that item [4,15]. Responses during recall could be corrupted by many sources of noise including sensory, perceptual, mnemonic, and/or motor noise [3,4]. More recently, cognitive modeling studies in human adults have established that visual WM capacity is constrained by the precision with which items are stored [15,16]. In particular, visual WM capacity has been formalized through distinct components such as the probability to guess at random [2,16], the probability of misremembering features of non-target items or binding errors [17,18], the precision of memory representation and its decline with load [15,16,19] and the variability of precision [20,21], rather than through a fixed limit to the number of objects that can be stored [3]. Importantly, most recent versions of flexible resource models suggest that WM resource is not equally but variably distributed across items and trials. Thus, precision itself is allowed to vary over time, across objects and across conditions within individuals [20,21]. To test these assumptions, different models were compared and fit to errors in recall (i.e., the difference between the participant's estimate and the true stimulus value) [22] measured with delayed-estimation tasks [19]. Results showed that model variants with a combination of several components, including a variable precision parameter, were most successful and outperformed models that did not consider variability in precision [22].

1.2. Variability in Working Memory Performance

The comparison of visual WM models revealed that human adults show substantial variability in WM precision across trials within a testing session, which is implicated to strongly contribute to capacity limitations [20–22]. Based on findings that visual cues during stimulus encoding can increase WM precision, shifts of attention could constitute a possible source of variability in precision [23]. By contrary, precision variability could result from random fluctuations in attention, when multiple items have to be remembered [21]. Further, variability in WM performance has been linked to dopamine activity [24], whereby dopaminergic stimulation in the prefrontal cortex can modulate visuospatial WM [25,26]. In addition to such rapid trial-to-trial variability in WM separated by milliseconds or seconds [20–22,27], intra-individual WM variability has also been reported for slower time scales, such as across sessions within days or even from day to day [28–32]. In these studies, memory span, updating, or delayed spatial recognition tasks were repeatedly administered to younger and older adults embedded in intensive microlongitudinal designs [32]. In this way, it has been demonstrated that WM fluctuations from day to day are related to fluctuations in motivation [33], mood states [29] and affect [34]. Moreover, trial-to-trial variability in measures of reaction time was shown to follow a u-shaped function across the lifespan where children and older adults were more variable in their WM performance than younger adults [35]. When evaluating day-to-day variability and measures of WM accuracy, however, older adults showed lower variability compared to younger adults and thus more stable performance [31]. Together, these findings highlight the importance to consider different time scales and different cognitive measures when evaluating intra-individual variability in WM functioning [31].

1.3. Development of Children's Working Memory

Studies on children's WM variability are scarce [35–39]. Moreover, thus far, only a few studies have investigated the contribution of children's WM precision for age- and load-related performance changes [40–45]. For example, Burnett Heyes and colleagues (2012) observed developmental increases in visual WM precision (the reciprocal of the standard deviation of a continuous response distribution) in 7 to 13 years old boys [40]. In comparison, Sarigiannidis and colleagues (2016) found reduced guessing behavior (i.e., height parameter of a discrete probability distribution) in older (aged 10–12) compared to younger (aged 7–9) children, rather than improvements in precision [42]. In addition to these mixed results, so far, it is not clear how WM precision and in particular the moment-to-moment variability of this precision changes across development. In a recent study from our own lab, fluctuations in children's WM updating performance were assessed over a period of four weeks in the school context. Results revealed that WM accuracy systematically fluctuates across and within days and across moments. Here, children strongly differed in their amount of reliable variability in accuracy at these different time scales whereby third graders were more variable within days than fourth graders [37].

1.4. Research Questions and Approach

Taken together, the existing research emphasizes a critical role of distinct WM components for visual WM capacity limitations in adults and children (e.g., [22,37,40,42]). Beyond temporally holding sensory information in visual WM, spatial WM updating requires children to constantly update the locations of multiple items. A precise representation of each item's location may be beneficial to successfully solve the task. However, updating performance has been typically indexed by response accuracy–a binary measure that only provides information whether children have correctly recalled the item or not. In addition, while environmental contexts and life conditions doubtlessly affect cognitive development [46], limitations in children's WM precision have been typically studied in the laboratory. Thus, an ecologically valid assessment of children's WM precision and its variability over time is still missing but may reveal further insights into cognitive processes in everyday contexts. To investigate such processes, microgenetic approaches and intensive longitudinal designs allow the assessment of rapidly changing processes with high density of observations within a given period of time [47]. In this regard, intensive longitudinal designs in combination with ambulatory assessment has proven to be a fruitful approach to measure WM updating fluctuations at different time scales in children's daily lives [37,38]. By adopting cognitive tasks for mobile devices, dynamics of behavior and developmental processes can be examined in a reliable and feasible way [48]. Based on these considerations, here we aimed at further identifying and comparing distinct components that limit visuospatial WM updating in children's natural environment. Because WM has been demonstrated to be an important predictor of academic attainment (e.g., [14,37]) and variance in WM performance related to age and years of schooling is expected to overlap considerably in the present study, we focused on grade differences instead of age-related changes. In particular, we measured spatial precision and estimated variability in spatial precision at different time scales in Grade 3 and Grade 4 students who performed a sequential visuospatial updating task three times daily over a period of four weeks using smartphones.

By taking into account recent developmental findings on visual and spatial WM capacity [40–44], we assumed that spatial precision declines as load on WM updating increases (i.e., from a memory load of two to a load of three) and that spatial precision increases with level of education (Grade 3 vs. 4). Following recent findings of variability in updating accuracy [37] and cognitive modeling of precision in adults [20,21], we tested whether spatial precision of WM updating systematically varies within children by considering different time scales (i.e., items, trials, occasions and days), effects of load and level of education. Specifically, by considering recent theoretical considerations of variable precision models [20,21], we assumed that the amount of rapid fluctuations in spatial precision may increase with load due to an increased level of children's internal noise. Finally, we explored individual differences in fluid intelligence and its relation to different variance components of spatial precision.

2. Materials and Methods

The present study is based on data from the FLUX project ('Assessment of Cognitive Performance FLUctuations in the School ConteXt') of the Individual Development and Adaptive Education (IDeA) Center in Frankfurt, Germany. The project followed an intensive microlongitudinal design with four daily assessments over a period of four weeks (28 or 31 consecutive days including weekend days) embedded in a pre- and posttest protocol. Within this project, cognitive performance [37,38], motivation, affect [49], sleep [38,50] and physical activity [51], amongst other variables, were assessed on a daily basis via smartphones (Dell Streak 5, with Android 2.2 operation system). In this study, we considered daily measures from a visuospatial WM updating task and background measures from a pretest session such as demographic variables, fluid intelligence (i.e., *CFT 20-R*, [52]) and school achievement including a mathematics test (i.e., *DEMAT*, [53] and reading comprehension test (i.e., *ELFE*, [54]). Pretest assessment took place in the classroom in groups of up to 20 students and started one week before the longitudinal study phase (see [37], for a description of study protocol).

2.1. Participants

Participants were 110 third- and fourth-graders aged between 8 and 11 years (65 boys, $M = 9.88$ years, $SD = 0.61$, *range* = 8.1). Fifty children of the sample were enrolled in Grade 3 (26 boys, $M = 9.40$ years, $SD = 0.46$, *range* = 2.3) and 60 in Grade 4 (39 boys, $M = 10.27$ years, $SD = 0.39$, *range* = 1.6). Children's fluid intelligence was in an average range with $M = 106.9$ ($SD = 12.8$) and $M = 109.3$ ($SD = 17.3$) for Grade 3 and Grade 4 students, respectively. Grade 4 students significantly differed in fluid intelligence from Grade 3 students (*CFT 20-R* raw scores: Grade 4: $M = 33.59$ ($SD = 7.31$) > Grade 3: $M = 29.84$ ($SD = 5.37$), $t = 3.05$, $df = 103.12$, $p < 0.05$). They were recruited from seven classes in one public elementary school in an average urban neighborhood in Frankfurt am Main, Germany. Participation was voluntary and could be canceled anytime without giving reasons. The children received a gift certificate or money for participation. Informed consent was obtained in accordance with a protocol approved by the local ethics review board.

2.2. Procedure

Children completed a visuospatial WM updating task on three daily sessions over a period of four weeks. WM performance was tested in the morning during class (Occasion 1), at noon at the end of school (Occasion 2) and in the afternoon (Occasion 3). School sessions were scheduled to fixed times for all children, afternoon sessions could be scheduled individually within a time window of ± 2 h and sessions were available up to 60 min. Within each occasion, the spatial updating session followed a numerical updating session in which children had to remember and update numbers in WM (cf. [37]). The spatial WM updating task comprised eight trials per session. Each session started with four trials of memory Load 2 (=2 items), followed by four trials of memory Load 3 (=3 items). Children's responses were consecutively measured for each item held and updated in WM. In each trial, two or three responses could be obtained for a manipulation of memory Load 2 or 3, respectively. Thus, in one session (occasion), children were able to give 20 responses in total. In the course of study period, a maximum of 91 sessions (Grade 3) or 84 sessions (Grade 4) could be completed. Thus, in total, a maximum of 364/336 responses (Grade 3/Grade 4) to the first, second, or third item within trials could be collected for each child.

2.3. Spatial Working Memory Updating Task

Children had to memorize and update locations of differentially colored and shaped cartoon creatures (=items) presented in a 4 × 4 grid. During the encoding phase, two or three items were presented simultaneously at different locations in the grid for 3000 ms. After an inter-stimulus-interval (ISI) of 500 ms, three or four updating cues were presented for Load 2 and Load 3 conditions, respectively. Updating cues were shown in the center of the grid and were presented sequentially. Each cue was shown for 2500 ms with an ISI of 500 ms. Each item of the sample display was assigned to one respective cue. Cues were cartoon arrows that matched the item's colors where the respective item was placed at the center of an arrow. The direction of the arrow prompted children to mentally shift the spatial position of the respective item to the adjacent location in the grid (= updating operation). Directions of arrows were horizontal (left, right), vertical (upper, below), or diagonal. No item's position could be updated twice in a row. Intermediate and end positions were never doubly assigned. After updating, children had to retrieve updated positions for each item within a trial. They responded by consecutively touching the remembered item location. Target locations were indicated by the corresponding item and a question mark sign that were shown left to the grid. A feedback followed by showing color-coded crosses at correct locations after the final response was given (Figure 1) (cf. [37]; task was adopted from [55]).

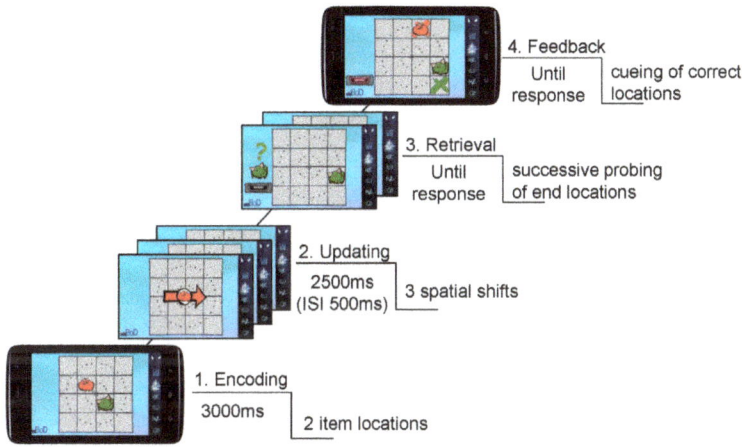

Figure 1. Visuospatial working memory updating task (example showing Load 2). Children had to encode, hold and update the locations of two or three items in visual WM. After updating operations (i.e., sequential mental shifts within a 4 × 4 spatial grid), children were prompted to retrieve the updated locations. Responses were consecutively given to each item by touching on the remembered location (cf. [37]).

2.4. Data Analysis

Behavioral data were analyzed using the *lme4* package [56] as well as core packages in R-statistics (https://www.r-project.org, R Core Team, 2016). Given the intensive longitudinal design, observations were inherently structured by repeated measures across items (Level 1) that were nested within trials (Level 2), measures across trials, in turn, were nested within occasions (Level 3) and assessment at occasions were nested within days (Level 4) (Figure 2a). Item responses were measured in terms of continuous spatial precision (i.e., Euclidean distance) in addition to discrete accuracy (i.e., correct vs. incorrect) (cf. Section 2.5). The hierarchical data structure allowed for decomposing the four different variance components of spatial precision for each individual (cf. Section 2.5).

With an intensive longitudinal study protocol, missing data were expected. Here, on average across load conditions and Grades, 67% of the maximum possible visual spatial WM updating data were available. Missing data resulted from, for example, illness, exams, technical problems such as empty batteries, or smartphones left at home. Based on available data, the average total number of responses from Grade 3 students was 232.98 (SD = 86.57) and 232.74 (SD = 86.58) for first and second items in Load 2 trials and 230.96 (SD = 87.97), 230.76 (SD = 87.94) and 230.58 (SD = 87.99) for first, second and third items of Load 3 trials, respectively. Grade 4 students responded on average 239.82 (SD = 67.18) and 239.72 (SD = 67.20) times to the first and second item in Load 2 trials and 238.75 (SD = 67.97), 238.63 (SD = 67.99) and 238.58 (SD = 67.98) to first, second and third items in Load 3 trials, respectively. Sufficient data for hierarchical modeling analysis and sufficiently reliable estimation of individual variance components were assumed for children with more than 20 days (cf. [37]). Thus, load effects on variability of spatial precision and individual differences in variance components were assessed based on data of 83 children for whom sufficient observations were available to estimate variance components at different timescales. All other analyses were based on data from the entire sample of 110 children.

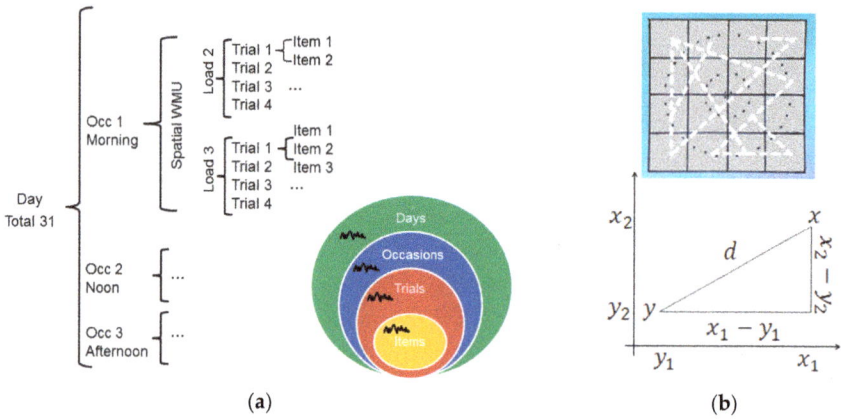

(a)   (b)

Figure 2. Hierarchical data structure and spatial precision: (**a**) Data were inherently structured by repeated measures at four different levels of time scale (i.e., Items, Trials, Occasions and Days) given the microlongitudinal study design; (**b**) Spatial precision was formalized in terms of the Euclidean Distance δ between presented (*y*) and reported location (*x*) within a 4 × 4 space grid (cf. upper panel). Dashed white lines represent possible distances in the space grid ranging from δ = 0 to a maximum of δ = 4.24.

2.5. Scoring Behavioral Performance

Spatial precision was formalized as Euclidean Distance between response location and original location for each item (cf. [57]). The Euclidean Distance is defined as the distance between two points in space that corresponds to the length of a straight line drawn between them, where the distance δ from *x* to *y* or *y* to *x* is given by the following Pythagorean formula:

$$\delta(x,y) = \sqrt{(x_1 - y_1)^2 + (x_2 - y_2)^2}, \tag{1}$$

Here, we assume that a higher δ may reflect more dissimilar representations between presented and reported item location, which may result from less spatially precise memory representations due to increased memory noise (e.g., [15]). The Euclidean metric works well for two-dimensional spaces and reflects a more sensitive measure of spatial recall precision as compared to the number of cells as a distance measure. For example, placing an item in a cell that touches the correct cell diagonally (δ = 1.41) is considered a somewhat larger error than placing it in a cell that touches the correct cell horizontally or vertically (δ = 1). The metric space of δ was a 4 × 4 cell grid where one cell reflects one of 16 different item locations. Specifically, we computed the square root of the sum of the squares of the difference between all corresponding values within a 4 × 4 matrix (e.g., *x*(1,2) and *y*(2,3)) by using the *dist* function in R. This resulted in nine distinct δ values ranging from δ = 0 to a maximum of δ = 4.24 and 120×(15×15 − 1)/2 possible pairs of presented and reported location (cf. Figure 2b).

For *response accuracy*, a given response was assigned a value of 1 for correct responses (when the correct location of the target item was chosen) and a value of 0 for erroneous responses (when any other location except the correct location was chosen).

For data analysis across trials (Level 2), spatial precision and accuracy scores were obtained by averaging across responses for each item within trials. For analysis at the occasion level (Level 3), the mean spatial precision and mean accuracy of all responses of the four trials per session and load condition was obtained. To test whether performance in mean spatial precision differs between morning, noon and afternoon sessions, we conducted paired t-tests between levels of *Occasion* (i.e., *morning, noon, afternoon*) separately for each load condition.

Variance components of spatial precision. Separately for each child and each load condition, a multilevel model was set up with the dependent variable being spatial precision, that is, the Euclidean Distance between presented and reported location for each item. The model's intercept parameter is composed of a fixed and random effects, the slope parameter has only a fixed effect. In particular, the model allowed for random intercepts of each time scale that were nested within each other. Running trial number was included as a continuous predictor and modeled as fixed effect to take into account individual longer-term trends. This general model resulted in four different variance components of spatial precision: A variance component of day-to-day variability across the n daily occasions (σ^2_{Days}), a component of occasion-to-occasion variability across the n trials within occasions divided by the number of occasions within days ($\sigma^2_{Occasion}$), trial-to-trial variance across the n item-responses within trials divided by the number of trials within days (σ^2_{Trial}) and the variance component of item-to-item variability, including also error variance, divided by the number of responses within days (σ^2_{Item}).

To test whether mean spatial precision and variability of spatial precision across different time scales change as a function of WM load (i.e., Load 3 vs. 2), we conducted paired t-tests separately for each performance component. Further, we assessed individual differences in children's estimated variance components of spatial precision at different time scales. We tested for differences in spatial precision performance between school classes using independent t-tests. Finally, we assessed the relationship between mean and variability of spatial precision and measures of fluid intelligence (i.e., *CFT 20-R* raw scores) and school achievement (i.e., *ELFE* and *DEMAT* raw scores) using correlation and hierarchical regression analyses. These analyses were based on subsamples of 82, 79, or 73 children (i.e., for *CFT, DEMAT, ELFE*, respectively) for whom scores and sufficient data for estimating variance components of spatial precision were available. Results were considered to be significant when $p < 0.05$ by applying a Bonferroni correction to take into account multiple comparisons.

3. Results

3.1. Relationship between Mean Spatial Precision and Mean Response Accuracy

For each trial, mean behavioral performance scores were computed by averaging across data from item-to-item responses. Note that mean response accuracy corresponds to the probability of remembering the correct target location, while mean spatial precision corresponds to participant's recall precision of spatial location in terms of the mean spatial distance δ between correct and reported location. A mean Euclidean distance δ of 0 corresponds to memory representations with perfect spatial precisions, while a mean δ of 4.24 reflects most imperfect or imprecise spatial representations within trial (which could result from a true location in one of the corners of the grid being remembered as the diagonally opposite corner). Trial-to-trial mean response accuracy ranged from 0 (i.e., incorrect remembered locations) to 1 (i.e., correct remembered locations). Figure 3 shows the relationship between these two parameters and indicates that trial-to-trial mean spatial precision δ varies widely when there was in fact no variation for mean response accuracy. For both grades of school, this variation in spatial precision was most pronounced for erroneous responses (i.e., mean response accuracy = 0) (Figure 3).

3.2. Daily Measures of Spatial Precision

To further assess the role of daily spatial precision in WM updating, we compared mean performance at different occasions, that is, average Euclidean distances δ in morning, noon and afternoon sessions within days in Grade 3 and Grade 4 students. Descriptive results demonstrated best performance in terms of lowest mean δ for Grade 4 students and Load 2 condition during morning sessions ($M = 0.30$, $SD = 0.23$), while lowest spatial precision was observed for Grade 3 students and Load 3 during noon ($M = 1.11$, $SD = 0.39$; cf. Table S1). Children showed highest mean spatial precision during sessions in the morning, while lowest performance was observed during noon sessions (Load 2/3: $t \leq -8.33$, $df = 109$, $p < 0.05$). Further, results demonstrated reduced spatial precision in noon compared to afternoon sessions (Load 2/3: $t \geq 4.29$, $df = 109$, $p < 0.05$) and higher spatial precision during morning than afternoon (Load 2/3: $t \leq -3.36$, $df = 109$, $p < 0.05$).

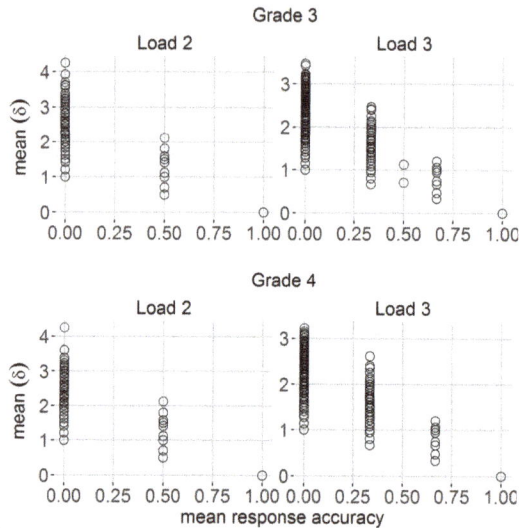

Figure 3. Trial-to-trial mean spatial precision (i.e., Euclidean distance δ) (y-axis) as a function of mean response accuracy (x-axis) for Grade 3 (first row) and Grade 4 students (second row) and separately for loads two and three.

3.3. Variability in Spatial Precision

For each child and load condition, we estimated variance components using hierarchical modeling to examine systematic within-person variability of spatial precision across different time scales. Figure 4a shows the children's average estimated variance components $\sigma^2(\delta)$ separately for school classes. The total size of each bar corresponds to the average amount of observed variability of spatial precision across days (i.e., the variance of mean spatial precision performance from day-to-day). This variability is decomposed into four variance components reflecting the contribution of item-to-item variability (yellow), trial-to-trial variability (red), occasion-to-occasion variability (blue) and true day-to-day variability (green) to observed day-to-day variability. Figure 4a shows that, on average across children, each variance component contributed to the observed total amount of variability across days within grades and load conditions (cf. Figure 4a). For each time scale and load condition, estimated spatial precision variance component was significantly different from zero within children from Grade 3 (Load 2, all: $t \geq 3.76$, $df = 33$, Load 3: $t \geq 4.02$, $df =$, $p < 0.05$) and Grade 4 (Load 2: $t \geq 3.41$, $df = 48$, Load 3: $t \geq 4.39$, $df = 48$, $p < 0.05$). Detailed summary statistics for each variance component can be found in Table S2 (see Online Supplement).

3.3.1. Effects of Working Memory Load on Mean and Variability of Spatial Precision

As expected, results showed a significant increase in mean Euclidean distance δ with increased load in Grade 3 students (Load 2: $M = 0.66$, $SD = 0.4$, Load 3: $M = 1.02$, $SD = 0.39$; $t = -17.31$, $df = 49$, $p < 0.05$) and Grade 4 students (Load 2: $M = 0.37$, $SD = 0.26$, Load 3: $M = 0.75$, $SD = 0.34$; $t = -14.66$, $df = 59$, $p < 0.05$), suggesting that children showed lower overall spatial precision as load on WM increased.

For the variability in spatial precision, the item-to-item variance component significantly increased with load in children from Grade 3 (Load 2: $M = 0.011$, $SD = 0.007$, Load 3: $M = 0.014$, $SD = 0.005$; $t = -5.95$, $df = 33$, $p < 0.05$) as well as in children from Grade 4 (Load 2: $M = 0.005$, $SD = 0.004$,

Load 3: $M = 0.012$, $SD = 0.004$; $t = -12.27$, $df = 48$, $p < 0.05$) (cf. Figure 4a, yellow bars). No differences between load conditions were found for spatial precision variability from trial-to-trial (Grade 3: $t = 1.58$, $df = 33$, $p = 0.12$; Grade 4: $t = -0.01$, $df = 48$, $p \geq 0.99$), occasion-to-occasion (Grade 3: $t = 2.16$, $df = 33$, $p \geq 0.04$; Grade 4: $t = 1.45$, $df = 48$, $p \geq 0.15$), or for true day-to-day variation in spatial precision (Grade 3: $t = 1.49$, $df = 33$, $p \geq 0.15$; Grade 4: $t = -0.33$, $df = 48$, $p \geq 0.74$) (see also Table S2, Online Supplement). These effects cannot be attributed to different trends of learning between the two load conditions, as we took into account individual longer-term trends separately for each child and load condition (cf. *Materials and Methods*, subsection *Variance components of spatial precision*). Thus, load-related differences in children's updating performance can only be observed for the fast item-to-item changes in spatial precision performance within trials but not for the slower variations across trials, occasions, or days.

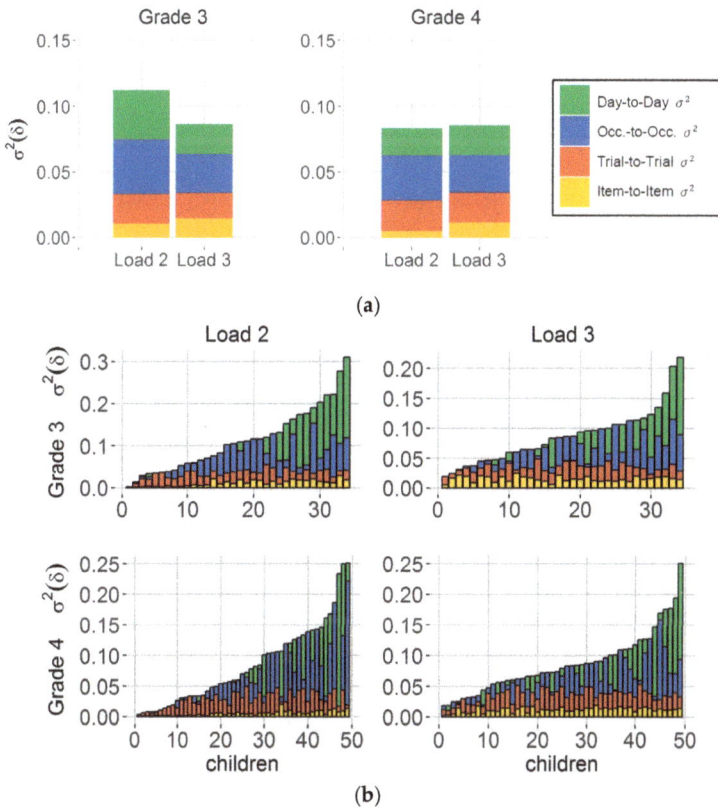

Figure 4. Variance components of spatial precision. (**a**) The size of each bar reflects the total amount of children's averaged observed day-to-day variability separately for Grade 3 and Grade 4 students and load conditions (i.e., Load 2 and 3). This variability is decomposed into four different variance components that were estimated for each individual in each load condition. Variance components reflect variability of spatial precision from item-to-item (yellow), trial-to-trial (red), across occasions (Occ.; blue) and true day-to-day variability (green); (**b**) Each bar corresponds to children's estimated item-to-item, trial-to-trial, occasion-to-occasion and day-to-day variance component of observed variability across days. Bars are ordered by their total size (i.e., variance of average performance across days) from very low (left) to very high (right) variability. $N = 34$ (Grade 3), $n = 49$ (Grade 4).

3.3.2. Individual Differences in Mean and Variability of Spatial Precision

Further, we examined whether Grade 3 students differ from Grade 4 students in their amounts of estimated variance components of spatial precision and to what degree individual spatial precision variability differs between time scales within each grade. Figure 4b summarizes individual differences in estimated variance components of spatial precision. Here, each bar refers to one child and the total size of the bars corresponds to the variance of average performance across days (i.e., observed day-to-day variability) for each child. Bars on the right at each panel correspond to the children who showed highest observed day-to-day variability of spatial precision. Descriptive results indicate that children considerably differ in their individual amount of estimated variance components at different time scales. For example, there are children who varied in spatial precision across all considered time scales where variation was most pronounced from day-to-day in these children. In contrast, there are also children who showed almost no variation across days but substantial variability in spatial precision across items, trials and/or occasions (cf. Figure 4b). In comparison to Grade 3, Grade 4 students showed significantly less item-to-item variability of spatial precision for memory Load 2 ($t = 4.02$, $df = 48.6$, $p < 0.05$) and Load 3 condition ($t = 2.90$, $df = 67.3$, $p < 0.05$). No differences between grades were found for trial-to-trial (Load 2/3: $p \geq 0.07$), occasion-to-occasion (Load 2/3: $p \geq 0.39$), or day-to-day variability (Load 2/3: $p \geq 0.16$). For the overall mean spatial precision, we observed improved performance (i.e., lower mean δ) in Grade 4 students compared to Grade 3 students for Load 2 (Grade 3: $M = 0.66$, $SD = 0.4$, Grade 4: $M = 0.37$, $SD = 0.26$; $t = 4.44$, $df = 79.57$, $p < 0.05$) and Load 3 (Grade 3: $M = 1.02$, $SD = 0.39$, Grade 4: $M = 0.75$, $SD = 0.34$; $t = 3.89$, $df = 97.94$, $p < 0.05$).

3.3.3. Relationship between Spatial Precision Components, Fluid Intelligence and School Achievement

Firstly, we assessed the relationship between fluid intelligence (i.e., *CFT-20-R* raw scores) and spatial precision components. For mean spatial precision, results demonstrated that children who had on average more spatially precise representations (i.e., lower mean δ) scored also higher in fluid intelligence (Load 2: $r = -0.47$, $p < 0.05$, Load 3: $r = -0.51$, $p < 0.05$). For the variance components of spatial precision, the item-to-item variability component was significantly related to fluid intelligence scores for both Load 2 ($r = -0.47$, $p < 0.05$) and Load 3 conditions ($r = -0.44$, $p < 0.05$) (cf. Figure 5, first row). No significant associations were observed for the trial-to-trial (Load 2: $r = 0.004$, $p = 0.97$; Load 3: $r = 0.19$, $p = 0.09$) and occasion-to-occasion variance component (Load 2: $r = -0.2$, $p = 0.08$; Load 3: $r = 0.09$, $p = 0.47$). The day-to-day variance component showed a significant relationship for Load 2 ($r = -0.37$, $p < 0.05$) but no significant association for Load 3 ($r = -0.03$, $p = 0.78$). Thus, children's fluid intelligence was significantly linked to both mean and variability of spatial precision. Notably, among variance components, variability from item to item showed most consistent associations with fluid intelligence, where lower variability under both loads was linked to higher fluid IQ.

Secondly, to examine convergent, divergent and predictive validity of item-to-item variability, we conducted additional correlation and hierarchical regression analyses. Results revealed a significant positive correlation between the item-to-item variability assessed on Load 2 and Load 3 conditions ($r = 0.76$, $p < 0.05$), which denotes high convergent validity of this construct. In addition, higher item-to-item variability was significantly linked to lower mean spatial precision (i.e., higher mean δ) (Load 2: $r = 0.96$, Load 3: $r = 0.95$, both $p < 0.05$) and to lower mean accuracy (Load 2: $r = -0.95$, Load 3: $r = -0.94$, both $p < 0.05$), which suggests low divergent validity between mean performance and item variability. To inspect the predictive validity of item-to-item variability of spatial precision compared to mean spatial precision on fluid intelligence, we compared three models including mean precision (Model 1), item-to-item variability (Model 2), or both mean and variability of spatial precision (Model 3) as predictor variables. We found a significant prediction of fluid intelligence by mean spatial precision (Load 2: $R^2 = 0.22$, Load 3: $R^2 = 0.26$, both $p < 0.05$) and item-to-item variability (Load 2: $R^2 = 0.22$, Load 3: $R^2 = 0.19$, both $p < 0.05$). Importantly, results demonstrated highest multiple R^2 for Model 3 including both mean and variability of spatial precision (i.e., Load 2: $R^2 = 0.23$, Load 3: $R^2 = 0.28$, both $p < 0.05$), whereby Model 3 showed a significantly higher R^2 than Model 2 for the Load 3 condition (Load 3: $F = 9.41$, $p < 0.05$). No such effect was observed for the Load 2 condition (Load 2: $F = 0.74$, $p = 0.39$), or when comparing Model 3 with Model 1 (Load 2: $F = 0.23$, $p = 0.63$; Load 3: $F = 2.24$, $p = 0.14$) (see also Figure S3 in the Supplement for a correlation matrix between mean and variability components and fluid intelligence).

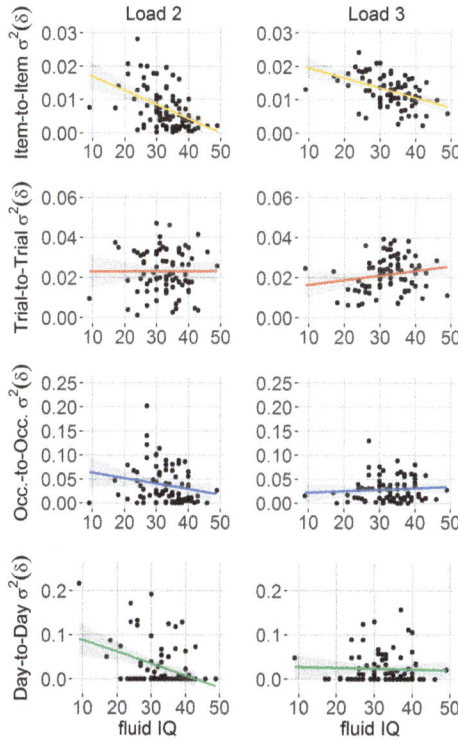

Figure 5. Relationship between fluid intelligence and variability of spatial precision. Children ($n = 82$) with higher scores of fluid intelligence measures (i.e., CFT 20-R raw scores) (x-axis) showed lower item-to-item variability of spatial precision (cf. first row, Load 2/3: $p < 0.05$). No such relationship was found for variability of spatial precision across trials (second row), occasions (third row), or days (fourth row).

Thirdly, we explored associations between children's mean and item-to-item variability of spatial precision and measures of school achievement. Correlation analysis revealed that children with lower precision variability scored higher in a test of mathematical skills (Load 2: $r = -0.30$, Load 3: $r = -0.35$, both $p < 0.05$) and in a test of reading comprehension (Load 2: $r = -0.54$, Load 3: $r = -0.51$, both $p < 0.05$). Also, mean spatial precision was significantly correlated with both academic abilities, whereby higher precision (i.e., lower mean δ) was associated with better math (Load 2: $r = -0.32$, Load 3: $r = -0.36$, both $p < 0.05$) and better reading skills (Load 2: $r = -0.53$, Load 3: $r = -0.53$, both $p < 0.05$). Results of hierarchical regression analyses revealed significant prediction of children's math skills by mean spatial precision (Model 1: Load 2: $R^2 = 0.10$, $p < 0.05$; Load 3: $R^2 = 0.13$, $p < 0.05$) as well as item-to-item variability (Model 2: Load 2: $R^2 = 0.09$, $p < 0.05$; Load 3: $R^2 = 0.12$, $p < 0.05$). Model 3 with both mean and variability of spatial precision as predictor variables showed a significant effect for Load 3 ($R^2 = 0.13$, $p < 0.05$) but not for Load 2 ($R^2 = 0.10$, $p = 0.01$). We observed no significant difference in R^2 between Model 3 and Model 2 (Load 2: $F = 1.39$, $p = 0.24$, Load 3: $F = 0.70$, $p = 0.40$), or Model 3 and Model 1 (Load 2: $F = 0.13$, $p = 0.72$; Load 3: $F = 0.05$, $p = 0.82$). Also, children's reading skills could be significantly predicted by mean spatial precision (Model 1: Load 2: $R^2 = 0.28$, $p < 0.05$; Load 3: $R^2 = 0.28$, $p < 0.05$) and item-to-item variability (Model 2: Load 2: $R^2 = 0.29$, $p < 0.05$; Load 3: $R^2 = 0.26$, $p < 0.05$). Model 3 with both mean and variability of spatial precision showed significant effects too (Load 2: $R^2 = 0.29$, $p < 0.05$; Load 3: $R^2 = 0.28$, $p < 0.05$). Model 3 did not differ from Model 2 (Load 2: $F = 0.11$, $p = 0.75$, Load 3: $F = 1.91$, $p = 0.17$) or from Model 1 (Load 2: $F = 1.36$, $p = 0.25$; Load 3: $F = 0.03$, $p = 0.86$).

In sum, these results suggest that variability of spatial precision is related to fluid intelligence as well as school achievement in children. In particular, children with more stable spatial precision representations from item-to-item within trials showed higher fluid intelligence and school achievement scores than children with less stable representations. The mean spatial precision component also showed a strong link to the measure of fluid intelligence and scholastic abilities. Further, the item-to-item variability construct showed high convergent validity and low divergent validity as compared to children's mean spatial precision. For the high load condition, we observed that item-to-item variability together with mean spatial precision showed higher predictive validity for fluid intelligence than item-to-item variability alone. Thus, there is currently no indication that the item-to-item variability component is better than mean spatial precision at predicting fluid intelligence or school achievement. Note, however, that high correlations between mean spatial precision and item-to-item variability in spatial precision implicate high communality between these two variables. High communality could indicate similar or the same processes that underlie children's mean and item-to-item variability of spatial working memory updating.

4. Discussion

By using cognitive ambulatory assessment, this study provides novel evidence that the spatial precision with which items are stored characterizes children's WM performance in real-world and real-time contexts. Hierarchical modeling revealed substantial within-person changes in spatial precision at different time scales. Importantly, higher memory load increased the amount of item-to-item variability in children's spatial precision but not any other variability component. Further, lower item-to-item variability of spatial precision was related to higher levels of education, higher fluid intelligence and higher school achievement. In sum, precise and transiently stable representations of spatial locations from moment to moment are associated with improved WM performance and thereby emphasize the importance to understand distinct components in contributing to WM updating development.

4.1. Spatial Precision as Continuous Quantitative Measure of Children's Updating Performance

To better understand how children mentally present and update visuospatial information in working memory, we measured spatial precision in terms of the spatial distance between presented and reported item location during a sequential spatial WM updating task. Children showed substantial differences from trial to trial in how far in space their estimate differed from the true item location. Importantly, this was most pronounced when within trial average performance of response accuracy was low. These findings are in line with previous studies on the precision of visual WM representations in adults (e.g., [15,16]) and children [40–44] and support flexible resource accounts of visual WM capacity (e.g., [4,15]). In contrast to fixed capacity or 'slot' models [2,5,58], resource models account for the presence of internal noise in memory, which has been suggested to increase as a function of set size (i.e., the number of to-be-remembered items) (e.g., [4,15,19]). Here, WM capacity has been described as a continuous resource that can be flexibly distributed across all items in the visual scene. The more resource an item receives, the less noise is present in its representation and the more precise is the recall of that item [4,15]. Based on these assumptions, cognitive modeling studies in adults observed a critical trade-off between the number of stored items and the precision of WM representation, that is, precision declined as load on WM increased [15,16,20–22]. These findings are consistent with our observation that mean spatial precision substantially decreased from memory loads two to three and thereby limited children's performance. Note that cognitive modeling studies on visual WM precision are typically based on a continuous recall paradigm which allows to measure behavioral performance (i.e., error) that is distributed along a continuous feature dimension (e.g., orientation, color) [19]. Our results are attributable to a spatial WM updating task which typically relies on a binary measure of each response, that is, correct vs. incorrect recall of item location. This task is well-established in the visual WM updating literature [37,55,59,60] but studies using fidelity measures of children's updating performance are still missing. Inspired from studies on visual WM capacity and the continuous recall paradigm, we could show that incorrect responses during WM updating do not necessarily mean that children had no memory representation of the target locations at all. Therefore, we suggest that continuous measures of spatial precision provide additional insights in children's response behavior during WM updating in addition to binary measures of response accuracy.

4.2. Systematic Variability in Children's Spatial Precision

More recently proposed resource models of visual WM suggest that mental resource is variably but not equally distributed across items. Therefore, mnemonic precision is itself variable over time within individuals and task conditions [20,21]. Factorial model comparison revealed that this within-person variability of precision accounts for a significant proportion of errors in recall whereby variable precision models outperformed models that did not consider variability in precision [22]. Following these assumptions, we examined whether children's spatial precision during WM updating varies over time and whether this variability depends on memory demands. Results of hierarchical modeling revealed substantial variability of spatial precision at different time scales including variation within and across days, while in particular item-to-item variability showed systematic increases from memory loads two to three. These results support the conception that specifically variability across items plays a role for variable memory precision within individuals [20,21]. Further, our findings are consistent with recent modeling results of visual WM performance impairments under high load due to increased variability of precision [20,22,61].

A growing body of evidence including our study found increased variability in cognitive performance with higher task demand or cognitive load [37,62–65]. The majority of these findings are based on developmental or lifespan research on variability of trial-to-trial reaction time (RT) measures. Here, we combined intensive longitudinal assessment of cognitive performance and hierarchical modeling which allowed us to directly test which time scales are most important for performance limitations. We identified that it is indeed the fast item-to-item variability which was increased with higher memory load and thereby affects performance limitations. Variability from item to item has been recently reported by measuring memory performance for all items in each trial of a continuous recall task and thereby claiming that guesses, not low-precision representations, determines visual WM limitations [66]. Here, we do not want to exclude the possibility that some portion of the incorrect responses were merely random guesses with a uniform distribution across all fields of the grid. However, the goal of the present study was to identify how variability in children's item-responses changes at different time scales, rather than to separate guessing from precision (for which a higher number of observations within a broader feature space would be necessary). Beyond this 'slot' vs. resource debate on WM capacity (for reviews see [3,67]), neurocognitive studies have proposed different potential mechanisms that may underlie variability in cognitive performance [23,24,61,68,69]. Possible sources of variability in spatial precision may result from internal process-related fluctuations (e.g., sleep quality based on circadian functions, cf. [38]) but also external factors such as environmental noise (cf. [68]). Variability in dopaminergic activity in prefrontal cortex was found to modulate visuospatial WM performance [24–26] and thus, may reflect a potential neural source underlying variability in spatial precision. The high correlation between mean performance and variability in performance suggests that similar or even the same processes may underlie the two components, while it will become necessary to use further experimental manipulations and/or neuroimaging methods to convincingly identify this proposed communality of underlying processes. Based on previous findings on visual WM precision, we speculate that attentional mechanisms constitute an important source underlying item-to-item variability of spatial precision [15,21,23,69]. One possibility is that such variation may result from random fluctuations in attention and that these fluctuations increase when multiple locations have to be processed, that is encoded, stored and updated and finally recalled. Another potential mechanism may be less controlled shifts in attention when demands on WM are high, while more controlled allocation of selective attention may stabilize WM performance and thereby improve spatial precision [15,23].

4.3. Individual Differences and Developmental Changes in Variability of Spatial Precision

Combining the concepts of short-term within-person variability such as performance variations across and within days and theories of long-term change during development has been proven to be a worthwhile concept of understanding individual dynamics in cognitive functions [31,70]. Following these calls, we attempted to measure short-term within-person variability in WM performance over a period of four weeks in third as well as fourth graders. Further, we measured children's performance with smartphones in typical settings, such as in school and after school to increase ecological validity [32,71]. We observed that third graders with mean age of approximately nine years showed higher item-to-item variability of spatial precision of WM performance compared to the around ten-year-old fourth graders. These results fall in line with previous developmental research on within-person variability of RT measures (i.e., SD of RTs) and variability in accuracy at faster time scales, which together found a reduction in performance variability with increasing age during childhood [37,65,72]. Moreover, not only younger but also older populations [72–74] and patients with attention-deficit hyperactivity disorder (ADHD) showed increased trial-to-trial RT variability [75,76], which has been suggested to reflect reduced resolution of information processing systems [73,74]. Our findings refine these results and point to the importance of transient within-person changes in spatial WM precision for long-term changes during development of educational competencies.

In addition to reduced item-to-item variability, we observed that Grade 4 students were on average more precise in spatial recall than Grade 3 students. This finding fits well to the results of recent developmental studies on age-related changes in visual WM capacity using the continuous recall paradigm [40–43]. These studies found reduced errors in recall over middle childhood development, while they came up with mixed conclusions whether this performance improvement is due to increases in WM precision [40,41] or reduced guessing behavior [42]. Developmental improvements in WM resolution have been observed already in younger children (i.e., between four and six years old) in experimental manipulations of the precision of colors within a color discrimination paradigm [44]. These as well as our findings support assumptions of the dynamic field theory which predicts that neuronal interactions in visuospatial WM become more spatially precise over development, resulting in more stable behavior (i.e., spatial precision hypothesis; [44,77]).

The observed grade differences in spatial precision performance may be associated with differences between children in their fluid intelligence and their school achievement [37]. More mature self-regulatory processes with increased age and level of education may also explain grade differences [37,78]. Further, we observed strong associations between mean and variability of spatial precision and fluid intelligence as well as school achievement. In particular, children with higher mean spatial precision and lower item-to-item variability showed higher fluid intelligence and higher math and reading abilities. These findings support and extend previous results on WM in predicting higher-level abilities such as learning and intelligence [11–14].

4.4. Future Perspectives and Limitations

The present study extends existing research in important ways by showing that children's spatial WM is not stable over time but substantially varies across days, occasions, trials and items. Specifically, the item-to-item variability systematically changes with memory load and level of education, thereby reflecting a new index of performance limitations in children's everyday life. It is however important to note that, in contrast to previous research on the variability of WM precision [20,21], we worked with a spatial WM updating task that is inherently different and more complex than the continuous recall paradigm [19]. To mentally shift multiple locations held in WM may reflect different cognitive functions than to briefly store visual features in WM, thus a direct comparison to previous cognitive modeling research using the variable precision model is restricted. To further test the assumptions of the variable precision model in children and their natural contexts, future studies could combine a continuous recall paradigm and ambulatory assessment which would allow to estimate and to compare variability at different time scales. In addition, it is important to note that with the current design we cannot distinguish whether the observed grade- (and age-)related differences in WM performance are due to effects of schooling, maturity, and/or other time-related variables. To fully understand the development of distinct components of WM capacity and to which extent WM improvements are driven by education versus maturation, further research is needed. As a future perspective, longitudinal methods and a broader age range could help to clearly separate the variance of WM components that is linked to these variables.

Moreover, whereas limits in attention reflect reasonable mechanisms of item-to-item variability in spatial precision (e.g., [21,23]), we cannot test these assumptions within the current study. Further work should focus on disentangling the mechanisms underlying variability of spatial precision and thereby limitations in children's updating performance. Variability in spatial precision from item to item may result from early perceptual and attentional limitations during encoding but could also stem from constraints in memorizing, mentally shifting, and/or retrieving information in WM. Thus, future studies should examine the specific WM sub-processes and how their interaction affects variability in spatial precision. For example, to better understand updating-related processes, one could measure children's estimates of remembered locations after each updating step by estimating spatial precision and its variability across updates. Further, technical advances in combining ambulatory assessment and neurocognitive methods such as mobile electroencephalography (EEG) (e.g., [79]) may reflect a fruitful approach to relate neural correlates of WM sub-processes to children's behavioral performance in real-life contexts.

In addition to variability from item to item, spatial precision showed substantial fluctuations also at slower time scales such as days and occasions within days. These fluctuations were independent of memory load and school grade, suggesting a less detrimental effect of these more enduring within-person changes for performance limitations. However, children considerably differed in their amount of day-to-day or occasion-to-occasion variability and also in whether they showed an increase, decrease or no change in these variabilities with load. To better understand these individual differences, the relationships of spatial precision variability at slower time scales with other daily varying constructs may shed light on some influential factors [37], such as sleep [38] or physical activity [51].

The combination of ambulatory assessment and hierarchical modeling allowed us to provide improved knowledge about short-term changes in children's behavior in everyday life settings. This may be specifically important for developmental and lifespan research, as cognitive development is a dynamic process which is not constrained to laboratory settings [32,71]. Following these calls, we were able to assess children's WM performance at different time scales with high density of observations in their natural contexts. Aside from these important aspects of ambulatory assessment, there are methodological constraints, for example regarding the compliance with and reactivity to study procedures during data collection [71]. Thus, an important future perspective is the improvement of such aspects, for example, by implementing reward systems within intensive longitudinal designs to enhance children's study motivation.

Supplementary Materials: The following are available online at http://www.mdpi.com/2079-3200/6/1/8/s1, Table S1: Summary statistics of daily measures of spatial precision in updating, Table S2: Descriptive statistics of spatial precision variance components at different time scales.

Acknowledgments: This research was funded by the German Institute for International Educational Research (DIPF), Frankfurt, Germany. We owe special thanks to Verena Diel, Philipp Wiesemann and a team of highly committed student assistants for their important roles in conducting this study.

Author Contributions: The reported study was part of the FLUX Project, which was designed by Florian Schmiedek and Judith Dirk. Elena M. Galeano Weber was responsible for the development of research questions and conducted the data analyses for this article. Elena M. Galeano Weber drafted the manuscript. All authors provided critical revisions and approved the final version of the manuscript.

Conflicts of Interest: The authors declare no conflict of interest.

References

1. Baddeley, A.D.; Hitch, G. Working memory. *Psychol. Learn. Motiv.* **1974**, *8*, 47–89.
2. Cowan, N. The magical number 4 in short-term memory: A reconsideration of mental storage capacity. *Behav. Brain Sci.* **2001**, *24*, 87–185. [CrossRef] [PubMed]
3. Ma, W.J.; Husain, M.; Bays, P.M. Changing concepts of working memory. *Nat. Neurosci.* **2014**, *17*, 347–356. [CrossRef] [PubMed]
4. Palmer, J. Attentional limits on the perception and memory of visual information. *J. Exp. Psychol. Hum. Percept. Perform.* **1990**, *16*, 332–350. [CrossRef] [PubMed]
5. Pashler, H. Familiarity and visual change detection. *Percept. Psychophys.* **1988**, *44*, 369–378. [CrossRef] [PubMed]
6. Alloway, T.P.; Passolunghi, M.C. The relationship between working memory, IQ and mathematical skills in children. *Learn. Individ. Differ.* **2011**, *21*, 133–137. [CrossRef]
7. Logie, R.H.; Gilhooly, K.J.; Wynn, V. Counting on working memory in arithmetic problem solving. *Mem. Cognit.* **1994**, *22*, 395–410. [CrossRef] [PubMed]
8. Swanson, H.L.; Beebe-Frankenberger, M. The relationship between working memory and mathematical problem solving in children at risk and not at risk for serious math difficulties. *J. Educ. Psychol.* **2004**, *96*, 471–491. [CrossRef]
9. Miyake, A.; Shah, P. *Models of Working Memory: Mechanisms of Active Maintenance and Executive Control*; Cambridge University Press: Cambridge, UK, 1999; ISBN 9780521587211.
10. Shah, P.; Miyake, A. The separability of working memory resources for spatial thinking and language processing: An individual differences approach. *J. Exp. Psychol. Gen.* **1996**, *125*, 4–27. [CrossRef] [PubMed]
11. Fukuda, K.; Vogel, E.; Mayr, U.; Awh, E. Quantity, not quality: The relationship between fluid intelligence and working memory capacity. *Psychon. Bull. Rev.* **2010**, *17*, 673–679. [CrossRef] [PubMed]
12. Giofrè, D.; Mammarella, I.C.; Cornoldi, C. The structure of working memory and how it relates to intelligence in children. *Intelligence* **2013**, *41*, 396–406. [CrossRef]
13. Swanson, H.L. Intellectual growth in children as a function of domain specific and domain general working memory subgroups. *Intelligence* **2011**, *39*, 481–492. [CrossRef]
14. Alloway, T.P.; Alloway, R.G. Investigating the predictive roles of working memory and IQ in academic attainment. *J. Exp. Child Psychol.* **2010**, *106*, 20–29. [CrossRef] [PubMed]
15. Bays, P.M.; Husain, M. Dynamic shifts of limited working memory resources in human vision. *Science* **2008**, *321*, 851–854. [CrossRef] [PubMed]
16. Zhang, W.; Luck, S.J. Discrete fixed-resolution representations in visual working memory. *Nature* **2008**, *453*, 233–235. [CrossRef] [PubMed]
17. Bays, P.M.; Catalao, R.F.; Husain, M. The precision of visual working memory is set by allocation of a shared resource. *J. Vis.* **2009**, *9*, 7. [CrossRef] [PubMed]
18. Oberauer, K. Binding and inhibition in working memory: Individual and age differences in short-term recognition. *J. Exp. Psychol. Gen.* **2005**, *134*, 368–387. [CrossRef] [PubMed]
19. Wilken, P.; Ma, W.J. A detection theory account of change detection. *J. Vis.* **2004**, *4*, 11. [CrossRef] [PubMed]
20. Fougnie, D.; Suchow, J.W.; Alvarez, G.A. Variability in the quality of visual working memory. *Nat. Commun.* **2012**, *3*, 1229. [CrossRef] [PubMed]
21. Van den Berg, R.; Shin, H.; Chou, W.C.; George, R.; Ma, W.J. Variability in encoding precision accounts for visual short-term memory limitations. *Proc. Natl. Acad. Sci. USA* **2012**, *109*, 8780–8785. [CrossRef] [PubMed]
22. Van den Berg, R.; Awh, E.; Ma, W.J. Factorial comparison of working memory models. *Psychol. Rev.* **2014**, *121*, 124–149. [CrossRef] [PubMed]

23. Lara, A.H.; Wallis, J.D. Capacity and precision in an animal model of visual short-term memory. *J. Vis.* **2012**, *12*, 13. [CrossRef] [PubMed]

24. Li, S.C.; Lindenberger, U.; Sikström, S. Aging cognition: From neuromodulation to representation. *Trends Cogn. Sci.* **2001**, *5*, 479–486. [CrossRef]

25. Cools, R.; D'Esposito, M. Inverted-U—Shaped dopamine actions on human working memory and cognitive control. *Biol. Psychiatry* **2011**, *69*, e113–e125. [CrossRef] [PubMed]

26. Müller, U.; Yves von Cramon, D.; Pollmann, S. D1-versus D2-receptor modulation of visuospatial working memory in humans. *J. Neurosci.* **1998**, *18*, 2720–2728. [PubMed]

27. Lecerf, T.; Ghisletta, P.; Jouffray, C. Intraindividual variability and level of performance in four visuo-spatial working memory tasks. *Swiss J. Psychol.* **2004**, *63*, 261–272. [CrossRef]

28. Li, S.C.; Aggen, S.H.; Nesselroade, J.R.; Baltes, P.B. Short-term fluctuations in elderly people's sensorimotor functioning predict text and spatial memory performance: The MacArthur Successful Aging Studies. *Gerontology* **2001**, *47*, 100–116. [CrossRef] [PubMed]

29. Riediger, M.; Wrzus, C.; Schmiedek, F.; Wagner, G.G.; Lindenberger, U. Is seeking bad mood cognitively demanding? Contra-hedonic orientation and working-memory capacity in everyday life. *Emotion* **2011**, *11*, 656–665. [CrossRef] [PubMed]

30. Schmiedek, F.; Lövdén, M.; Lindenberger, U. On the relation of mean reaction time and intraindividual reaction time variability. *Psychol. Aging* **2009**, *24*, 841–857. [CrossRef] [PubMed]

31. Schmiedek, F.; Lövdén, M.; Lindenberger, U. Keeping It Steady Older Adults Perform More Consistently on Cognitive Tasks Than Younger Adults. *Psychol. Sci.* **2013**, *24*, 1747–1754. [CrossRef] [PubMed]

32. Sliwinski, M.J.; Smyth, J.M.; Hofer, S.M.; Stawski, R.S. Intraindividual coupling of daily stress and cognition. *Psychol. Aging* **2006**, *21*, 545–557. [CrossRef] [PubMed]

33. Brose, A.; Schmiedek, F.; Lövdén, M.; Molenaar, P.C.; Lindenberger, U. Adult age differences in covariation of motivation and working memory performance: Contrasting between-person and within-person findings. *Res. Hum. Dev.* **2010**, *7*, 61–78. [CrossRef]

34. Brose, A.; Lövdén, M.; Schmiedek, F. Daily fluctuations in positive affect positively co-vary with working memory performance. *Emotion* **2014**, *14*, 1–6. [CrossRef] [PubMed]

35. Mella, N.; Fagot, D.; De Ribaupierre, A. Dispersion in cognitive functioning: Age differences over the lifespan. *J. Clin. Exp. Neuropsychol.* **2016**, *38*, 111–126. [CrossRef] [PubMed]

36. Astle, D.E.; Luckhoo, H.; Woolrich, M.; Kuo, B.C.; Nobre, A.C.; Scerif, G. The neural dynamics of fronto-parietal networks in childhood revealed using magnetoencephalography. *Cereb. Cortex* **2015**, *25*, 3868–3876. [CrossRef] [PubMed]

37. Dirk, J.; Schmiedek, F. Fluctuations in elementary school children's working memory performance in the school context. *J. Educ. Psychol.* **2016**, *108*, 722–739. [CrossRef]

38. Könen, T.; Dirk, J.; Schmiedek, F. Cognitive benefits of last night's sleep: Daily variations in children's sleep behavior are related to working memory fluctuations. *J. Child Psychol. Psychiatry* **2015**, *56*, 171–182. [CrossRef] [PubMed]

39. Mella, N.; Fagot, D.; Lecerf, T.; De Ribaupierre, A. Working memory and intraindividual variability in processing speed: A lifespan developmental and individual-differences study. *Mem. Cognit.* **2015**, *43*, 340–356. [CrossRef] [PubMed]

40. Burnett Heyes, S.; Zokaei, N.; van der Staaij, I.; Bays, P.M.; Husain, M. Development of visual working memory precision in childhood. *Dev. Sci.* **2012**, *15*, 528–539. [CrossRef] [PubMed]

41. Burnett Heyes, S.; Zokaei, N.; Husain, M. Longitudinal development of visual working memory precision in childhood and early adolescence. *Cogn. Dev.* **2016**, *39*, 36–44. [CrossRef] [PubMed]

42. Sarigiannidis, I.; Crickmore, G.; Astle, D.E. Developmental and individual differences in the precision of visuospatial memory. *Cogn. Dev.* **2016**, *39*, 1–12. [CrossRef] [PubMed]

43. Simmering, V.R.; Miller, H.E. Developmental improvements in the resolution and capacity of visual working memory share a common source. *Atten. Percept. Psychophys.* **2016**, *78*, 1538–1555. [CrossRef] [PubMed]

44. Simmering, V.R.; Patterson, R. Models provide specificity: Testing a proposed mechanism of visual working memory capacity development. *Cogn. Dev.* **2012**, *27*, 419–439. [CrossRef] [PubMed]

45. Zokaei, N.; Burnett Heyes, S.; Gorgoraptis, N.; Budhdeo, S.; Husain, M. Working memory recall precision is a more sensitive index than span. *J. Neuropsychol.* **2015**, *9*, 319–329. [CrossRef] [PubMed]

46. Baltes, P.B. Theoretical propositions of life-span developmental psychology: On the dynamics between growth and decline. *Dev. Psychol.* **1987**, *23*, 611–626. [CrossRef]

47. Siegler, R.S. Microgenetic analyses of learning. In *Handbook of Child Psychology*, 6th ed.; Kuhn, D., Siegler, R.S., Eds.; Wiley: Hoboken, NJ, USA, 2006.

48. Sliwinski, M.J.; Mogle, J.A.; Hyun, J.; Munoz, E.; Smyth, J.M.; Lipton, R.B. Reliability and validity of ambulatory cognitive assessments. *Assessment* **2018**, *25*, 14–30. [CrossRef] [PubMed]

49. Leonhardt, A.; Könen, T.; Dirk, J.; Schmiedek, F. How differentiated do children experience affect? An investigation of the within-and between-person structure of children's affect. *Psychol. Assess.* **2016**, *28*, 575–585. [CrossRef] [PubMed]

50. Könen, T.; Dirk, J.; Leonhardt, A.; Schmiedek, F. The interplay between sleep behavior and affect in elementary school children's daily life. *J. Exp. Child Psychol.* **2016**, *150*, 1–15. [CrossRef] [PubMed]

51. Kühnhausen, J.; Leonhardt, A.; Dirk, J.; Schmiedek, F. Physical activity and affect in elementary school children's daily lives. *Front. Psychol.* **2013**, *4*. [CrossRef] [PubMed]

52. Jacobs, C.; Petermann, F.; Weiß, R. Grundintelligenztest (CFT 20-R)[German Culture Fair Intelligence Test]. *Diagnostica* **2007**, *53*, 109–113. [CrossRef]

53. Gölitz, D.; Roick, T.; Hasselhorn, M. *Deutscher Mathematiktest für Vierte Klassen (DEMAT 4) [German Mathematics Test for Fourth Grades (DEMAT 4)]*; Beltz: Göttingen, Germany, 2006.

54. Lenhard, W.; Schneider, W. *ELFE 1–6: Ein Leseverständnistest für Erst- bis Sechstklässer [A Reading Comprehension Test for First to Sixth Graders]*; Hogrefe: Göttingen, Germany, 2006.

55. Göthe, K.; Esser, G.; Gendt, A.; Kliegl, R. Working memory in children: Tracing age differences and special educational needs to parameters of a formal model. *Dev. Psychol.* **2012**, *48*, 459–476. [CrossRef] [PubMed]

56. Bates, D.; Maechler, M.; Bolker, B. Linear mixed-effects models using S4 classes. R package version 0999375-42. In *R: A Language and Environment for Statistical Computing*; The R Foundation for Statistical: Vienna, Austria, 2011.

57. Noack, H.; Lövdén, M.; Schmiedek, F.; Lindenberger, U. Age-related differences in temporal and spatial dimensions of episodic memory performance before and after hundred days of practice. *Psychol. Aging* **2013**, *28*, 467–480. [CrossRef] [PubMed]

58. Luck, S.J.; Vogel, E.K. The capacity of visual working memory for features and conjunctions. *Nature* **1997**, *390*, 279–281. [CrossRef] [PubMed]

59. Oberauer, K.; Kliegl, R. A formal model of capacity limits in working memory. *J. Mem. Lang.* **2006**, *55*, 601–626. [CrossRef]

60. Salthouse, T.A.; Babcock, R.L.; Shaw, R.J. Effects of adult age on structural and operational capacities in working memory. *Psychol. Aging* **1991**, *6*, 118–127. [CrossRef] [PubMed]

61. Galeano Weber, E.M.; Peters, B.; Hahn, T.; Bledowski, C.; Fiebach, C.J. Superior intraparietal sulcus controls the variability of visual working memory precision. *J. Neurosci.* **2016**, *36*, 5623–5635. [CrossRef] [PubMed]

62. Bunce, D.; MacDonald, S.W.; Hultsch, D.F. Inconsistency in serial choice decision and motor reaction times dissociate in younger and older adults. *Brain Cogn.* **2004**, *56*, 320–327. [CrossRef] [PubMed]

63. Dixon, R.A.; Garrett, D.D.; Lentz, T.L.; MacDonald, S.W.S.; Strauss, E.; Hultsch, D.F. Neurocognitive markers of cognitive impairment: Exploring the roles of speed and inconsistency. *Neuropsychology* **2007**, *21*, 381–399. [CrossRef] [PubMed]

64. Fozard, J.L.; Vercruyssen, M.; Reynolds, S.L.; Hancock, P.A.; Quilter, R.E. Age differences and changes in reaction time: The Baltimore Longitudinal Study of Aging. *J. Gerontol. B Psychol. Sci. Soc. Sci.* **1994**, *49*, 179–189. [CrossRef]

65. MacDonald, S.W.; Nyberg, L.; Bäckman, L. Intra-individual variability in behavior: Links to brain structure, neurotransmission and neuronal activity. *Trends Neurosci.* **2006**, *29*, 474–480. [CrossRef] [PubMed]

66. Adam, K.C.; Vogel, E.K.; Awh, E. Clear evidence for item limits in visual working memory. *Cogn. Psychol.* **2017**, *97*, 79–97. [CrossRef] [PubMed]

67. Luck, S.J.; Vogel, E.K. Visual working memory capacity: From psychophysics and neurobiology to individual differences. *Trends Cogn. Sci.* **2013**, *17*, 391–400. [CrossRef] [PubMed]

68. Dirk, J.; Schmiedek, F. Variability in children's working memory is coupled with perceived disturbance: An ambulatory assessment study in the school and out-of-school context. *Res. Hum. Dev.* **2017**, *14*, 200–218. [CrossRef]

69. Goris, R.L.; Movshon, J.A.; Simoncelli, E.P. Partitioning neuronal variability. *Nat. Neurosci.* **2014**, *17*, 858–865. [CrossRef] [PubMed]

70. Nesselroade, J.R.; Salthouse, T.A. Methodological and theoretical implications of intraindividual variability in perceptual-motor performance. *J. Gerontol. B Psychol. Sci. Soc. Sci.* **2004**, *59*, 49–55. [CrossRef]

71. Ram, N.; Brinberg, M.; Pincus, A.L.; Conroy, D.E. The questionable ecological validity of ecological momentary assessment: Considerations for design and analysis. *Res. Hum. Dev.* **2017**, *14*, 253–270. [CrossRef]

72. Williams, B.R.; Hultsch, D.F.; Strauss, E.H.; Hunter, M.A.; Tannock, R. Inconsistency in reaction time across the life span. *Neuropsychology* **2005**, *19*, 88–96. [CrossRef] [PubMed]

73. Hultsch, D.F.; MacDonald, S.W.; Dixon, R.A. Variability in reaction time performance of younger and older adults. *J. Gerontol. B Psychol. Sci. Soc. Sci.* **2002**, *57*, 101–115. [CrossRef]

74. Lövdén, M.; Li, S.C.; Shing, Y.L.; Lindenberger, U. Within-person trial-to-trial variability precedes and predicts cognitive decline in old and very old age: Longitudinal data from the Berlin Aging Study. *Neuropsychologia* **2007**, *45*, 2827–2838. [CrossRef] [PubMed]

75. Bellgrove, M.A.; Hawi, Z.; Kirley, A.; Gill, M.; Robertson, I.H. Dissecting the attention deficit hyperactivity disorder (ADHD) phenotype: Sustained attention, response variability and spatial attentional asymmetries in relation to dopamine transporter (DAT1) genotype. *Neuropsychologia* **2005**, *43*, 1847–1857. [CrossRef] [PubMed]

76. Kuntsi, J.; Oosterlaan, J.; Stevenson, J. Psychological mechanisms in hyperactivity: I response inhibition deficit, working memory impairment, delay aversion, or something else? *J. Child Psychol. Psychiatry* **2001**, *42*, 199–210. [CrossRef] [PubMed]

77. Schutte, A.R.; Spencer, J.P.; Schöner, G. Testing the dynamic field theory: Working memory for locations becomes more spatially precise over development. *Child Dev.* **2003**, *74*, 1393–1417. [CrossRef] [PubMed]

78. Barrett, L.F.; Tugade, M.M.; Engle, R.W. Individual differences in working memory capacity and dual-process theories of the mind. *Psychol. Bull.* **2004**, *130*, 553–573. [CrossRef] [PubMed]

79. Debener, S.; Emkes, R.; De Vos, M.; Bleichner, M. Unobtrusive ambulatory EEG using a smartphone and flexible printed electrodes around the ear. *Sci. Rep.* **2015**, *5*. [CrossRef] [PubMed]

Journal of
Intelligence

MDPI

Brief Report

Children's Allocation of Study Time during the Solution of Raven's Progressive Matrices

Patrick Perret * and Bruno Dauvier

Aix Marseille Univ, PSYCLE, Aix-en-Provence, France; bruno.dauvier@univ-amu.fr
* Correspondence: patrick.perret@univ-amu.fr

Received: 14 November 2017; Accepted: 8 February 2018; Published: 28 February 2018

Abstract: The acuity of reasoning on Raven's Progressive Matrices is strongly influenced by strategic determinants. Building on metamemory studies that highlight the influence of study-time allocation on memory development, we investigated children's allocation of study time while solving these matrices. A total of 170 children aged 6–12 years completed a computerized short-form version of the standard matrices featuring items selected to represent a broad range of difficulties. Beyond analyzing changes in mean latencies and performances with age, we used generalized additive mixed models to explore within-participant variability in response times as a function of both item complexity and overall individual efficiency. Results revealed that individual differences in performances were significantly associated with children's adaptive modulation of response times. Mediation analysis further indicated that response-time modulation contributed to age-related changes in performance. Taking account of study-time allocation in reasoning tasks may open up new avenues for the study of reasoning development and the assessment of intellectual functioning.

Keywords: reasoning; allocation of study time; cognitive development; Raven's Progressive Matrices

---

1. Introduction

Raven's Progressive Matrices (RPM) are considered to be one of the best measures of reasoning, as attested by the ongoing presence of matrix completion tasks in most cognitive assessment batteries and by their lasting use in most research on fluid intelligence (Gf). Identifying the variables that contribute to individual differences and age-related changes in RPM performance thus offers the opportunity to broaden our understanding of reasoning development. The current study explores the hypothesis that children's ability to adaptively modulate their study times as a function of matrix complexity constitutes a driving force for RPM performance. Our review of the literature will bring together arguments in favor of this hypothesis. Next we will present the results of an experiment in which response time's variability was analyzed in order to reveal the adaptive modulation of study time and its relationship with age and performance. We then discuss the implications of these results with regard to theories of reasoning development and reasoning assessment practices.

When confronted with RPM items, participants have to find the missing element that completes a series of perceptually or analogically organized abstract patterns. To do so, participants have to engage in the inductive abstraction of the rules governing the organization of the successive designs. Both the nature and number of these rules contribute to the relative difficulty of the items [1].

The available age norms for the test clearly show that children's reasoning abilities increase with age, but surprisingly few studies have directly addressed the question of what develops in children's processing of matrices. Carpenter, Just and Shell [2]'s seminal study shed light on two main cognitive processes required by RPM solution: The ability to induce abstract relations and the ability to maintain and articulate sub-results. Indeed, one of the main sources of variation in RPM difficulty is the number of rules that have to be combined in order to grasp the overall structure of an item.

Therefore, the solution of RPM draws heavily on working memory attentional resources and a body of empirical results supported the view that working memory development extends the scope and complexity of the items that children can solve [3,4].

Another line of hypotheses focuses on the role of processing strategies. Snow [5] identified two contrasting strategies: a constructive matching strategy that consists in mentally preparing an ideal response and then comparing it with the options that are actually available, and an elimination strategy that consists in comparing the features of the matrix elements with those of the possible responses, arriving at a default response through a process of elimination. Analyzing response times, coupled with eye movements, Vigneau, Caissie, and Bors [6] were able to confirm that individual variations in RPM efficiency are closely linked to these strategic factors, as participants with the best performances spent proportionately more time studying the matrix than they did analyzing the response options. Mitchum and Kelley [7]'s experiments also indicated that relying on a constructive matching strategy improves monitoring accuracy, with the presence of the anticipated answer among the response options providing a cue for confidence judgments. Furthermore, the processing strategies used by participants not only affect their performance, but also the validity of the test itself. When the cognitive components involved in the processing of the items differ from one strategy to another, reasoning resources are differentially engaged. For example, Arendasy and Sommer [8] showed that when participants rely on a response elimination strategy, the test's Gf loading is reduced. Chen, Honomichl, Kennedy, and Tan [9]'s cross-sectional and microgenetic study indicated that children's thinking becomes increasingly relational with age and experience. However, it also suggested that many children tend to underperform, insofar as minor changes in the administration procedure (e.g., verbal feedback) can help them implement more efficient strategies. This led the authors to suggest intensifying research efforts in that direction. Identifying which mechanisms facilitate the efficient processing of analogical matrices can inform the design of dynamic assessment procedures that are better able to reveal children's core reasoning abilities [10].

The strategic dimension, therefore, seems to determine how efficiently individuals cope with the cognitive demands of RPM. However, the available literature is narrowly focused on Snow [5]'s initial distinction between constructive and elimination strategies. The present study examined another strategic dimension that might contribute to both developmental change and individual differences in performance, namely the adaptive modulation of study time. Research on human memory has consistently shown that adults regulate the study time they allocate to material as a function of both (objective) item difficulty and (subjective) judgments of learning [11]. In the absence of time pressure, items that are more difficult to memorize tend to induce longer study times, and this modulation has been found to enhance learning [12]. In the wake of Flavell's pioneering work [13], these metacognitive processes have also been investigated from a developmental perspective. In a study by Destan, Hembacher, Ghetti, and Roebers [14], children as young as 5 years exhibited an emergent ability to differentiate between easy and difficult items, as both their judgments of learning (before the test) and their confidence judgments (after the test) varied according to the items' complexity. However, the translation of judgments of learning into the strategic differential allocation of study times was only observed for 6- and 7-year-olds. Dufresne and Kobasigawa [15], as well as Lockl and Schneider [16], have also found similar developmental trends toward a more adaptive allocation of study time with age. In order to translate this into performances, metacognitive judgments have to be converted into effective strategic adaptations. Schneider and Pressley [17] referred to this hypothetical difficulty as an implementation deficit. Such a discrepancy between young children's emergent abilities and their limited spontaneous use of strategies has previously been observed in other research areas, and was referred to as production deficiencies [18].

Ackerman and Thompson [19] recently proposed that these metacognitive regulatory processes, identified in research on memory, might have analogical counterparts in reasoning. As we have seen, intermediate judgments of learning help people monitor the time they allocate to memorizing material. The discrepancy reduction model [20] predicts that people will devote extra study time when they perceive the need to reduce a discrepancy between learning goals and actual judgments of learning. Ackerman and Thompson [19] suggested that, when confronted with reasoning tasks, people use similar subjective estimates of understanding to regulate the time they devote to processing information, and continue to invest efforts until a threshold of confidence is reached. Transposed to the RPM context, a first hypothesis could be that responding more slowly should promote success, as longer explorations allow for more advanced information processing. However, Vigneau, Caissie, and Bors [6]'s analyses of response times revealed a more complex pattern of data. First, speed and eye-tracking strategic indicators made distinct and complementary contributions to predicting performance. Second, the mean item latency was not related to performance. Third, only response times on easy items significantly contributed to the prediction of RPM scores. Taken together, these results led the authors to the following conclusion: "At one level, spending more time encoding critical features is an appropriate approach to solving Raven items; at another level, not spending too much time on (easy) items is a feature of efficient performance" (p. 271). More recently, Goldhammer, Naumann, and Greiff [21] examined this issue further and also found that response time effects were moderated by item difficulty. One interpretation of this result is that it is only worth devoting extra time to the processing of matrices when the item requires deeper examination, owing to the complexity of its underlying rules, and that high RPM performances are achieved through the modulation of study times according to item difficulty. In the cognitive development literature, at least one experiment suggests that children and adults may differ in the extent to which they strategically allocate different study times to different items. In a functional MRI study comparing children's and adults' functioning on RPM, Crone, Wendelken, van Leijenhorst, Honomichl, Christoff, and Bunge [22] incidentally observed that whereas children exhibited longer response times than adults for simple problems, this was not the case for complex ones, suggesting that children failed to allocate sufficient time to solving harder items.

Against this background, the present study was designed to provide us with a finer-grained analysis of children's study-time variability on RPM. More specifically, we hypothesized that an adaptive modulation of study time according to matrix complexity could contribute to individual and developmental differences in performance.

2. Method

Participants were 170 children (93 girls) aged 6–12 years (*M* = 9.25 years, *SD* = 1.14). They were drawn from two elementary schools located in southeastern France. Most participants were Caucasian and came from middle- to upper-class backgrounds, although data on ethnicity and socioeconomic status were not collected. Written consent to take part in this study was given by their parents, the school's principal, and the regional supervisory school authority.

The children had to solve a computerized short-form version of the standard matrices (SRPM). We selected 24 items (6 per series B to E) to represent the various rule types and degrees of difficulty of the SRPM. The task was administered on a laptop computer (15' screen with 1024 × 768 resolution) and the experiment was run using E-Prime 2 software (PST Inc., Sharpsburg, PA, USA).

Participants were tested individually in a quiet room provided by their school, with the experimenter seated slightly to the side of the child. Before completing the 24 test items, children were given a standard set of instructions and completed five (unselected) matrices of the SRPM as practice items. In each matrix, the bottom right-hand figure was missing, and the children were instructed to use the computer mouse to select the piece that best completed the pattern from among the response options. Accuracy and response time (RT) were registered for each item.

3. Results

We began by investigating the correlations between children's age, SRPM performances, and response times (RTs). The latter, initially expressed in milliseconds, showed a highly skewed distribution (skewness = 5.06). RTs were then log transformed, and the new variable (Log.RT) showed close to normal distribution (skewness = 0.4). The log transformation is known as an efficient way to deal with reaction times asymmetrical distributions [23] and was preferred to the inverse transformation because it does not reverse the scale, which makes it easier to read the graphs. Descriptive statistics in Table 1 shows that SRPM performances increased as a function of age, with comparable levels of between-subject variability from grade 2 to 5. The correlational analysis includes the individual mean overall Log.RT, as well as individual mean Log.RTs for easy items, intermediate items, and difficult items. Items were ranked according to the item difficulty parameter, which was one minus the success rate for the whole dataset. A modulation index was also computed as the within-participant correlation between the individual RT by item and item difficulty. A participant with short RTs for easy items and longer RTs for difficult items was thus characterized by a high positive correlation reflecting high modulation. Conversely, the absence of modulation led to an index close to zero. This individual modulation index was then correlated with the children's age and total score on the short-form SRPM, as shown in Table 2.

Table 1. Descriptive statistics mean (standard deviation) of age, short-form version of the standard matrices (SRPM) performances, response times (RTs) by grade group.

Grades	2	3	4	5
N	46	38	43	43
Age	95.3 (5.04)	105.6 (3.7)	117.3 (4.38)	129.3 (4.09)
SRPM perf.	0.49 (0.17)	0.6 (0.13)	0.63 (0.13)	0.7 (0.1)
Log.RT	9.76 (0.88)	9.71 (0.84)	9.83 (0.93)	9.58 (0.86)

Table 2. Descriptive statistics and correlations between age, SRPM performances, RTs and the modulation index.

	Mean (SD)	Modul.	Perf.	Log.RT	Log.RT-e	Log.RT-i	Log.RT-d
Age (months)	111.8 (13.71)	0.31 **	0.45 **	−0.07	−0.22 **	−0.14	0.12
Modulation	0.52 (0.24)	—	0.63 **	0.15 *	−0.27 **	−0.03	0.56 **
SRPM perf.	0.6 (0.15)	0.63 **	—	0.24 **	−0.1	0.07	0.53 **

Note: SRPM perf.: individual success rate; Log.RT-e (-i, -d): individual mean Log.RT for easy (-e), intermediate (-i), or difficult (-d) items. * $p < 0.05$. ** $p < 0.01$.

As expected, age and SRPM performance were correlated ($r = 0.45$, $p < 0.01$), and no correlation was found between age and overall Log.RT ($r = 0.07$, *ns*). There was a significant negative correlation between age and Log.RT for the set of easy items ($r = -0.22$, $p < 0.01$), meaning that older children spent slightly less time on these items. However, Log.RTs were positively correlated with performance, meaning that the more efficient children spent more time inspecting the items, especially the more difficult ones ($r = 0.53$, $p < 0.01$). The modulation index was positively correlated with age ($r = 0.31$, $p < 0.01$) and strongly correlated with performance ($r = 0.63$, $p < 0.01$). Children who achieved the best performances on the SRPM were also those who showed the clearest RT modulation as a function of item difficulty. Moreover, we conducted a mediation analysis to test the hypothesis that RT modulation mediated the relation between age and performance (Figure 1). The indirect effect was 0.18 (Sobel test: $z = 4$, $p < 0.01$), supporting the idea that the age-related improvement in RPM performances may be partially attributable to the development of modulation abilities.

One limitation of our modulation index is that it could only capture linear relations between item difficulty and RT at the individual level, whereas nonlinear changes could be expected if a child gave up trying to do the more difficult items. An inverted U-shaped relation would then be observed, with the child spending more time inspecting intermediate items than either easier or harder ones. To investigate the potentially nonlinear relationship between RT and item difficulty as a function of individual efficiency, we fitted a generalized additive mixed model (GAMM) to the data, using the mgcv [24] library in R [25] [1], with Log.RT as response variable, item difficulty, individual performance and the interaction between the two as explanatory variables, and an individual random intercept. GAMM models automatically identify significant nonlinear multivariate relations between variables, adopting a cross-validation approach to select the most suitable empirical degree of freedom of a nonlinear function of the predictors [27]. Random effects are also allowed within a multilevel framework [28].

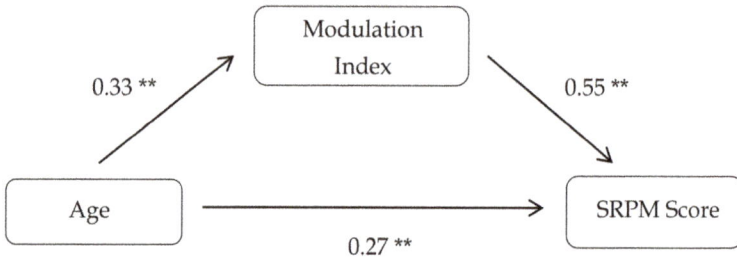

Figure 1. Mediation analysis of the relation between age and SRPM scores mediated by the modulation index. ** *p* < 0.01.

The model showed that the relationship between item difficulty and Log.RT was nonlinear and moderated by individual performance (interaction *edf* = 12.5, *p* < 0.01, R^2 = 0.3). A graphical representation of this interaction, based on the model's predictions for a set of representative levels of individual mean efficiency (success rate: 0.4–0.8), is provided in Figure 2. On the whole, Log.RT increased as a function of item difficulty. For the most complex items, the most efficient children spent around 11 log units (i.e., approximatively 1 min) inspecting each item, while the least efficient children spent fewer than 9.8 log units (i.e., 20 s) on each one. The increase was nearly linear for children with an SRPM success rate of around 0.8 (i.e., most efficient children), but nonlinear for children with a success rate of around 0.4. It seems that for the less efficient children in our sample, RTs increased between the easy and intermediate items, but then stayed the same for the most difficult items.

Further investigations were carried out using a relative item difficulty index that took the children's age into account. RT modulation is supposed to be an individual mechanism that is applied as a function of item difficulty relative to the child's own aptitude. Spending more time on a relatively difficult item than on a relatively easy item is supposed to reflect adaptive modulation, whereas spending the same amount of time on all the items corresponds to lack of modulation. Our hypothesis was that less efficient children of a given age would exhibit poorer RT regulation skills. We therefore modeled RTs in terms of (a) item difficulty relative to age, and (b) child's aptitude compared with other children of the same age. Whereas in Figure 2 developmental and individual differences were mixed, this complementary analysis aimed at controlling for the effect of age and focusing more precisely on individual differences.

---

[1] The mgcv library in R was used to fit the binomial GAMM model with the tensor (te) function to test for nonlinear interactions.

The model formula, expressed in Wilkinson and Rogers 's notation [26], was LogIT~te (ItemDifficulty, IndividualPerformance) + (1 | Subject).

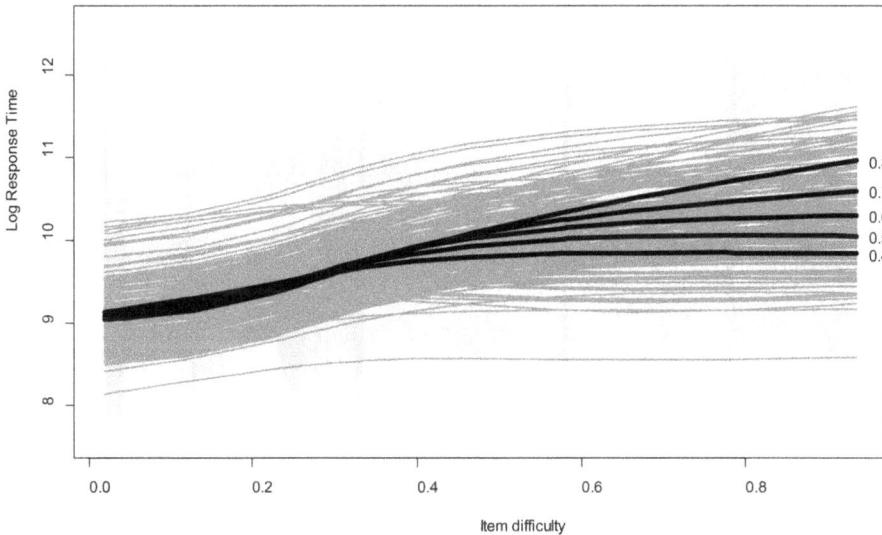

Figure 2. Log.RTs by item difficulty and children's performance, with predicted values illustrating the generalized additive mixed model (GAMM) results. Light-gray dotted lines: observed values; gray lines: individual fitted values; bold black lines: predicted values for a representative subset of individuals with success rate between 0.4 and 0.8.

First, a Rasch model [2] was fitted to the accuracy data to obtain estimates of item difficulty and individual ability parameters on the latent continuum. This approach allowed item difficulty relative to the child's ability to be directly estimated by subtracting the two parameters, as they were expressed on the same scale. A simple linear model was used to determine the ability level expected for each age, which then allowed us to compute the difficulty of each item relative to age. This relative item difficulty index therefore reflected how difficult an item was supposed to be at a given age, such that the higher the value, the more difficult the item. We also computed a relative child ability index reflecting the difference between a child's expected ability given his/her age and his/her actual ability. Positive values therefore corresponded to children who performed better than expected for their age, and negative values to children who did not. A GAMM model was then fitted with Log.RT as the response variable, the relative item difficulty index, relative individual ability index and the interaction between the two as explanatory variables, and random effects allowing for a two-degree individual nonlinear trend [3].

The model showed a significant effect of the interaction between the two age-related indices on Log.RT (interaction *edf* = 10.4, $p < 0.01$, R^2 = 0.26). Predicted values for a representative set of relative abilities ranging from −3 to +3 are plotted in Figure 3. One point on the age-related child ability index approximatively corresponds to one standard deviation for the group distribution (SD = 1.05). As the distribution was leptokurtic, extreme values around −3 and 3 were present in the sample. RT profiles only differed for difficult items. For easy items, no regulation skills were necessary, and the children gave their responses within 15 s on average (fewer than 9.5 log units).

---

2   The Rasch model was fitted using the eMr package [29] in R, which allows for maximum likelihood estimation of individual parameters.

3   LogTI~te(RelativeItemDifficulty,RelativeChildAbility) + (ns(RelativeItemDifficulty, 2) | Subject). The ns (.. , 2) function gives the natural splines with two degrees of freedom, and allows for nonlinear random effects.

By contrast, when the difficulty of the items exceeded the ability level expected for their age, only some of the children modulated their RTs. For underachievers who performed far below expected levels (relative ability index = −3), RTs remained constant at around 10 s (9.3 log units) whatever the items' relative difficulty. By contrast, the more difficult the items, the longer the overachievers (relative ability index = +3) spent on them, with RTs longer than 2 min (11.7 log units) for the most difficult items. Children who performed at their expected level (relative ability index = 0) exhibited a less pronounced modulation pattern, with RTs of around 30 s (10.3 log units) for the most difficult items. For these especially difficult items (relative item difficulty > 4), underachievers' RTs were even shorter than they were for intermediate items, whereas overachievers never seemed to give up, as their RTs continuously increased as a function of item difficulty.

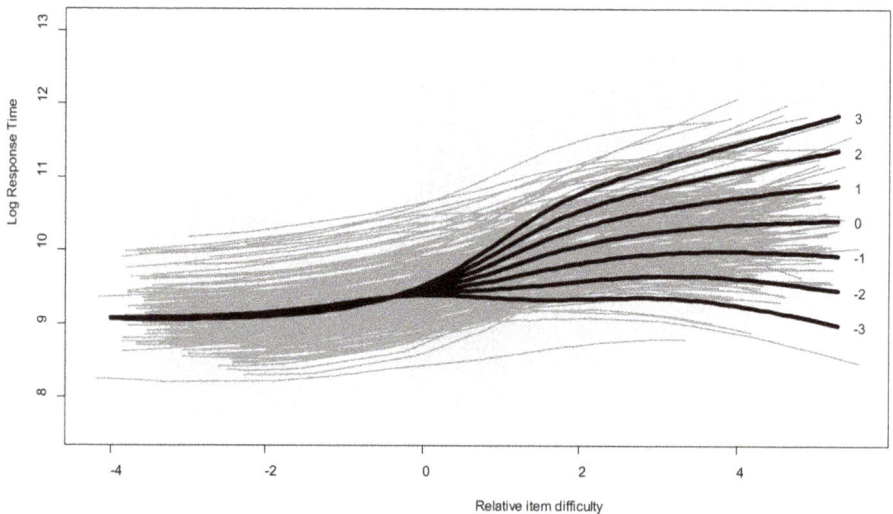

Figure 3. Log.RTs by item difficulty and children's expected ability for their age, with predicted values illustrating the GAMM results. Light-gray dotted lines: observed values; gray lines: individual fitted values; bold black lines: predicted values for a representative subset of individual relative ability parameters on the Rasch scale ranging from −3 to 3.

4. Discussion

In this study, we sought to examine the relationship between children's performances on the SRPM and the time they spent studying the matrices. Drawing on memory development research, we hypothesized that children's performances are influenced by their ability to adaptively modulate the amount of time they spend on processing matrices of different levels of difficulty. To this end, we analyzed intra-individual RT variability and computed a study-time modulation index, derived from the correlation between RT and item difficulty for each participant. Four major findings emerged from the analyses we conducted.

First, the examination of mean RTs as a function of age did not provide any insight into the mechanisms responsible for developmental change. Whereas performance showed a marked improvement with age, mean RTs did not vary significantly, suggesting an apparent (and misleading) independence of the two variables. This result clearly illustrates the need to go beyond mean-based analyses in order to further our understanding of the processes mediating developmental change and individual differences [30].

Second, contrary to mean RTs, the modulation index reflecting intraindividual RT variability, was significantly associated with age and performance. Older or more efficient children adjusted their study times more to the complexity of the items. Additionally, mediation analyses revealed that the age-related changes in performance were partly explained by children's increasing modulation efficiency. Third, the relationship between RTs and item difficulty took different forms as a function of children's level of performance. Whereas more efficient children exhibited a linear relationship between RT and difficulty (i.e., they always spent more time processing more difficult items), less efficient children tended to exhibit a nonlinear relationship. These children correctly adjusted their RTs as a function of complexity, providing the items were not too difficult, but seemed to suspend the modulation process beyond a certain threshold of difficulty. Fourth and last, when we took age-related performance expectations into account, we found evidence that underachievers and overachievers clearly displayed contrasting RT modulation profiles.

One limitation of the present study is that the strategic nature of RT modulation can still be discussed. RT modulation can be seen as a deliberate goal-oriented behavior intended to improve performance, but it could also be regarded as the byproduct of qualitatively different processing approaches, that is, as a consequence rather than a cause. For example, Dual Process Theories of reasoning [31] advocate the categorization of inferences as either produced by System 1 (intuitive and fast elicited responses) or by System 2 (analytic and time-consuming responses). These processing approaches could correspond to the recruitment of elimination and constructive matching strategies in the processing of Raven's matrices. It could also be that RT modulation and processing approaches constitute two sides of the same coin and will be difficult to disentangle: Children cannot recruit a System 2 approach unless they accept to devote time and efforts to the processing of complex matrices, and constructive-matching strategies are themselves time-consuming. Thompson, Prowse Turner and Pennycook [32] argued that reasoning theories should integrate metacognitive components in order to address the monitoring issues that emerge from such questions: "For a given participant of a given cognitive capacity, operating under a given set of task instructions, in a given environment, what predicts the degree of Type 2 engagement?" (p. 108). With regard to the present results, this raises the straightforward research question of why some children adaptively modulate their study time while others either do not, or do so less effectively. Several hypotheses can be put forward about the nature and psychological determinants of these different profiles.

4.1. Role of Metacognitive Judgments

Younger or less efficient children may fail to modulate their study time because of their inability to discriminate between the items' levels of difficulty. In the metacognitive literature, the ease of learning judgment concept refers to the estimation of difficulty that an individual can produce after brief exposure to material that has to be learned. In reasoning tasks, deliberate processing efforts and strategies may be driven by these estimations [19]. A child's lack of study-time modulation may stem from an inability to adequately assess the difficulty of the RPM items and to discriminate between their inner complexities. Future research should try to disambiguate this issue by assessing children's ability to produce relevant judgments of reasoning complexity.

4.2. Discrepancy Reduction or Region of Proximal Reasoning?

The metamemory literature that drove the hypotheses of the present study may also shed light on our results. Two main theoretical models can be used to predict children's learning strategies. As mentioned earlier, the discrepancy reduction model predicts that children will devote more study time to items perceived as more difficult, in order to reduce the discrepancy between a desired state of learning and its actual estimation. Transposed to a reasoning context, the idea is that extra-time allocation reduces negative judgments of understanding for more complex matrices. However, Metcalfe [33] argued that a more rational learning attitude consists in concentrating resources not on more difficult items per se, but on those located in the child's region of proximal learning, that is "those items with the smallest distance from being learned" (p. 350). The third result of our study, concerning the linear/nonlinear relationship between RTs and difficulty has several possible explanations with regard to these alternative interpretive frameworks. Should the less efficient children in Figure 2 be regarded as having a modulation deficit (i.e., not trying enough to reduce the discrepancy for the most difficult items, as the more efficient children seemed to try to do), or should they be regarded as adaptively not spending too much time and effort on the items they rapidly perceive of as being clearly out of reach? The concept of utilization deficiencies [34] describes situations in which an elaborated strategy, though available in children's repertoire, cannot (yet) help them cope with the task at hand. Here, children may fall back to the use of simpler and faster strategic approaches when the inner complexity of an item obviously exceeds their working memory capacities, and makes the constructive-matching strategy ineffective. Future research should try to document the validity of each of these interpretations by articulating the analyses of modulation profiles with external measures of cognitive ability indicating participants' region of proximal reasoning.

4.3. The Role of Thinking Dispositions

Metamemory researchers have shown that children sometimes display adequate metaknowledge, while failing to appropriately capitalize on the information it provides (e.g., [35]). The term thinking dispositions [36] refers to individual inclinations toward the effective use of available cognitive resources. The motivational aspect of research on intelligence indicates that cognitive sophistication results from both processing abilities and thinking dispositions (e.g., [37]), such that skills are not enough: "However technically adroit a person may be at problem solving, decision making, reasoning, or building explanations, what does it matter unless the person invests himself or herself energetically in these and other kinds of thinking on occasions that invite it?" [36] (p. 276). In order to solve the SRPM, children have to engage in a reiterated and effortful process of induction that draws heavily on (limited) relational integration abilities in working memory. In the test manual, Raven, Raven, and Court [38] highlighted this dispositional dimension, claiming that one of the main sources of error is the reluctance to devote mental energy to solving abstract problems. Vodegel-Matzen, van der Molen, and Dudink [1] found that high-scoring individuals typically spent more time solving the items than low scorers. In a similar vein, Kagan, Pearson, and Welch [39] had earlier highlighted the influence of cognitive style (impulsive vs. reflective) on reasoning test performances. The fourth result of our study indicated that age-related expectancies of success/failure on a given item could be contradicted by actual performances as a function of the time (and certainly the effort) a child devotes to exploring the matrix. As shown in Figure 3, underachievers tended to invest equivalent amounts of time in processing the items, whatever their attainability. Overachievers showed the opposite pattern, persevering proportionally to the magnitude of the challenge the items represented for them. This last result points to the need to consider thinking dispositions (e.g., effort willingness, need for cognition, cognitive style) in future research exploring modulation profiles.

Overall, the findings of the present study provide evidence that study-time modulation constitutes one of the key strategic factors for developmental and individual differences in reasoning performances. Additional research is now needed to further explore the determinants of children's modulation profiles and to gain a deeper understanding of their actual contribution to intelligent behaviors. On the clinical front, which is moving toward the digitization of cognitive assessment procedures, taking account of study-time modulation during the solution of matrix reasoning tasks could greatly enrich analysis of the processes behind the scores. These analyses could guide both clinical assessment and cognitive remediation: Children displaying obviously dysfunctional RT modulation, such as the underachievers in Figure 3, could benefit from dynamic assessment procedures designed to increase the validity of Gf measures [40].

Acknowledgments: The authors would like to thank Thomas Arciszewski, Emilie Chaouch and Jean-Rémi Lagier for their assistance in data collection.

Author Contributions: Patrick Perret conceived and designed the experiment; Bruno Dauvier analyzed the data; Patrick Perret and Bruno Dauvier wrote the paper.

Conflicts of Interest: The authors declare no conflict of interest.

References

1. Vodegel Matzen, L.B.; van der Molen, M.W.; Dudink, A.C. Error analysis of Raven test performance. *Personal. Individ. Differ.* **1994**, *16*, 433–445. [CrossRef]
2. Carpenter, P.A.; Just, M.A.; Shell, P. What one intelligence test measures: A theoretical account of the processing in the Raven Progressive Matrices test. *Psychol. Rev.* **1990**, *97*, 404–431. [CrossRef] [PubMed]
3. Pennings, A.B.; Hessels, M.G.P. The measurement of mental attentional capacity: A neo-Piagetian developmental study. *Intelligence* **1996**, *23*, 59–78. [CrossRef]
4. Dauvier, B.; Bailleux, C.; Perret, P. The development of relational integration during childhood. *Dev. Psychol.* **2014**, *50*, 1687–1697. [CrossRef] [PubMed]
5. Snow, R.E. Aptitude processes. In *Aptitude, Learning, and Instruction: Cognitive Process Analyses of Aptitude*; Snow, R.E., Federico, P.-A., Montague, W.E., Eds.; Lawrence Erlbaum Associates: Hillsdale, NJ, USA, 1980; pp. 27–63.
6. Vigneau, F.; Caissie, A.F.; Bors, D.A. Eye-movement analysis demonstrates strategic influences on intelligence. *Intelligence* **2006**, *34*, 261–272. [CrossRef]
7. Mitchum, A.L.; Kelley, C.M. Solve the problem first: Constructive solution strategies can influence the accuracy of retrospective confidence judgments. *J. Exp. Psychol. Learn. Memory Cognit.* **2010**, *36*, 699–710. [CrossRef] [PubMed]
8. Arendasy, M.E.; Sommer, M. Reducing response elimination strategies enhances the construct validity of figural matrices. *Intelligence* **2013**, *41*, 234–243. [CrossRef]
9. Chen, Z.; Honomichl, R.; Kennedy, D.; Tan, E. Aiming to complete the matrix: Eye-movement analysis of processing strategies in children's relational thinking. *Dev. Psychology* **2016**, *52*, 867–878. [CrossRef] [PubMed]
10. Resing, W.C.M.; Bakker, M.; Pronk, C.M.E.; Elliott, J.G. Progression paths in children's problem solving: The influence of dynamic testing, initial variability, and working memory. *J. Exp. Child Psychol.* **2017**, *153*, 83–109. [CrossRef] [PubMed]
11. Son, L.K.; Metcalfe, J. Metacognitive and control strategies in study-time allocation. *J. Exp. Psychol. Learn. Memory Cognit.* **2000**, *26*, 204–221. [CrossRef]
12. Metcalfe, J. Metacognitive judgments and control of study. *Curr. Dir. Psychol. Sci.* **2009**, *18*, 159–163. [CrossRef] [PubMed]
13. Flavell, J.H.; Wellman, H.M. Metamemory. In *Perspectives on the Development of Memory and Cognition*; Kail, R.V., Hagen, J.W., Eds.; Erlbaum: Portland, OR, USA, 1977; pp. 3–33.
14. Destan, N.; Hembacher, E.; Ghetti, S.; Roebers, C. Early metacognitive abilities: The interplay of monitoring and control processes in 5- to 7-year-old children. *J. Exp. Child Psychol.* **2014**, *126*, 213–228. [CrossRef] [PubMed]
15. Dufresne, A.; Kobasigawa, A. Children's spontaneous allocation of study time: Differential and sufficient aspects. *J. Exp. Child Psychol.* **1989**, *47*, 274–296. [CrossRef]
16. Lockl, K.; Schneider, W. The effects of incentives and instructions on children's allocation of study time. *Eur. J. Dev. Psychol.* **2004**, *1*, 153–169. [CrossRef]
17. Schneider, W.; Pressley, M. *Memory Development between Two and Twenty*, 2nd ed.; Erlbaum: Mahwah, NJ, USA, 1997.
18. Bjorklund, D.F.; Miller, P.H. New themes in strategy development. *Dev. Rev.* **1997**, *17*, 407–410. [CrossRef]
19. Ackerman, R.; Thompson, V.A. Meta-reasoning: What can we learn from metamemory. In *Reasoning as Memory*; Feeney, A., Thompson, V.A., Eds.; Psychology Press: Abingdon, UK, 2014; pp. 164–182.
20. Nelson, T.O.; Narens, L. Metamemory: A theoretical framework and new findings. In *The Psychology of Learning and Motivation*; Bower, G.H., Ed.; Academic: New York, NY, USA, 1990; Volume 26, pp. 125–173.
21. Goldhammer, F.; Naumann, J.; Greiff, S. More is not always better: The relation between item response and item response time in Raven's Matrices. *J. Intell.* **2015**, *3*, 21–40. [CrossRef]

22. Crone, E.A.; Wendelken, C.; van Leijenhorst, L.; Honomichl, R.D.; Christoff, K.; Bunge, S.A. Neurocognitive development of relational reasoning. *Dev. Sci.* **2009**, *12*, 55–66. [CrossRef] [PubMed]

23. Ratcliff, R. Methods for dealing with reaction time outliers. *Psychol. Bull.* **1993**, *114*, 510–532. [CrossRef] [PubMed]

24. Wood, S.N. Fast stable restricted maximum likelihood and marginal likelihood estimation of semiparametric generalized linear models. *J. R. Stat. Soc.* **2011**, *73*, 3–36. [CrossRef]

25. R Core Team. *R: A Language and Environment for Statistical Computing*; R Foundation for Statistical Computing: Vienna, Austria, 2017; Available online: https://www.R-project.org/ (accessed on 21 August 2017).

26. Wilkinson, G.; Rogers, C. Symbolic description of factorial models for the analysis of variance. *Appl. Stat.* **1973**, *22*, 392–399. [CrossRef]

27. Wood, S.N. Stable and efficient multiple smoothing parameter estimation for generalized additive models. *J. Am. Stat. Assoc.* **2004**, *99*, 673–686. [CrossRef]

28. Wood, S.N. *Generalized Additive Models: An Introduction with R*; CRC Press: Boca Raton, FL, USA, 2017.

29. Mair, P.; Hatzinger, R. Extended Rasch modeling: The eRm package, for the application of IRT models in R. *J. Stat. Softw.* **2007**, *20*, 1–20. [CrossRef]

30. Mella, N.; Fagot, D.; Lecerf, T.; de Ribaupierre, A. Working memory and intraindividual variability in processing speed: A lifespan developmental and individual differences study. *Mem. Cognit.* **2015**, *43*, 340–356. [CrossRef] [PubMed]

31. Evans, J.S.B.T. The heuristic-analytic theory of reasoning: Extension and evaluation. *Psychon. Bull. Rev.* **2006**, *13*, 378–395. [CrossRef] [PubMed]

32. Thompson, V.A.; Prowse Turner, J.A.; Pennycook, G. Intuition, reason, and metacognition. *Cognit. Psychol.* **2011**, *63*, 107–140. [CrossRef] [PubMed]

33. Metcalfe, J. Is study time allocated selectively to a region of proximal learning? *J. Exp. Psychol. Gen.* **2002**, *131*, 349–363. [CrossRef] [PubMed]

34. Miller, P.H. Individual differences in children's strategic behaviors: Utilization deficiencies. *Learn. Individ. Differ.* **1994**, *6*, 285–307. [CrossRef]

35. Metcalfe, J.; Finn, B. Metacognition and control of study choice in children. *Metacognit. Learn.* **2013**, *8*, 19–46. [CrossRef]

36. Perkins, D. *Outsmarting IQ: The Emerging Science of Learnable Intelligence*; The Free Press: New York, NY, USA, 1995.

37. Toplak, M.E.; West, R.F.; Stanovich, K.E. Rational thinking and cognitive sophistication: Development, cognitive abilities, and thinking dispositions. *Dev. Psychol.* **2014**, *50*, 1037–1048. [CrossRef] [PubMed]

38. Raven, J.; Raven, J.C.; Court, J.H. *Manual for Raven's Progressive Matrices and Vocabulary Scales. Section 1: General Overview*; Harcourt Assessment: San Antonio, TX, USA, 1998.

39. Kagan, J.; Pearson, L.; Welch, L. Conceptual impulsivity and inductive reasoning. *Child Dev.* **1966**, *37*, 584–594. [CrossRef]

40. Elliott, J. Dynamic assessment in educational settings: Realizing potential. *Educ. Rev.* **2003**, *55*, 15–32. [CrossRef]

Journal of
Intelligence

MDPI

Article

A Solution to the Measurement Problem in the Idiographic Approach Using Computer Adaptive Practicing

Abe D. Hofman [1,*,†], Brenda R. J. Jansen [2], Susanne M. M. de Mooij [3], Claire E. Stevenson [1] and Han L. J. van der Maas [1]

1   Department of Psychological Methods, University of Amsterdam, 1018 WS Amsterdam, The Netherlands;
    c.e.stevenson@uva.nl (C.E.S.); h.l.j.vandermaas@uva.nl (H.L.J.v.d.M.)
2   Department of Developmental Psychology, University of Amsterdam,
    1018 WS Amsterdam, The Netherlands; b.r.j.jansen@uva.nl
3   Department of Psychological Sciences, Birkbeck, University of London, London WC1E 7HX, UK;
    sdemoo01@mail.bbk.ac.uk
*   Correspondence: a.d.hofman@uva.nl
†   Current address: Nieuwe Achtergracht 129-B, 1018 WS Amsterdam, The Netherlands.

Received: 22 December 2017; Accepted: 27 February 2018; Published: 2 March 2018

Abstract: Molenaar's manifesto on psychology as idiographic science (Molenaar, 2004) brought the $N = 1$ times series perspective firmly to the attention of developmental scientists. The rich intraindividual variation in complex developmental processes requires the study of these processes at the level of the individual. Yet, the idiographic approach is all but easy in practical research. One major limitation is the collection of short interval times series of high quality data on developmental processes. In this paper, we present a novel measurement approach to this problem. We developed an online practice and monitoring system which is now used by thousands of Dutch primary school children on a daily or weekly basis, providing a new window on cognitive development. We will introduce the origin of this new instrument, called Math Garden, explain its setup, and present and discuss ways to analyze children's individual developmental pathways.

Keywords: idiographic approach; computerized adaptive practicing; intraindividual variation; cognitive development; mathematics

1. Introduction

The human cognitive system, and especially its development in the first 10 years, is inconceivably complex. Of all complex systems that are now studied in science, such as ecosystems, the climate, the immune system, and stock markets, the developing human cognitive system is by far the most challenging [1]. One common element in the study of the dynamic complex systems is the focus on high quality and highly frequent measurements. Such data, collected within an individual, are required to study individual development in detail and to answer fundamental questions on cognitive development and learning [2,3]. This idiographic approach is also important for educational approaches based on personalized learning. To adapt education to the individual, highly frequent samples of reliable data on learning processes are required. Within developmental psychology, Siegler [4] stressed the importance of frequent sampling to collect longitudinal data (the microgenetic method). The idiographic and microgenetic approach share many ideas and concepts, although the latter does not necessarily imply using only intra-individual data. The microgenetic method is defined by three key components: (1) observations span the full period of the developmental process;

(2) the density of observations is high, relative to the rate of change; (3) and the analysis aims to infer the process that gives rise to both quantitative and qualitative changes [4].

Figure 1 provides an illustration of the importance of idiographic analysis for qualitative changes. Here we consider the case of a sudden transition in some developmental process for 30 simulated children. Suppose this process can be described by a switching regression model per individual, where each child goes through a similar sudden change in development. Up until some age (the precise age differs per subject and is sampled from a normal distribution with mean $M = 6$ and standard deviation $SD = 0.5$) the developmental curve is based on a low intercept ($M = 0.5; SD = 0.1$). After this age the intercept changes abruptly ($M = 2.5; SD = 0.1$). Slopes before and after this sudden jump are rather flat ($M = 0.1; SD = 0.02$). Some measurement error is added ($M = 0; SD = 0.2$). Figure 1 clearly shows within subject sudden changes for all 30 children. The darker line, however, representing the group's average performance at each point in time, suggests a more continuous developmental process. Such between subject data would have been collected in a typical cross-sectional study. Although, in this case a more advanced between subject analysis—a mixture approach for instance [5]—would reveal the discontinuous character of the developmental process.

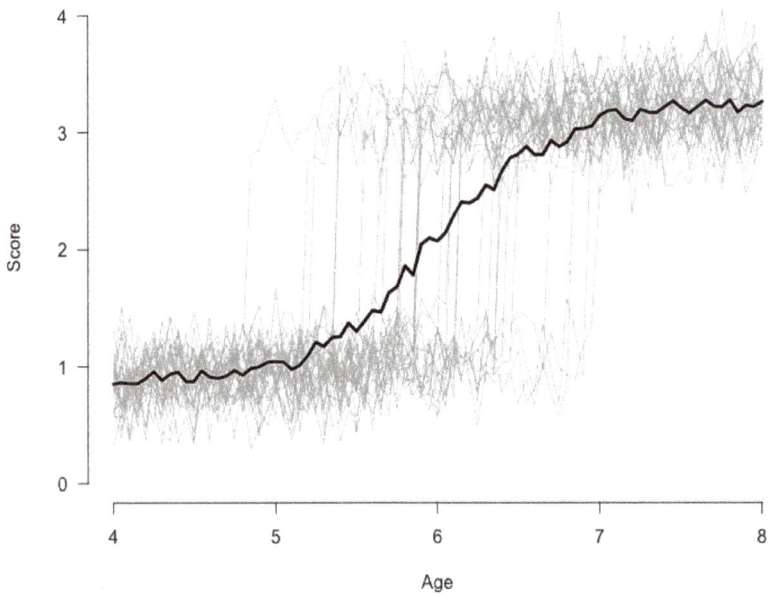

Figure 1. The (misleading) average of multiple individual curves.

Idiographic analyses are thus essential in revealing the dynamics of development. However, it has been very difficult to develop reliable and valid measurement instruments for cognitive development that can be used for the full period of developmental processes. It is even more difficult to construct these instruments in such a way that they can be used in high frequent measurements, say once a week or once a day. Moreover, even if such tests were available, recruiting subjects would be very hard. Most schools would not agree to daily or weekly test sessions for say an hour per session for long periods of time.

Over the last 10 years we developed a new system meeting both scientific and educational objectives, that solves these problems. With this system, the main application being Math Garden (in Dutch: Rekentuin) [6,7] we have collected high-frequency time series of thousands of subjects over multiple years in many scholastic and cognitive domains. We first describe and explain the basic technology underlying Math Garden. Second, we present examples of analysis of intraindividual data. Third, we discuss some limitations of our approach.

1.1. Computer Adaptive Practice

The inspiration for the system that solves an important number of the measurement problems of the idiographic approach to development was the observation that children solve many practice exercises in math and language almost daily. Actually, school children spend about 50% of their time on reading, writing, and arithmetic [8]. A substantial part of this time is devoted to practice exercises. If we could obtain the data of these practice exercises, a new measurement system could be in reach. However, the diversity of practice materials, which are not setup as measurement instruments, makes such an approach impractical.

To acquire measurements that are scientifically useful, we developed a new exercise approach for education that is both educationally and scientifically valuable. Understanding this approach requires some knowledge of modern test theory. Modern test theory provides techniques for educational measurement, among them computerized adaptive testing [9]. Modern test theory involves various item response models that specify the probability of a correct answer given characteristics of the person and the items, in the simplest case the ability of a person and the difficulty of the item. The person ability and item difficulty are expressed on the same latent scale. In the most basic model, the Rasch model [10], the probability is 0.5 when the ability of the person equals the item difficulty. If a person's ability is much higher the probability approaches 1, and vice versa 0 Person abilities and item difficulties are related to the more traditional test indices such as sum scores for persons and p-values for items. However, there are important advantages of the Rasch model compared to the more traditional test indices. The main advantage relevant for our approach concerns adaptive testing. In computerized adaptive testing (CAT), people do not have to solve all items in a test; they are only presented with a limited set of informative items, depending on their successes and failures on earlier items. More difficult items follow successes and easier items follow failures. Tests are much shorter since uninformative (too easy or too difficult) items are not administered, which results in a quicker estimation of a person's ability. In CAT the item bank consists of hundreds or even thousands of items.

Computer adaptive testing is however not directly applicable to computer adaptive practice. In order to use CAT in an educational practice system, we had two problems to solve. The first problem concerns the pretesting of items. Note that CAT assumes that all item difficulties are known. This means that all items in the item bank should be pretested on many subjects before one can start CAT. Since our computer adaptive practice systems (Math Garden and Language Sea) consist of about 40 games, with in total more than 50.000 items, pretesting is impractical.

The second problem is more technical but important. In CAT based on the Rasch model the most informative subsequent item is an item for which the expected probability correct is about 0.5. This implies that subjects fail on about 50% of the items. In an educational practice system this is unacceptable and unethical. Although selection of easier items is possible in CAT, the speed of convergence in estimating a person's ability drops considerably [11]. Clearly, if a large majority of answers is correct we do not learn much about a person's ability.

We solved the problem of pretesting by using an online estimation method that originates from the world of chess. In the Elo rating system, ratings (abilities) of players are updated after each game by a simple update formula [12]. In this update formula, the difference between the expected outcome computed from the ratings of the players prior to the game and the actual outcome of the chess game is used to compute the new ratings. The advantage of Elo's dynamic estimation method is that it does not depend on pretesting, it can start with arbitrary initial ratings. We can set all players' ratings to 1500, let players play chess, update ratings and the ratings will converge after some time to values that accurately represent (differences in) playing strength (in chess, ratings vary between 1000 and 3000).[1]

In Math Garden we apply the same system with some important modifications. First, people play against items (and not other people). A person's ability (ratings) increases when they solve the item correctly, and decreases when they fail, and vice versa for the item difficulties. Mathematical details of our adaptation of the Elo system can be found in [6] and especially [13].

We solved the second problem by integrating response times into the scoring of responses. As mentioned, correct performance on very easy items is not very informative about a person's ability, however speed of responding is [14]. Yet, children may have different speed accuracy trade-off strategies; some may favour accuracy over speed while others favour speed over accuracy. For instance, the ability of children who play cautiously may be underestimated. To minimize the influence of differences in speed accuracy trade-off we developed an explicit scoring rule for the weighing of accuracy and speed. This scoring rule, called item residual time rule, weighs accuracy $(+1, -1)$ with the remaining time for an item [13]. Given a time limit of, for instance 20 s, a correct answer in 8 s gives a score of +12, whereas an error in 5 s yields a score of −15. Thus fast guessing is discouraged. Maris and van der Maas [13] show that this scoring rule implies the two parameter logistic item response model [15] with the item time limit as a discrimination parameter. The integration of response times into the response scores enables us to present children with items for which they have an average probability of 0.75 of solving the items correctly. Given a person's current ability estimates a set of items is selected with a 0.75 expected probability correct. From this set a random item is selected that has not been played recently by the child [6].

This scoring rule forms the basis of the extended Elo system used in Math Garden and other applications in the system. In the games, the scoring rule is represented by virtual coins, equal to the time in seconds available for the item. Each second a coin disappears. In case of a correct answer, the child wins the remaining coins. In case of an error, the remaining coins are subtracted from the total coins won. In this way, the scoring rule is understandable for young children and adds a gamifying element to the task, keeping the children motivated. Children can buy virtual prizes, such as flags and trophies, using the collected coins. Because the games are adapted to player ability level, the coins and prizes they win are independent of ability and only depend on the frequency of playing. Hence, the possibility to win by mainly playing, also encourages weak players to practice a lot. If children do not want to answer an item for any reason, they can click a question mark, which replaces the item with another item and no coins are won or lost.

1.2. Math Garden

These innovations are applied in Math Garden, and later other learning platform websites for children such as Language Sea, a language learning program; Words and Birds, a learning platform for learning English as a secondary language and Type Garden, an adaptive e-learning environment that teaches children to touch type [16]. In Math Garden each plant represents a math game that grows as ability increases. Currently Math Garden contains games for many different mathematical skills, such as basic arithmetic operations, but also counting, series, fractions, and clock reading. Other games concern more general cognitive abilities, such as working memory, deductive reasoning, and perceptual abilities.

These online games allow children to practice intensely at their own ability level with direct feedback, two important requirements for deliberate practice [17]. Teachers are provided with learning analytics for each individual child. Each online learning platform is a self-organizing learning tool that does not require extra effort from teachers. Note that these websites are not teaching methods.

---

[1]   Given the current large number of Math Garden players item ratings converge within about a week.

They take over practicing and monitoring tasks, but not the instruction (although some games give intelligent feedback).

Math Garden and Language Sea are popular in the Netherlands. About two thousand schools have bought subscriptions for some classes or the whole school. Schools agree with the use of anonymized data for scientific research. At the end of 2017, more than 200,000 primary school children in the Netherlands use these websites regularly. On weekdays about 1.5 million item responses are collected per day. About 25% of the response are collected after school hours.

2. Scientific Analysis

This type of 'big' data is extremely promising. It contains highly frequent 'modern test theory' measurements of the development of numerous abilities from children of a wide range of ages. In a sense, it provides a new window on intellectual development.

On the other hand, new problems arise. First there is the issue of user privacy. It is crucial to de-identify the data carefully. Second, data are collected with a variety of devices, at home or at school, children might receive help, use each other's accounts, etc. Third, big data analyses are often exploratory with all of the associated risks, such as accidental relations between variables. Finally, in the analysis of Math Garden data many, often rather arbitrary, choices have to be made about data selection and handling of missing data. Our general approach is to check the robustness of results with different data selections and different types of analyses.

In the last 5 years about 25 papers using Math Garden and Language Sea data have been published (for example, see [18–32]. For instance the development of the ability to solve three-term arithmetic expressions (such as $3 + 4 \times 6$) was studied [33]. The question was whether the development in the domain of mathematics involves a shift from non-formal mechanisms to formal rules and axioms or, alternatively, involves an increase in reliance on non-formal mechanisms. Math Garden data from about 50,000 children were analyzed. So-called foil errors were more common for problems in which formally lower-priority sub-expressions were spaced close together. These effects increased with the children's grade level, suggesting that these mechanisms do not vanish but actually become more important over development.

A second example concerns the inversion error when writing down number words in symbolic notation (also called "transcoding") [34]. In Dutch and many other languages, transcoding is complicated by decade-unit inversion: 24, for instance, is pronounced as 'four-and-twenty'. It was shown, using Math Garden data, that the incidence of these errors declined but did not disappear in later elementary school. In addition, transcoding ability mediated the relationship between visuospatial working memory and mathematics performance, a strong effect that declined with age.

Many of these papers center on interindividual differences and item effects. In this paper, we will focus on the analysis of intraindividual data.

2.1. Intraindividual Analysis

Mathematical proficiency is essential for functioning in today's society. Higher proficiency levels are associated with higher levels of employment [35,36] and are, for example, necessary for making well-informed choices about health and health care [37]. Despite the importance of mathematics, relatively little is known about the intraindividual development of mathematical abilities [38].

Here we explore how to visualize, describe, and analyze data at the detailed level of an individual's responses to single math problems. In this specific illustration, a subset of Math Garden's addition and multiplication data is used. These data stem from children who have visited Math Garden almost daily and who played frequently for prolonged periods. The data consists of a large set of person-by-item time-series: time-series of responses of a single child to a single item. The large amount of data on learning of individual children that is unlocked by these time-series is illustrated in Figure 2. Figure 2 shows the development of an individual child's multiplication skills from weeks 1 to 15 (horizontal axis). The vertical axis represents the difficulty of the attempted multiplication problems. A dot in the graph shows that the child has attempted to solve this problem, whereas the color shows the accuracy of the response. Figure 2 shows that the difficulty of the attempted problems increases in time.

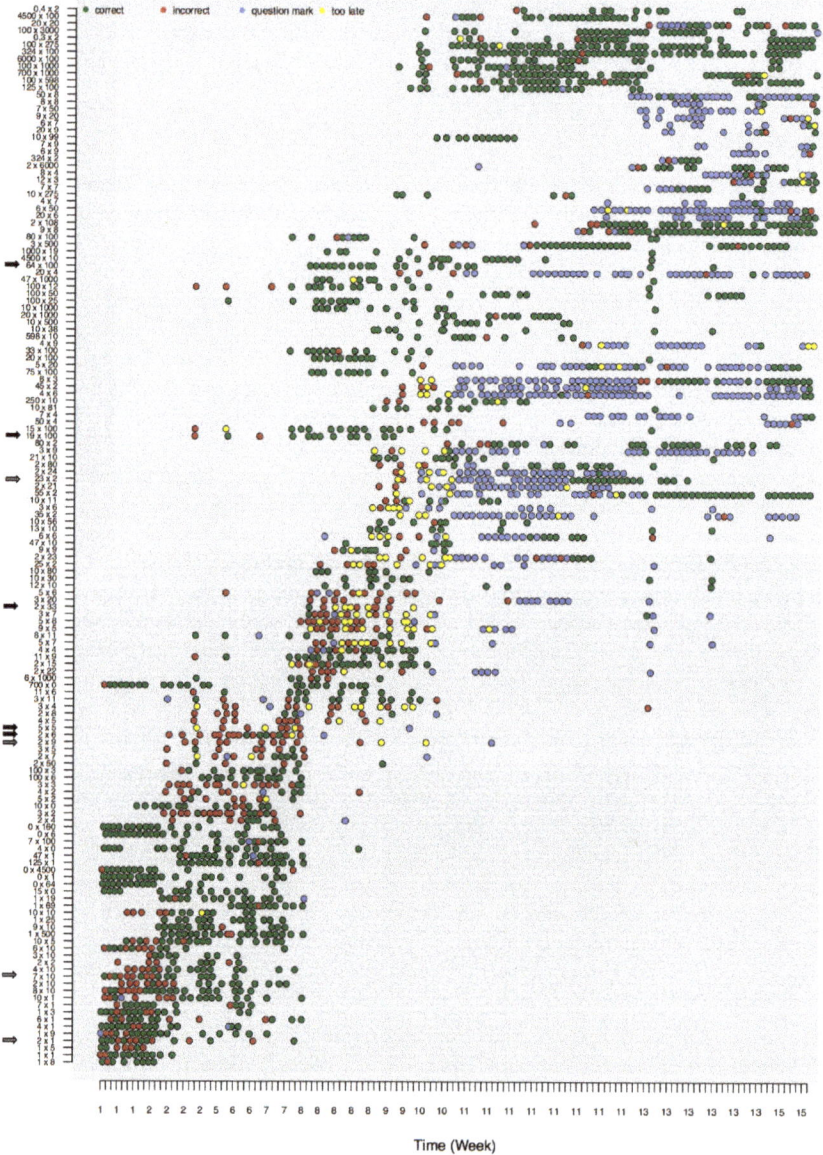

Figure 2. One player's development in learning to solve multiplication problems correctly. The colors refer to correct (green), incorrect (red), question mark (blue) or responses that were too late (yellow). The minimum number of responses for each time-series was 5. The items are sorted by item difficulty (low = easy and high = difficult). Plots for other players, providing different patterns, are available on www.abehofman.com/papers. The arrows along the Y axis indicate the items that are further described in the text (black arrows illustrate different response patterns; grey arrows indicate different trajectories of mastery).

The child whose data are plotted in Figure 2 starts, in week 1, with correct and some incorrect responses to easy multiplication items. Due to the CAT routine, only a subset of available items are presented at each time-point. Around week 2, this child seems to master items with a times 10 operator. As a consequence the child's ability estimate increases (not represented in Figure 2) and more difficult items are presented. Responses to the more difficult set of items (e.g., 2×6 and 5×5) are more often incorrect, as is predicted from the measurement model. Around weeks 8, 9, and 10 even more difficult items are presented (e.g., 2×33 and 19×100), but now the child consistently succeeds at quite difficult problems but fails at easier problems, indicating some model misfit. This misfit is especially prominent for the long series of only correct responses to more difficult items (e.g., 64×100 and 100×12). The most difficult items (at the top of the figure) are almost always solved correctly, while the easier items—including some items that belong to the standard multiplication tables—are still solved incorrectly.

Furthermore, the trajectory of mastery differs remarkably between items. Whereas some items seem to be learned slowly (e.g., 7×10), other items are mastered suddenly, from one attempt to the next (e.g., 23×2). For other items it is even unclear whether they are mastered at all, since the player continues to switch between correct and incorrect responses (e.g., 2×1). Also, other items are no longer presented to the child even though the last responses to the items were incorrect (e.g., 2×9).

The visual inspection of these figures highlights many interesting patterns. However, the large number of users in these systems, combined with the fast rate with which responses are collected, makes it impossible to inspect these plots for all users. Hence, learning analytics are needed to characterize different patterns of learning, to highlight users who show interesting (deviating) developmental patterns, and in the end to use such analytics to provide teachers and children with person-specific support on their learning process.

3. Study 1: Learning Analytics

We developed and investigated learning analytics to characterize different learning patterns. These analytics are aimed to describe per item: (1) whether the child learned the item; (2) the learning pattern; (3) the stability and variability of responses over time. We focus on learning analytics that are feasible in a big data setting. The learning analytics should thus be fairly simple and easy to compute.

For the first analysis, we collected responses of frequent players from the addition and multiplication games between 1 September 2013 and 1 July 2017. To this end, we first selected players with more than 1500 responses (N is 5339 and 4714, respectively). We only used data of subjects that played at the most difficult level (with an expected probability correct of 0.6, see [25]). In both games so-called mirror items exist. Mirror items are items that only differ in the order of the operands (e.g., $1 + 2$ and $2 + 1$). Since these mirror items are closely related, responses to both mirrors were combined within a single time-series. In a second step, we omitted all responses to (mirror) items with less than five observations and only included players when they provided at least 250 responses to 25 different items.

The data selection procedure resulted in a data set of 2287 (mean age = 8.12, SD = 2.01) and 2867 players (mean age = 8.89, SD = 1.73) for the domains of addition and multiplication respectively. The data included in total 1,040,321 and 2,090,822 responses to 1169 and 740 mirror items.

To characterize individual learning curves, a number of candidate learning statistics were computed for each person-by-item time-series. These were the following:

1. Response probabilities of the last two responses.
2. Transition probability matrix of correct and incorrect responses.
3. Coefficients of a logistic regression model.

These statistics were computed for correct and incorrect responses only, excluding question mark and late responses. The percentage of correct responses in the last two responses informs us whether users are able to answer an item correctly at the end of a time-series. The transition probability matrix is a 2 by 2 transition matrix, where the probability of switching from an incorrect to a correct response and the probability of remaining at a correct response are particularly informative. Since the remaining two probabilities are complementary, these are redundant and will be omitted. The transition matrix indicates persistence from incorrect to correct responses. Parameters of the logistic regression provide information on the person-by-item learning curve. The logistic function is:

$$P(x = 1|t) = 1/(1 + e^{-\beta_0 + \beta_1 x_t})$$ (1)

where β_0 is the intercept and β_1 is the slope (steepness) of the learning curve. We used the position in the time-series as the explanatory variable (x_t). The slope of the learning curve reflects the learning speed. A flat curve indicates that an item was already mastered at the start of data collection, or that an item was not mastered during data collection, the value of the intercept (β_0) indicates when learning occurred.

We use Bayesian logistic regression instead of regular logistic regression, because the latter cannot handle complete separation [39]. Complete separation occurs when a developmental trajectory involves a perfect step-like function between different states [3]. The models were fit using the arm package [40] in R [41] using default priors. BIC differences were calculated between models with and without a slope parameter to compare the contribution of this parameter to model fit.

Results

In the addition data set 35% of the series ended with two correct responses. This percentage is close to the implied probability by the measurement model of 0.36 (0.6^2).[2] For the multiplication data set 47% of the series ended with two correct responses, higher than the expected probability of 0.36.

Figure 3 shows histograms of the switching probabilities between an incorrect (0) and correct response (1) (learning probability), indicating learning, and the probabilities of remaining at a correct response, for each domain. The upper histograms of Figure 3 show that for the learning probabilities of both domains there is a clear peak at one (bar on the right), indicating that in about 30% of the addition series and 25% of the multiplication series the learning probability is one. This probability of one indicates that an incorrect response is followed by a correct response. The lower histograms of Figure 3 show the probabilities of remaining at a correct response. For both addition and multiplication, there is a large peak at zero, indicating that in 20% of the series for addition and 15% of the series for multiplication a correct response is always followed by an incorrect response. The low frequency of remaining in the learned state implies that the switch from incorrect to correct responses is not very stable. Furthermore, a comparison of the probabilities of remaining in the learned state ($1 \rightarrow 1$) between the addition and multiplication data shows that for addition these probabilities are lower than for multiplication.

Third, we investigate the evidence for learning in the time-series by fitting learning curves with logistic regression models. To explore the fit of these models to the observed time-series we plotted the observed and predicted responses of three series of the same player, shown in Figure 4.

For the addition data set 19% of the models fitted to the time-series included significant slope (i.e., learning speed) parameters (as indicated by the BIC difference between the model with only an intercept and the model with both a slope and an intercept parameter). Of these time-series that included a significant slope, 70% of the slopes were positive. For the multiplication data set 36% of the series were best described with a model including a slope parameter, and 86% of these were positive. Negative slopes occur, for instance, when children answer numerous item administrations correctly, but fail on the item once or twice at the end of the series. So for both data sets only a minority of

---

2   For many results in this section, formal significance tests could be provided. However, we refrain from doing so because: (1) no clear a priori hypothesis could be formulated and (2) due to the large data sets very small and uninteresting results become significant in a null-hypothesis testing framework. For example, the 35% did significantly differ from the expected 36% according to a simple proportion test ($X^2(1) = 58.60$, $p = 1.936 \times 10^{-14}$)

learning curves show an increase in mastery. Yet, the slope parameters for multiplication were higher (average $\beta_1 = 0.25$) than the slope parameters for addition (average $\beta_1 = 0.08$), see also the left panel of Figure 5. Furthermore, for both data sets the time-series length was negatively correlated with slopes and learning probability in the transition matrix, indicating that learning speed was negatively related to the number of times a child spent solving an item. This negative effect can be explained by the adaptivity of the learning program. If children learn and their ability estimates increase accordingly, more difficult items will be selected. Hence, long time-series can only be collected if children do not show large changes in their ability.

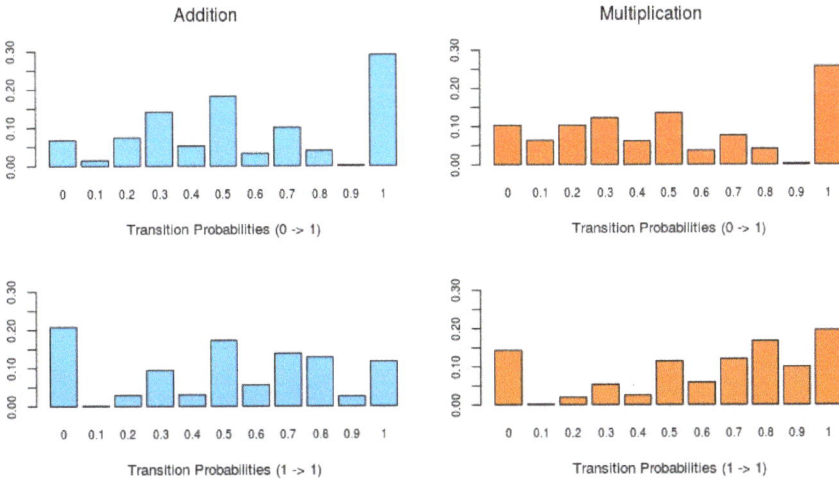

Figure 3. The distribution of the transition probabilities of switching from incorrect to correct responses (**top**) and remaining at a correct response (**bottom**) for addition (**left**) and multiplication (**right**) for all collected time-series. For, example, the transition (learning) probability $(0 \to 1)$ of 0.7 indicates that 70% of incorrect responses are immediately followed by a correct response. The bar at 0.7 in the upper-left panel indicates that this is the case in about 10% of all the collected series in the addition game.

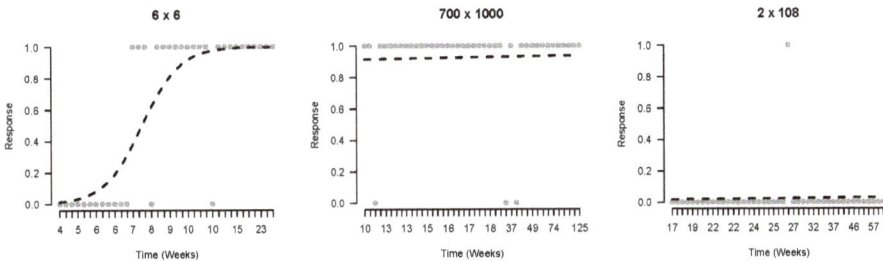

Figure 4. An example of three different developmental patterns of responses to different items by the same player. The left panel shows a time-series with a clear increase in the probability of a correct response. The middle and right panel respectively show a series of a previously learned item and a series that indicates no learning.

For a better understanding of these learning curves, we investigated differences between children's estimated learning speeds (i.e., slopes). First, a positive correlation was found between the average learning speed of the addition and multiplication domains ($\rho(826) = 0.345, p < 0.001$; only players with more than five time-series in both domains were included). Second, we investigated the correlations between the slopes on different items within the multiplication domain. Based on the patterns of Figure 2 and the results of [42] two different item clusters can be defined: items that belong to multiplication tables 2 through 9 (*table* items) and items with a times 10, 100 or 1000 operator (*times 100* items). Within the multiplication domain no significant correlation was found between these two item clusters ($\rho(185) = -0.003$, $p = 0.964$). We tested whether the correlation between these two sets of multiplication items is indeed lower compared to correlations based on more similar items within the domain. To this end, we used a permutation test[3] to calculate the correlation between learning curves of two random sets of *table* and *times 100* items. The average (within cluster) correlation for *table* items was 0.471 ($SD = 0.067$) and for times 100 items was 0.420 ($SD = 0.050$). These results indicate that players who show steeper learning curves on *table* (*times 100*) items also show steeper learning curves on other *table* (*times 100*) items, but learning speed measured by the learning slopes between items sets is unrelated. These results are surprising and will be further explored in the next analyses.

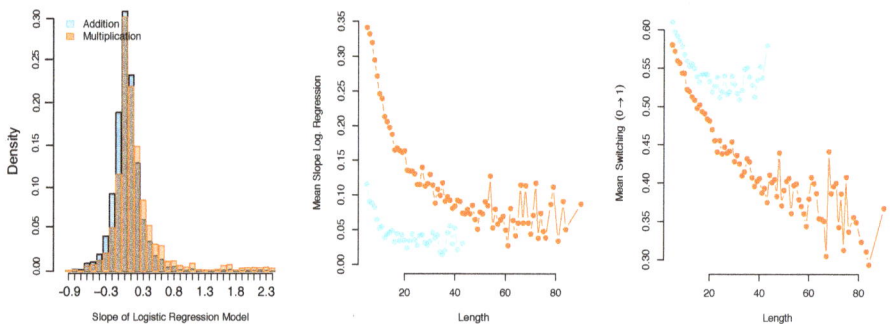

Figure 5. The distribution of the estimated slope parameters, i.e., indicator of learning speed, for both data sets (**left**-panel), and the relation between the length of the series and learning speed (**middle**-panel) and the probability of switching from an incorrect to a correct response (**right**-panel).

To conclude, the results about learning, stability, and change show that significant learning occurs on only a small set of the time series in these Math Garden games. Although large variations in learning can be expected [43], some variability is caused by the manner of data collection in an adaptive learning environment. In this adaptive learning environment children are presented with items that match their ability, which removes the start of the learning curve (when items are still too difficult) as well as the end of the learning curve (when items have become too easy). A second explanation for the limited observation of significant learning may be possible violations of unidimensionality. This will be the topic of the next section.

4. Study 2: The Problematic Assumption of Unidimensionality

Math Garden allows for the massive collection of high-frequent intraindividual data. Children might display all kinds of personal developmental trajectories, which in principle can be detected and analyzed. One limitation with regard to the implementation of the Rasch model in the system is the use of a common scale of item difficulties. In the self-organizing algorithm of Math Garden children's responses together determine the difficulty of items. This only works when item ordering is similar for all children. Basically this is the assumption of unidimensionality in IRT. One might argue that a principled idiographic measurement approach would not assume unidimensionality [44]. It is possible

---

[3]   For the permutation test we used 5000 replications where in each replication all items were randomly distributed between two sets. For each set we calculated each player's average slopes (i.e., mean learning speed) and the correlation between both of these averages values.

that each child requires his or her own measurement scale, e.g., a person specific ordering of items. This would be highly impractical of course and probably unnecessary. Fortunately, it is possible to investigate this matter empirically.

In this section, we investigate the dimensionality of the item scales using different analytics based on an item clustering approach. This clustering approach - based on an extended measurement model [45]—is aimed to classify items into subsets of related mathematical constructs. These subsets are defined by stronger (positive) correlations within the item sets and weaker (or negative) correlations with items in other sets. These sets possibly relate to different skills within a game.

In Pelánek et al. [45], different extensions of Elo models are presented. One of these extensions, called the networked model, is especially suited for estimation of item clusters. In the networked model, local and global skills are differentiated and estimated separately. The global skill is derived from all item responses whereas the local skill is derived from the responses to just a single item. Hence, the global skill can be interpreted as a general skill for the domain (e.g., addition skill or multiplication skill), where the local skills can be interpreted as skills to solve a specific item (e.g., the skills to solve $3 + 4$). However, it is expected that local skills cluster as various items will tap into the same skill (e.g., adding small numbers). The finding that (clusters of) local item skills are necessary to describe the abilities of children, next to a global skill, would actually be a violation of the assumption of unidimensionality.

For the estimation of the networked model, we selected the responses (accuracies) of the 200 most played items of players who completed at least 20 sessions of 15 responses between 1 September 2014 and 1 June 2017 for both the addition and the multiplication game. This resulted in 5144 users for the addition game (mean age = 7.17, $SD = 1.20$) and 8,180 users (mean age = 8.92, $SD = 1.31$) for the multiplication game. These users provided in total 2,708,027 and 4,557,333 responses for the addition and the multiplication game, respectively. In a first step, the correlation matrix of the local skills was inspected. In a second step the clustering of local item skills was explored using a hierarchical clustering algorithm. To interpret the results of the empirical data, we compared them to results of simulated data. For this simulation we generated responses with an unidimensional IRT model. In the generated data no local skills were present. Hence, when fitting the networked model to the generated data, we expected that extending the model by estimating local skills would merely result in capturing random fluctuations (error), and the correlation matrix of the local skills would be centered around zero with no specific patterns between items.

Results

As shown in Figure 6, the estimated correlations strongly differ between the simulated data set and the two empirical data sets. Whereas the estimated correlations for the simulated data set are around zero (as expected), the correlations of the empirical data sets show much more variation, as indicated by the large tails of both distributions in Figure 6.

To interpret the results of the clustering of local item skills, we produced heatmaps for the simulated data set (Figure 7) and the empirical data sets (multiplication in Figure 8; addition in Figure 9). The heatmap based on the correlation matrix of the simulated data shows no clear patterns (see Figure 7). Although the clustering metric seems to be sensitive to patterns of missing data, no clear clustering structure was found on the estimated correlations.

The heatmap based on the multiplication data set (see Figure 8) shows clear clusters of items with related content. First, replicating the results of Study 1, a large cluster of items that involve a times 10, 100 or 1000 operator was found (*times 100* items). As expected, the items in this cluster have a strong negative correlation with the items from multiplication tables 2 through 9 (*table* items). The *table* items are not clearly represented in a single cluster. However, based on the content of the items the clustering solutions seem clearly interpretable. For example, items 700×80, 3000×80 and 80×6000 are placed close to items 8×7 and 8×6. A third weaker cluster seems to be present that included items that involve larger, more complicated, calculations without any times 10, 100, or 1000 operator.

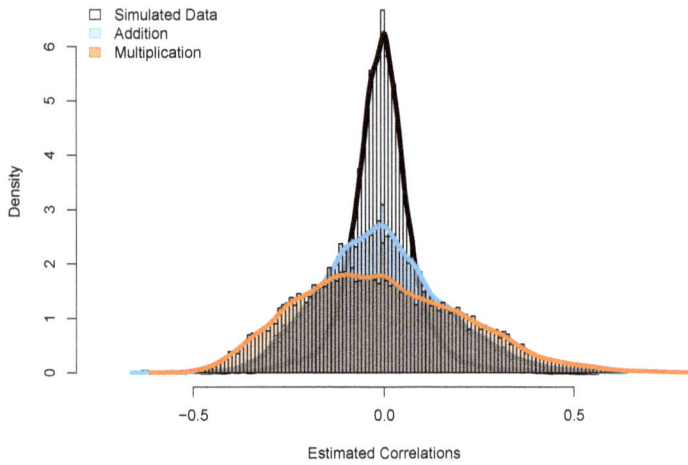

Figure 6. The distributions of the estimated correlations between the local skills in the addition, multiplication and simulated data.

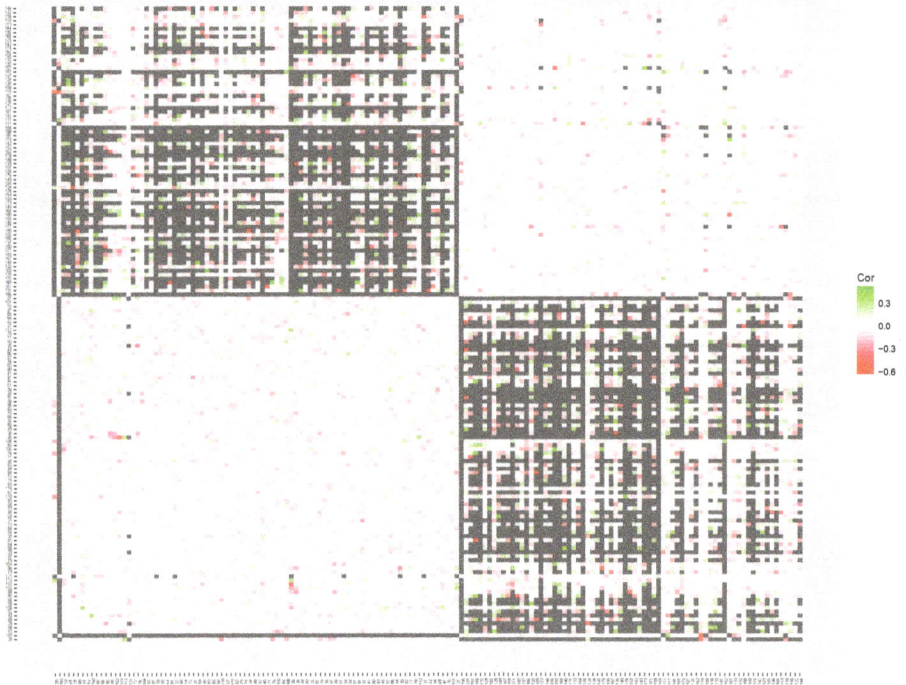

Figure 7. A heatmap based on the correlation matrix of the local skills estimated on a simulated data set based on the unidimensional model. Gray squares indicate missing values in the correlation matrix, resulting from adaptive item selection. The figure can also be found on www.abehofman.com/papers allowing for more detailed inspection.

For the addition data set (see Figure 9) the cluster solution appears less prominent, but certain item clusters are present and can be interpreted. First, a cluster of addition items with relatively small solutions is present (add 2, 3, 4 or 5), which correlate negatively with items with large solutions that involve adding tens (e.g., $40 + 10$ and $6 + 90$). A clear third small cluster is present with items that involve adding zero. However, a large set of addition items cannot be clearly assigned to a cluster. This indicates that the violation of unidimensionality may be less severe than for for the addition data set than the multiplication data set.

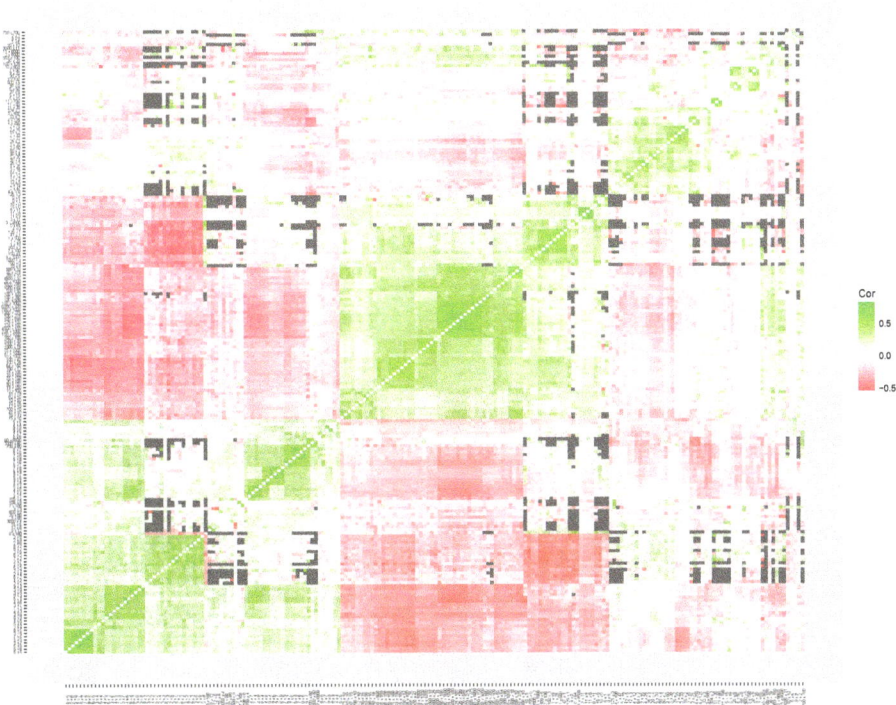

Figure 8. A heatmap based on the correlations matrix of the local skills of 200 multiplication items. Gray squares indicate missing values in the correlation matrix, resulting from the adaptive item selection. The figure can also be found on www.abehofman.com/papers allowing for more detailed inspection.

To conclude, the different analytics show that *table* and *times 100* multiplication items are best described by two different skills. Furthermore, the results based on the networked model shows that local skills can be estimated that provide important additions to the global skills currently used in the Math Garden. The correlations between these local skills should be described by multiple clusters that could be interpreted based on the item content. Future follow-up analyses using cross-validation techniques can determine both the weights in the expected score formula and the optimal number of clusters.

Figure 9. A heatmap based on the correlations matrix of the local user abilities of 200 addition items. Gray squares indicate missing values in the correlation matrix. See www.abehofman.com/papers for a downloadable version.

5. Discussion

The idiographic approach is essential in uncovering the rich dynamics of cognitive development. This is important for fundamental research, but also of practical relevance, especially in the educational context. The idiographic approach, however, requires highly frequent, psychometrically solid measurements of an individual. Once such data are collected, analyzing these data to gain insight into developmental and learning processes poses new challenges. We presented a new method to collect intensive time series to study intraindividual cognitive development using an innovative application of computerized adaptive testing to online learning platforms that schools can use for their students daily or weekly practice of various subjects, including language and mathematics. We then showed promising possibilities to analyze such intraindividual data, all concerning the development of mathematical skills. We explored different learning analytics based on time-series data of responses of children to single items. The results of Study 1 show that learning patterns in mathematics are irregular, with both relapses to lower ability and sudden changes to improved ability. In Study 2, different analyses indicated that mathematical skills consist of both global and local skills and that learning one local skill is not necessarily linked to learning another.

J. Intell. **2018**, *6*, 14

The results add to the main findings that result from microgenetic research [4]. Microgenetic research shows that cognitive development differs considerably between children and that strategy-usage is highly variable within children when a problem is repeatedly presented close in time [43]. According to Siegler and Crowley [4] multiple strategies are available to an individual and new more advanced strategies are not consistently applied. Over time more advanced strategies will replace older less adequate strategies. Hence, developmental change is not sudden, from strategy A to strategy B, but characterized by continuous shifts in the distribution of use of multiple (in)correct solution strategies [46], which Siegler refers to as the overlapping waves theory [47]. Moreover, this variability in strategy-use is often found in mathematics learning [48,49]. For example, children start with mostly simple counting strategies [50,51] and after they gain experience these will be replaced with more complex strategies, such as repeated addition for solving single digit multiplication [38]. For example, Lemaire and Siegler [52] showed that children often progress to more frequent use of complex strategies, but at each time point children use a mixture of strategies. The analyses in Study 1 add to these insights on development in mathematical abilities and show intraindividual and interindividual differences in learning trajectories.

The results of Study 2 also support this view on development in mathematics. Although each game consists of items that belong to a clearly defined domain (e.g., multiplication), we found multiple indications of multidimensionality. This might be surprising at first sight as tests consisting of very similar items (e.g., 4×6 and 12×3) are expected to be unidimensional. However, the enormous size of this data set yields very high power to detect interpretable sources of multidimensionality. What we found is that global skills in, for example multiplication, are supported by local skills, which can be interpreted as strategies for tackling specific items. Such strategies can exist next to each other and can be employed when applicable. As Straatemeier ([7], p. 174) proposed, ideally ability estimates would be based on unidimensional small item clusters within large item banks. We expect that separate ability estimates for these clusters will provide detailed insights into students' skills. This would provide a middle way between the current Math Garden approach based on one common scale and a full idiographic approach with a measurement scale per person.

The presented approach is very promising for the domain of intelligence. In the current system, games already exist that tap abilities that are related to intelligence, such as deductive reasoning and working memory. Hence, a platform to collect high frequent data on a regular basis, in an environment that is attractive for children, is available and has been shown successful. The presented techniques can be applied to such data as well. Intelligence is also often assumed to be a general ability supported by local skills, such as working memory or perception. The suggested analyses provide insights into the stability of intelligence, components of intelligence, and their interrelations, on an individual level. This way we would come closer to a full idiographic measurement approach.

Acknowledgments: Abe D. Hofman is supported by a NWO research talent grant (406-11-163) and Han L. J. van der Maas is supported by a NWO Creative Industries grant (314-99-107). We would like to thank Timo Fernhout for working on parts of the data analyses.

Author Contributions: Abe D. Hofman, Brenda R. J. Jansen and Han L. J. van der Maas conceived and designed the studies; Abe D. Hofman and Han L. J. van der Maas analyzed the data; Abe D. Hofman, Susanne M. M. de Mooij, Han L. J. van der Maas and Claire E. Stevenson wrote the paper.

Conflicts of Interest: The authors declare no conflict of interest.

Abbreviations

The following abbreviations are used in this manuscript:

IRT   Item response theory
CAT   Computer adaptive testing

References

1. Van der Maas, H.L.J.; Kan, K.J.; Hofman, A.D.; Raijmakers, M.E.J. Dynamics of Development: A complex systems approach. In *Inductive Developmental Systems*; Guilford Press: New York, NY, USA, 2013; pp. 270–286.
2. Molenaar, P.C.M. A manifesto on psychology as idiographic science: Bringing the person back into scientific psychology, this time forever. *Measurement* **2004**, *2*, 201–218.
3. Adolph, K.E.; Robinson, S.R.; Young, J.W.; Gill-Alvarez, F. What is the shape of developmental change? *Psychol. Rev.* **2008**, *115*, 527.
4. Siegler, R.S.; Crowley, K. The microgenetic method: A direct means for studying cognitive development. *Am. Psychol.* **1991**, *46*, 606–620.
5. Dolan, C.V.; van der Maas, H.L.J. Fitting multivariage normal finite mixtures subject to structural equation modeling. *Psychometrika* **1998**, *63*, 227–253.
6. Klinkenberg, S.; Straatemeier, M.; van der Maas, H.L.J. Computer adaptive practice of maths ability using a new item response model for on the fly ability and difficulty estimation. *Comput. Educ.* **2011**, *57*, 1813–1824.
7. Straatemeier, M. Math Garden: A New Educational and Scientific Instrument. PhD Thesis, University of Amsterdam, Amsterdam, The Netherlands, 2014.
8. OECD. *Education at a Glance: OECD Indicators*; OECD: Paris, France, 2006.
9. Wainer, H. *Computerized Adaptive Testing: A Primer*; Lawrence Erlbaum: Hillsdale, MI, USA, 2000.
10. Rasch, G. *Probabilistic Models for Some Intelligence and Achievement Tests*; Danish Institute for Educational Research: Copenhagen, Denmark, 1960.
11. Eggen, T.J.H.M.; Verschoor, A.J. Optimal testing with easy or difficult items in computerized adaptive testing. *Appl. Psychol. Meas.* **2006**, *30*, 379–393.
12. Elo, A.E. *The Rating of Chessplayers, Past and Present*; Arco Pub: New York, USA, 1978.
13. Maris, G.; van der Maas, H.L.J. Speed-accuracy response models: Scoring rules based on response time and accuracy. *Psychometrika* **2012**, *77*, 615–633.
14. Van Der Maas, H.L.J.; Wagenmakers, E.J. A psychometric analysis of chess expertise. *Am. J. Psychol.* **2005**, *118*, 29–60.
15. Birnbaum, Z.W.; Saunders, S.C. A new family of life distributions. *J. Appl. Probab.* **1969**, *6*, 319–327.
16. Van den Bergh, M.; Hofman, A.D.; Schmittmann, V.D.; van der Maas, H.L.J. Tracing the development of typewriting skills in an adaptive e-learning environment. *Percept. Mot. Skills* **2015**, *121*, 727–745.
17. Ericsson, K.A. The influence of experience and deliberate practice on the development of superior expert performance. In *The Cambridge Handbook of Expertise and Expert Performance*; Cambridge University Press: Cambridge, UK, 2006; Volume 38, pp. 685–705.
18. Gierasimczuk, N.; Van der Maas, H.L.J.; Raijmakers, M.E.J. An analytic tableaux model for deductive mastermind empirically tested with a massively used online learning system. *J. Log. Lang. Inf.* **2013**, *22*, 297–314.
19. Jansen, B.R.J.; De Lange, E.; Van der Molen, M.J. Math practice and its influence on math skills and executive functions in adolescents with mild to borderline intellectual disability. *Res. Dev. Disabil.* **2013**, *34*, 1815–1824.
20. Jansen, B.R.J.; Hofman, A.D.; Straatemeier, M.; Bers, B.M.C.W.; Raijmakers, M.E.J.; Maas, H.L.J. The role of pattern recognition in children's exact enumeration of small numbers. *Br. J. Dev. Psychol.* **2014**, *32*, 178–194.
21. Jansen, B.R.J.; Louwerse, J.; Straatemeier, M.; Van der Ven, S.H.G.; Klinkenberg, S.; Van der Maas, H.L.J. The influence of experiencing success in math on math anxiety, perceived math competence, and math performance. *Learn. Individ. Differ.* **2013**, *24*, 190–197.
22. Nyamsuren, E.; van der Maas, H.L.J.; Taatgen, N.A. How does prevalence shape errors in complex tasks? In Proceedings of the International Conference on Cognitive Modeling, Groningen, The Netherlands, 9–11 April 2015; Volume 13, pp. 160–165.
23. Hofman, A.D.; Visser, I.; Jansen, B.R.J.; van der Maas, H.L.J. The balance-scale task revisited: A comparison of statistical models for rule-based and information-integration theories of proportional reasoning. *PLoS ONE* **2015**, *10*, e0136449.
24. Van Der Ven, S.H.G.; Van Der Maas, H.L.J.; Straatemeier, M.; Jansen, B.R.J. Visuospatial working memory and mathematical ability at different ages throughout primary school. *Learn. Individ. Differ.* **2013**, *27*, 182–192.

25. Jansen, B.R.J.; Hofman, A.D.; Savi, A.O.; Visser, I.; van der Maas, H.L.J. Self-adapting the success rate when practicing math. *Learn. Individ. Differ.* **2016**, *51*, 1–10.

26. Kadengye, D.T.; Ceulemans, E.; Van den Noortgate, W. A generalized longitudinal mixture IRT model for measuring differential growth in learning environments. *Behav. Res. Methods* **2014**, *46*, 823–840.

27. Buwalda, T.A.; Borst, J.P.; van der Maas, H.J.L.; Taatgen, N.A. Explaining mistakes in single digit multiplication: A cognitive model. In Proceedings of the 14th International Conference on Cognitive Modeling, University Park, PA, USA, 11–18 September 2016; pp. 131–136.

28. Hofman, A.D.; Visser, I.; Jansen, B.R.J.; Marsman, M.; van der Maas, H.L.J. *Fast and Slow Strategies in Multiplication*; PsyArXiv: Grand Rapids, MI, USA, 2017.

29. Brinkhuis, M.J.S.; Savi, A.O.; Hofman, A.D.; Coomans, F.; van der Maas, H.L.J.; Maris, G. Learning as It Happens: A Decade of Analyzing and Shaping a Large-Scale Online Learning System; PsyArXiv 2018. Available online: https://osf.io/hfnxg/ (accessed on 22 December 2017)

30. Savi, A.; Ruijs, N.; Maris, G.; van der Maas, H. *Online Learning Solves Sturdy Problems in Education*; PsyArXiv: Grand Rapids, MI, USA 2017.

31. Coomans, F.; Hofman, A.D.; Brinkhuis, M.J.S.; van der Maas, H.L.J.; Maris, G. Distinguishing fast and slow processes in accuracy-response time data. *PLoS ONE* **2016**, *11*, e0155149.

32. De Bree, E.; van der Ven, S.H.G.; van der Maas, H.L.J. The voice of Holland: Allograph production in written Dutch past tense inflection. *Lang. Learn. Dev.* **2017**, *13*, 215–240.

33. Braithwaite, D.W.; Goldstone, R.L.; van der Maas, H.L.J.; Landy, D.H. Non-formal mechanisms in mathematical cognitive development: The case of arithmetic. *Cognition* **2016**, *149*, 40–55.

34. Van der Ven, S.H.G.; Klaiber, J.D.; van der Maas, H.L.J. Four and twenty blackbirds: How transcoding ability mediates the relationship between visuospatial working memory and math in a language with inversion. *Educ. Psychol.* **2017**, *37*, 487–505.

35. Hoyles, C.; Wolf, A.; Molyneux-Hodgson, S.; Kent, P. *Mathematical Skills in the Workplace: Final Report to the Science Technology and Mathematics Council*; Institute of Education, University of London; Science, Technology and Mathematics Council: London, UK, 2002.

36. Finnie, R.; Meng, R. *The Importance of Functional Literacy: Reading and Math Skills and Labour Market Outcomes of High School Drop-Outs*; Technical Report; Business and Labour Market Analysis Division: Ottawa, ON, Canada, 2006.

37. Reyna, V.F.; Brainerd, C.J. The importance of mathematics in health and human judgment: Numeracy, risk communication, and medical decision making. *Learn. Individ. Differ.* **2007**, *17*, 147–159.

38. Van der Ven, S.H.G.; Kroesbergen, E.H.; Boom, J.; Leseman, P.P.M. The development of executive functions and early mathematics: A dynamic relationship. *Br. J. Educ. Psychol.* **2012**, *82*, 100–119.

39. Gelman, A.; Jakulin, A.; Pittau, M.G.; Su, Y.S. A weakly informative default prior distribution for logistic and other regression models. *Ann. Appl. Stat.* **2008**, *2*, 1360–1383.

40. Gelman, A.; Su, Y.S.; Yajima, M.; Hill, J.; Pittau, M.G.; Kerman, J.; Zheng, T.; Dorie, V. *Arm: Data Analysis Using Regression and Multilevel/Hierarchical Models*; R Package, Version 9.01; Cambridge University Press: Cambridge, UK, 2006.

41. R Core Team. *R: A Language and Environment for Statistical Computing*; R Core Team: Vienna, Austria, 2013.

42. Van der Ven, S.H.G.; Straatemeier, M.; Jansen, B.R.J.; Klinkenberg, S.; van der Maas, H.L.J. Learning multiplication: An integrated analysis of the multiplication ability of primary school children and the difficulty of single digit and multidigit multiplication problems. *Learn. Individ. Differ.* **2015**, *43*, 48–62.

43. Siegler, R.S. Microgenetic analyses of learning. In *Handbook of Child Psychology*; John Wiley & Sons, Inc.: Hoboken, NJ, USA, 2006.

44. Nesselroade, J.R.; Gerstorf, D.; Hardy, S.A.; Ram, N. Focus article: Idiographic filters for psychological constructs. *Measurement* **2007**, *5*, 217–235.

45. Pelánek, R.; Papoušek, J.; Řihák, J.; Stanislav, V.; Nižnan, J. Elo-based learner modeling for the adaptive practice of facts. *User Model. User-Adapt. Interact.* **2016**, *27*, 89–118.

46. Kuhn, D.; Garcia-Mila, M.; Zohar, A.; Andersen, C.; White, S.H.; Klahr, D.; Carver, S.M. Strategies of knowledge acquisition. In *Monographs of the Society for Research in Child Development*; John Wiley & Sons, Inc.: Hoboken, NJ, USA, 1995.

47. Siegler, R.S. *Emerging Minds: The Process of Change in Children's Thinking*; Oxford University Press: Oxford, UK, 1996.

48. Lemaire, P. Executive functions and strategic aspects of arithmetic performance: The case of adults' and children's arithmetic. *Psychol. Belg.* **2010**, *50*, 335–352.

49. Ambrose, R.; Baek, J.; Carpenter, T.P. Children's invention of multidigit multiplication and division algorithms. In *The Development of Arithmetic Concepts and Skills: Constructive Adaptive Expertise*; Routledge: Mahwah, NJ, USA, 2003; pp. 305–336.

50. Dowker, A. *Individual Differences in Arithmetic: Implications for Psychology, Neuroscience and Education*; Psychology Press: East Sussex, UK, 2005.

51. Ashcraft, M.H.; Guillaume, M.M. Mathematical cognition and the problem size effect. *Psychol. Learn. Motiv.* **2009**, *51*, 121–151.

52. Lemaire, P.; Siegler, R.S. Four aspects of strategic change: Contributions to children's learning of multiplication. *J. Exp. Psychol. Gen.* **1995**, *124*, 83.

Sample Availability: Interested researchers can contact the first author or last author to request parts of the data for research purposes.

Journal of
Intelligence

MDPI

Article

Intraindividual Variability in Inhibition and Prospective Memory in Healthy Older Adults: Insights from Response Regularity and Rapidity

Emilie Joly-Burra [1,*], Martial Van der Linden [1,2,3] and Paolo Ghisletta [1,4,5]

[1] Faculty of Psychology and Educational Sciences, University of Geneva, CH-1211 Geneva, Switzerland; Martial.VanDerLinden@unige.ch (M.V.d.L.); Paolo.Ghisletta@unige.ch (P.G.)
[2] Swiss Centre for Affective Sciences, University of Geneva, CH-1211 Geneva, Switzerland
[3] Department of Psychology, University of Liège, B-4000 Liège, Belgium
[4] Faculty of Psychology (French), Swiss Distance Learning University, CH-3900 Brig, Switzerland
[5] Swiss National Centre of Competence in Research LIVES—Overcoming Vulnerability: Life Course Perspectives, Universities of Lausanne and of Geneva, CH-1211 Geneva, Switzerland
* Correspondence: Emilie.Joly@unige.ch; Tel.: +41-22-379-8177

Received: 30 November 2017; Accepted: 27 February 2018; Published: 1 March 2018

Abstract: Successful prospective memory (PM) performance relies on executive functions, including inhibition. However, PM and inhibition are usually assessed in separate tasks, and analytically the focus is either on group differences or at most on interindividual differences. Conjoint measures of PM and inhibition performance that take into account intraindividual variability (IIV) are thus missing. In the present study, we assessed healthy older adults' level of performance and IIV in both inhibition and PM using a classical Go/NoGo task. We also created a prospective Go/NoGo version that embeds a PM component into the task. Using dynamic structural equation modeling, we assessed the joint effects of mean level (μ), an indicator of amplitude of fluctuations in IIV (or net IIV; intraindividual standard deviation, *iSD*), and an indicator of time dependency in IIV (the autoregressive parameter ϕ) in reaction times (RTs) on inhibition and PM performance. Results indicate that higher inhibition failure, but not IIV, predicted PM errors, corroborating the current literature on the involvement of prepotent response inhibition in PM processes. In turn, fastest RT latency (μ) and increased net IIV (*iSD*) were consistently associated with prepotent response inhibition failure, while coherence in RT pattern (ϕ) was beneficial to inhibition performance when the task was novel. Time-dependent IIV (ϕ) appears to reflect an adaptive exploration of strategies to attain optimal performance, whereas increased net IIV (*iSD*) may indicate inefficient sustained cognitive processes when performance is high. We discuss trade-off processes between competing tasks.

Keywords: intraindividual variability; prospective memory; prepotent response inhibition; Go/NoGo SART task; amplitude of fluctuations; autoregressive parameter; random process fluctuation; functional adaptability; functional diversity

---

1. Introduction

1.1. IIV as a Tool to Study Cognitive Aging

Aging is associated with a broad range of functional changes in cognition and structural changes in the brain [1]. For decades, the bulk of cognitive and developmental studies have focused on interindividual differences in mean level of performance, regarding reaction time (RT) latency and error rates [2]. In that context, short-term variations in response within the same individual have mainly been considered error measurement, or noise, in the data. Early works from psychologists such as Fiske and Rice, nevertheless, stressed the importance of considering short-term fluctuations as valuable information to further the understanding of interindividual differences [3]. However, the substantial growth of intraindividual variability (IIV) as a tool to describe cognitive functioning, or, as Hultsch and MacDonald put it, "as a theoretical window onto cognitive aging," is fairly recent [4–6]. Because assessing short-term fluctuations requires many repeated assessments for each participant, this recent expansion of IIV as a tool to study human behavior and cognition was largely made possible by advanced statistical tools implemented in software that can handle large datasets.

Two broad types of IIV are often distinguished [7]: dispersion, defined as amplitude of fluctuations across multiple tasks (e.g., variability in global performance across a battery of attentional tasks), and inconsistency, amplitude of fluctuations across trials from the same task (e.g., variability in response latency across the items within a single sustained attentional task). Of these, the latter has probably received more attention in empirical research [4]. The present study focuses on the latter. This within-task trial-to-trial variability, which we will call IIV throughout the paper, has been shown to increase with age [8,9], even after controlling for mean level of performance [10]. Thus, even if individuals of different ages (e.g., younger and older adults) are rendered statistically equivalent with respect to their level of performance, such that there is no longer a difference between their mean performance because of a statistical control, the two age groups remain different with respect to their fluctuations around their means. These fluctuations are at the heart of IIV and thus provide complementary information about cognitive functioning with respect to the mean. Furthermore, IIV is greater in individuals with neurological disorders than in healthy subjects [11] and, far from being noise in the data, has been shown to be a good indicator of the integrity of neuroanatomical functioning in older adults [12,13]. In addition, individual differences in IIV predict level of cognitive performance such that increased IIV in RT has been linked to decreased executive control and resistance to distractor inhibition processes both in the general population and in patients with frontal lesions [11,14]. It has therefore been suggested that increased IIV reflects fluctuant executive control processes along the task and/or sustained attention lapses [14,15]. Moreover, IIV has been shown to predict not only short-term performance within a task, but also long-term cognitive decline [16,17], everyday problem-solving [18], psychopathology [19], and mortality [20,21]. In sum, the detrimental effects of increased IIV are observed on both specific cognitive task performance and more broad functional outcomes. Thus, IIV appears to be a fundamental marker of cognitive aging [22].

1.2. Prospective Memory and Cognitive Control in Older Adults

1.2.1. Automatic and Controlled Processes in Prospective Memory

While the relationship between IIV and general age-related cognitive decline has been studied for decades, other research fields in psychology are now turning to the study of IIV to deepen the understanding of cognitive processing underpinning performance. This is currently the case for prospective memory. Prospective memory (PM) is defined as the realization of delayed intentions in response to a given situation or cue [23], and is known to overall decrease with age [24–26]. PM enables us to remember to ask a friend a question the next time we see him or to post a letter while passing by the mailbox on our way to work. PM requires four phases: (1) intention formation; (2) intention retention; (3) intention initiation, and (4) intention execution [27]. Critically, PM differs from dual-task or mere action monitoring by (a) the presence of a delay between intention formation and action plan execution, during which the intention leaves the focus of attention; (b) the absence of explicit prompts to switch from the current activity (ongoing task) to the realization of the delayed intention; and (c) the fact that the prospective task is to be performed intermittently and less frequently than the ongoing task [28,29].

The successful realization of delayed intention relies on both prospective and retrospective components of PM. The prospective component is responsible for remembering that something has to be done when a given cue is encountered, while the retrospective component refers to remembering what has to be done. At first, it was suggested that the prospective component, which requires effective cue detection, is supported by automatic processes, while the retrospective component relies on more controlled processes [30]. Automatic prospective retrieval is proposed to rely on a reflexive association between the PM cue and the intended action [31], such that when the cue appears, the intended action is automatically retrieved from memory through recollection. Opposite to that idea is the preparatory attentional and memory process model, which posits that prospective remembering relies on strategic monitoring [32]. This monitoring process involves sustained attention and working memory capacity allocated to detection of the cue, which is no longer available for the ongoing task [33,34]. In line with this idea, brain regions involved in sustained attention and maintained intention are activated in participants expecting a PM cue, indicating anticipatory processing of PM cues, which may reflect monitoring for prospective cue and intention retrieval while performing the ongoing task [35]. From another standpoint, the multiprocess framework states that prospective intention retrieval occurs on either an automatic or controlled basis, depending on a series of task characteristics (importance of the prospective task, nature of the PM cue, its relationship with the intention, degree of absorption in the ongoing task, etc.) and individual differences in personality characteristics. One major determinant of the involvement of controlled monitoring processes is the focality of the PM cue: a task can be either focal, when the target cue feature for PM retrieval is to be processed in the ongoing task, or nonfocal, when the critical feature cuing for the PM task is not directly processed for ongoing task completion. A typical example of a focal PM task is a lexical decision task (word vs. nonword), in which the prospective cue is a certain category of words (e.g., fruits). In contrast, a nonfocal cue can be, for instance, a certain allocated target position on the screen or a particular color of a frame around the item to be processed for the ongoing task [36]. Importantly, the multiprocess framework predicts that nonfocal PM tasks require more controlled processes of strategic monitoring of the PM cues, whereas cue detection in focal PM tasks can efficiently rely on automatic recollection processes.

1.2.2. Age-Related PM Decline and Cognitive Control

Although retrospective memory plays an important role in effective PM performance, it does not appear to explain the observed age differences in performance. Instead, the distinction between controlled and automatic processes seems to be a better candidate to explain age decline in PM. Indeed, age effects are generally more pronounced for controlled than automatic processes [37,38]. Therefore, older adults' performance is substantially more impaired when attentional load is high and correct task execution requires controlled processes [39,40]. Accordingly, PM impairment with age seems to be particularly exacerbated for nonfocal as compared to focal PM tasks, the former requiring sustained attention and working memory capacity allocation to monitor for the target [31,41–43]. However, PM performance that relies on automatic intention retrieval processes can still, to a lesser extent, be affected by age, given that dividing attention between the ongoing task and the prospective requirements may increase the working memory demands anyway [44]. For this reason, Zuber and colleagues recently suggested that controlled and automatic processes always coexist within the same PM task, whether focal or nonfocal [45]. The predominance of control over automatic processes would therefore vary according to the nature of the task and to the PM phase within that task (see also [42]). Even if intention retrieval relied on automatic processes in focal PM tasks, correct intention execution may still require controlled processes.

Considering that retrieving and/or executing the intention entails self-initiating processes, PM processes and several facets of executive functioning can be considered to be somewhat intertwined [45–47]. Accordingly, the influence of executive functions on PM performance appears to be more pronounced in older than younger adults [47]. Most of the previous work on the involvement of executive functions in PM performance was based on global measures rather than specific facets of executive functioning [14,47,48]. However, it is now commonly accepted that executive function is not a unitary construct. As demonstrated by Miyake and coworkers, executive functions can be split into related but distinct facets: shifting, updating, and inhibition [49]. Friedman and Miyake showed that inhibition itself can further be divided into three related subprocesses: prepotent (or dominant) response inhibition, distractor-response inhibition, and resistance to proactive interference [50]. More specifically, they showed that prepotent response and distractor response inhibitions are closely related, hence considered a single construct, distinct from proactive interference inhibition. The few studies formally investigating the role of these specific facets of executive functioning in PM processes are therefore relatively recent. More precisely, diminished PM performance seems to be mediated by working memory, prepotent response inhibition, and shifting [43,45,48,51], more so as prepotent inhibition, shifting, and working memory are known to decline with increasing age [40,52–54].

1.2.3. The Specific Role of Prepotent Response Inhibition in PM

While the role of working memory (e.g., [51,55]) and shifting [32,56,57] in successful PM has received substantial attention, less is known concerning the specific role of prepotent response inhibition. It has been proposed that prepotent response inhibition plays a role both during monitoring for the cue, because one has to regularly inhibit the ongoing task in order to check for the PM cue [45,56], and during intention execution, because one has to inhibit the current ongoing task to be able to engage in effective execution of the PM intention [58]. Accordingly, Kliegel and colleagues showed that PM performance is particularly impaired in older adults when a task requires high inhibitory control [58].

However, the aforementioned studies focused on mean level of performance on PM and executive control. They therefore provide insights only on the role of interindividual differences in average performance on various facets of executive functions on PM global performance. Another approach to understanding the cognitive processes underlying PM performance is to consider IIV in tasks assessing cognitive processes supposedly involved in PM, such as prepotent response inhibition.

1.3. IIV in Prepotent Response Inhibition and PM

Building upon the idea that IIV in cognitive performance may reflect lapses of attention and controlled processes, Manly and colleagues used the Go/NoGo (GNG) task, a sustained attention-to-response task, to relate prepotent response inhibition performance to both mean level and IIV in RT [59]. In this task, sustained attention is required to maintain the task set between trials, while inhibition is needed to stop, or override, the inappropriate dominant response when an infrequent target is shown [60]. Both mean RT and IIV in this task independently predicted inhibition failure. Furthermore, when constraining participants to respond at a given pace (i.e., controlling for mean RT and variations in RT), IIV was still associated with increased error rates, thereby ruling out a speed/accuracy trade-off as the sole reason for inhibition failure. These results further corroborate the claim that IIV reflects fluctuations in executive processes, leading to inhibition failure independent of response latency. Similarly, Bellgrove and co-workers reported that lower IIV in GNG was associated with greater inhibitory performance in young to middle-age adults [61]. Using functional magnetic resonance imaging, they showed that IIV was positively correlated with activation in brain regions involved in sustained attention and inhibition. The authors therefore suggested that IIV reflects a greater demand for executive control in order to maintain task performance. In older adults, similar behavioral results were obtained by Rochat and colleagues [62]. While healthy older adults and older adults with dementia did not differ on their mean RT, IIV in GNG was higher in older adults diagnosed with Alzheimer's disease than in healthy controls. Critically, inhibition errors in GNG were once again associated with larger variability in RT, even after controlling for working memory capacity and shifting. Together, these studies suggest that variability in RT predicts inhibitory performance beyond the effect of mean-level RT; thus, IIV may reflect cognitive impairments that mean-level RT alone does not reveal.

A few studies very recently investigated IIV as predictive of PM performance. Loft and colleagues reported that a slowing in mean RT on nonprospective trials and increased variability in these RTs are beneficial to prospective performance in a nonfocal, but not in a focal, PM task [36]. Loft and co-workers thus suggested that increased mean RT and variability reflect regular monitoring for the prospective target. In contrast, Haynes et al. consistently found increased IIV in independent working memory and processing speed tasks to be predictive of lower performance on a composite PM score [63]. These authors speculated that the shared association between IIV and PM performance may arise from fluctuations in focus on the task and target monitoring. Similarly, Ihle and colleagues focused on costs to IIV as an outcome variable [64]. Costs to IIV are operationalized as the difference, computed for each participant, in amplitude of fluctuations as indicated by an increase in intraindividual standard deviation (*iSD*) between the pure ongoing task compared to the ongoing task plus embedded prospective task. In other words, costs to IIV assess the extent to which IIV increases when adding the PM task to the ongoing task. Ihle et al. showed that increased costs to IIV in nonfocal PM tasks correlate with lower PM, prepotent response inhibition, and working memory performance; these correlations did not emerge in focal PM tasks. They found no association between costs to mean RT (i.e., increase in mean RT between the pure ongoing task versus the ongoing task with embedded prospective task) and PM performance. Thus, it is not quite clear yet (a) whether IIV in RT reflects adaptive monitoring for target or maladaptive executive-control fluctuations, or (b) the extent to which IIV in prepotent response inhibition specifically predicts PM performance. In that respect, we believe it is useful to consider the distinction between two components of IIV: amplitude of fluctuations and temporal dependency.

1.4. Temporal Dependency in IIV

Although amplitude of fluctuations in RT, or the net size of IIV, is unquestionably valuable to study executive control fluctuations and explain cognitive performance, it does not consider the temporal aspects in the data, also called time-structured IIV [65,66]. Whereas amplitude in IIV, or net IIV, captures the range of RTs, time-structured IIV reflects dynamic aspects of cognitive functioning, such as adaptation, regulation, or search for strategies over time. Gilden argued that time dependency in RT is a signature of cognitive complexity and can reflect psychological processes involved in task solving [67]. Autoregressive models are one framework to operationalize temporal dependency in IIV [65,68]. These models assess the effect of the variable of interest at the previous measurement occasion on itself at the present occasion. In the case of RT, a positive autoregressive parameter (ϕ) signifies that if one had a slow RT at a given trial, one is likely to also have a slow RT at the next trial. Conversely, if one had a fast RT at a given trial, one is likely to also have a fast RT at the next trial. Hence, with a positive autoregressive effect, RTs tend to stay above or below one's mean level of RT for multiple trials before coming back to the mean RT level. The stronger the autoregressive parameter value, the longer it will take for the RTs to return back to the mean level. In other words, when one deviates from mean RT at a given trial, the higher the autoregressive parameter, the longer this deviation is likely to persist [68]. As a consequence, a positive autoregressive coefficient is interpreted as short-term coherence in response pattern, because it indicates alternation between periods of rather slow and rather fast trials in respects to one's mean RT. For instance, in studies considering day-to-day affective regulation, a positive autoregressive parameter has been interpreted as inertia to return to affective equilibrium [69]. The higher the autoregressive parameter, the longer it took for participants to recover from an emotional shock. In contrast, a null autoregressive parameter indicates that the RT for a given trial is independent from the RT for the previous trial, thereby indicating an absence of response patterns. In the case of affective regulation, this would mean that yesterday's affect will not impact today's affect. In other words, a participant with a null autoregressive parameter would display a random pattern of affect scores, hence a total lack of affective regulation. Finally, a negative autoregressive parameter signifies that if one had a slow RT at a given trial, one is likely to have a fast RT at the next trial. Conversely, one would have a slow RT at a given trial when the previous RT was fast. Negative autoregressive parameters, therefore, produce a back-and-forth pattern of RTs with consecutive fast and slow responses, as if participants tried to compensate from one trial to the next. Again, in the case of affective regulation, a negative autoregressive parameter would mean that if one was depressed yesterday, one is likely to feel better today, and probably depressed again tomorrow. A graphic illustration of the impact of autoregressive parameter and amplitude of fluctuations variations on time-series distributions is presented in Figure 1.

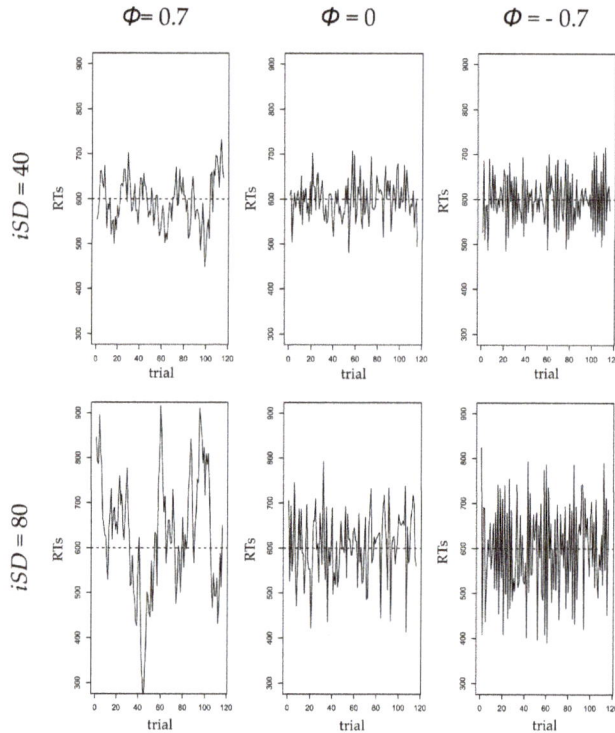

Figure 1. Simulated distributions of time series as a function of the values of the autoregressive parameter (ϕ, representing the time-structured component of intraindividual variation, IIV) and amplitude of fluctuation (intraindividual standard deviation, *iSD*, representing net IIV). From left to right, column panels represent time series for a positive ($\phi = 0.7$), null ($\phi = 0$), and negative ($\phi = -0.7$) autoregressive parameter. Top line panel represents time series for low amplitude of fluctuations (*iSD* = 40), and bottom line panel represents time series for a high amplitude of fluctuations (*iSD* = 80). Mean reaction time (RT) = 600 ms does not vary across time series.

Both amplitude of fluctuations and temporal dependency in IIV, therefore, may shed light on complementary information for understanding psychological functioning. Indeed, Ghisletta and colleagues reported that greater amplitude of fluctuations in a simple RT task predicted decline in fluid intelligence two years later, whereas higher consistency in time-structured variability in the same task predicted maintenance of the same outcome two years later [16]. Analyzing longitudinal data on negative affect, Wang and colleagues showed that net IIV predicted health complaints, while time-structured IIV further predicted chronic health problems; interestingly, mean level predicted neither outcome [68]. Similarly, using multilevel autoregressive models, Hamaker and co-workers recently reported that higher time dependency in older adults' negative affect was positively related to a higher mean level of negative affect, thereby suggesting a detrimental outcome of the carryover effect of negative affect [70]. These and similar results should therefore spur further research aimed at gauging the respective contributions of mean level of performance and both net and time-structured IIV to PM functioning.

1.5. Objectives of This Study

The aims of the present work are threefold. First, we seek to extend previous results indicating that IIV in GNG and PM tasks predicts, respectively, inhibition and PM performance in older adults. To do so, we investigated RT in terms of mean level, as well as amplitude of fluctuations in IIV and time-structured IIV modeled within the autoregressive framework. We assessed level of performance and IIV in inhibition performance in 100 healthy older adults using a classical GNG task. We then modified the task to embed a PM component and likewise estimated level of and variability in performance. In line with previous studies, we predicted that faster and more variable RTs would result in increased inhibition errors in GNG. Second, in an exploratory fashion, we compared IIV patterns across the two versions of the tasks. Given that we expected the prospective version of GNG to have a higher demand for controlled executive processes than the classical version of the task, we anticipated slower and more variable RTs in the former than in the latter. Finally, the third aim of this study is to test whether inhibitory performance in the modified GNG task predicts PM performance within the same task, given that previous literature strongly suggests that inhibition mediates age differences in PM [43,47,71]. We expected increased inhibition errors to predict poorer PM performance, even after controlling for working memory capacity. We are not aware of any other study using an inhibition task as an ongoing task for a PM task.

Here, we propose at least two interpretations of the autoregressive parameter (assessing the time-dependent aspect of IIV): on the one hand, coherence in RT patterns (i.e., a strong positive autoregressive parameter) could be associated with a strong activation of task set and better cognitive control, hence better performance in the task. On the other hand, strong coherence in RT patterns could reflect strong activation of the dominant response, rendering successful inhibition of this response less likely. In the first case, we would expect a negative relation between the autoregressive parameter and the number of inhibition and/or PM errors. In the second case, that relation would be positive. In both cases, a positive autoregressive parameter indicates persistence, or consistency, in RT patterns over time.

2. Materials and Methods

2.1. Participants

The initial sample for this study included 100 French-speaking healthy retired adults over 65 years of age, living independently at home, among the general population (62% women, age: 65–92 years). Exclusion criteria were dementia diagnosis, neurological antecedents, severe motor or sensory disability, and known psychiatric disorders. All participants gave their informed consent to participate. The study was conducted in accordance with the Declaration of Helsinki, and the protocol was approved by the Ethical Committee of the Faculty of Psychology and Educational Sciences at the University of Geneva. Participants were financially remunerated for the study.

Eight participants were excluded prior to statistical analysis, because they either did not complete all the cognitive task analyzed here (2 participants), reported not complying with prospective instructions on purpose (in order to maximize their inhibition performance; 3 participants), pressed the wrong response keys (2 participants), or did not remember the correct prospective cue (1 participant).

2.2. Procedure and Material

The present study was part of a wider project using a mixed qualitative and quantitative methodology to assess the nature of the relationships among cognitive functioning, goal-directed behaviors, and well-being in healthy older adults. Participants completed various cognitive tasks, including a classical Go/NoGo task and a modified version of the task in order to include a PM component, the Mini Mental State Examination (MMSE) [72], and Letter-Number Sequencing (LNS, *Wechsler Adult Intelligence Scale III*) [73]. Participants also completed the French versions of the Center for Epidemiologic Studies (CES-D) Depression Scale and the Lack of Initiative and Interest Scale

(IIS) as fillers between the two Go/NoGo tasks [74,75]. The purpose was to set a delay between the instructions of the PM task and performance of the task.

2.3. Classical and PM Go/NoGo Tasks

The classical Go/NoGo Task (CGNG, also known as Sustained Attention to Response Task, adapted from Rochat et al. [62]), is a computer-based task in which participants have to inhibit a prepotent motor response when an infrequent target stimulus appears on the screen. In this task, participants viewed one digit (between 1 and 9) at a time and were instructed to press the J key on the keyboard when they were shown any digit except 3. When the digit 3 appeared on the screen, participants were instructed to do nothing and wait for the next digit to appear. Each digit was displayed for 1500 ms against a black background, followed by a mask (a white cross in a circle), for 900 ms. Digits varied randomly in font size (5 font sizes between 63 and 135 points) and color (blue, pink, yellow, light green, dark green, gray, brown, and orange); both dimensions were irrelevant in CGNG. Before beginning the task, participants completed an 18-trial practice block that included 4 NoGo (i.e., digit 3) targets. In case of error, they received immediate feedback before the next trial. After the practice block, the CGNG task included 2 blocks of 117 trials each, during which participants did not receive feedback on their performance. Each digit, including 3, was presented 13 times in each block, thus giving a ratio of 104 Go trials (89%) to 13 NoGo trials (11%). Digits appeared randomly, so as to avoid consecutive NoGo trials. Participants were instructed to respond as quickly and accurately as possible. A short break of 5 min separated the two blocks.

After completing the CGNG task, participants were given instructions for the Prospective Go/NoGo (PGNG) task. They were told that now the digit color was relevant for successful task completion. Participants had to continue the previous task (i.e., press the J key when presented with any digit but 3) and additionally perform a second action (i.e., press the space bar after pressing the J key) when a digit in blue appeared (prospective cue). After instruction, participants filled out the CES-D and IIS (not analyzed here), in order to introduce a 10 min delay between prospective instructions and PGNG, preventing rehearsal of the prospective intention in working memory. Participants were not reminded of prospective instructions before beginning the PGNG.

The PGNG also contained 2 blocks of 117 trials each, but no practice block. Each block comprised 91 Go trials (78%), 13 NoGo trials (11%), and 13 Prospective trials (11%) in which prospective items were blue digits. There was no overlap between Prospective and NoGo trials (i.e., no blue digit 3). Again, item order was pseudo-randomized such that there were no consecutive NoGo or Prospective trials.

In order to design the PGNG task based on CGNG, we followed Einstein and McDaniel's guidelines for the creation of a typical laboratory paradigm for studying PM [76]. These include first presenting participants with instructions for the ongoing task and practicing this task (i.e., CGNG), then giving them the PM instructions (i.e., press the space bar when the digit is blue) and introducing a delay so that the prospective intention leaves the focus of awareness, then, after the delay, reintroducing the task (i.e., PGNG) without reminding the participants of the prospective instructions. Accordingly, CGNG is not a prospective task in itself, because (a) there is no delay between instructions for CGNG and completion of the task, and (b) NoGo trials in CGNG require inhibiting a prepotent response and not remembering to perform an additional action or to replace the regular action from the ongoing task with an alternative prospective action. PGNG, therefore, assesses inhibition performance in the NoGo trials and PM performance in the Prospective trials, where participants have to remember to perform this additional action.

Measures of interest for CGNG were reaction times (RTs) for correct Go trials and number of commission errors (incorrectly pressing the J key on a NoGo trial), the latter reflecting inhibition failure. For PGNG, we considered RTs for correct Go and Prospective trials, number of commission (inhibition) errors, and number of prospective omissions (forgetting to press the space bar on a Prospective trial). RTs were treated as trial-by-trial time series at an intraindividual (within-person) level, whereas commission errors and prospective omissions were summed for each block and treated as scores at an interindividual (between-persons) level. The analyses kept track of the actual trial number (i.e., NoGo trials in CGNG were considered missing and were part of the time series).

2.4. Analyses

2.4.1. Data Preprocessing

Suppression of Extreme RTs and Log Transformation

The first trial for each block was excluded from analysis, given that it consistently presented a very high RT. On the remaining 116 trials, RTs of correct trials below or above 3 standard deviations from the intraindividual mean were excluded from analysis and replaced with missing values for each subject (1.18% and 1.51% of trials in CGNG and PGNG, respectively). RTs were log-transformed to reduce skewness [77–79]. We thus obtained a total of 368 time series across 92 participants: four time series of log(RTs) for each subject, corresponding to blocks 1 and 2 of both CGNG and PGNG.

Amplitude of Fluctuations (iSD) Calculation and Stationarity Assessment

In order to compute an indicator of intraindividual amplitude of fluctuations, also referred to as net IIV [66], within each block, we calculated the intraindividual standard deviation (*iSD*) of log(RTs) for each individual's time series. *iSD* reflects the amount of fluctuation for an individual but does not consider the temporal dynamics of the fluctuation.

While *iSD* provides information on the amplitude of intraindividual fluctuations, time-series analyses further model the time dependency in the data, or time-structured IIV [66], via autoregressive models. In other words, a time-series analysis tests whether the RT at time t (from 1 to T) is influenced by previous RTs at time t-k, thereby capturing the temporal dynamic effects in the data up to a lag k ($k < T$) (for further details, see Section 2.4.2). However, time series can display general trends, such as learning effects across trials, resulting in decreasing RTs (negative trends), or fatigue effects, resulting in increasing RTs (positive trends). Such trends are known to potentially bias time-dependency estimation and thus must be removed from the data [68]. To screen for possible trends in the data, we visually inspected the time series and performed the Augmented Dickey-Fuller (ADF) test for each of the 368 time series [80]. This test formally assesses whether time series are stationary around zero, around a constant value (mean), or around a constant value plus a regular change pattern (mean and trend). The ADF test assesses the constancy of the mean and the variance of the dependent variable across repeated assessments. In our data, we expected the time series to be stationary around a mean (i.e., the mean RT). In the case of stationarity around a mean plus a trend, data must be detrended prior to any further analysis.

2.4.2. Dynamic Structural Equation Modeling with First-Order Autoregressive Parameter

Classically, autoregressive models are used to model time dependency in single-case time series. Such models estimate the lagged effects of RTs at previous trials t-k on the current RT at trial t. Autoregressive models thus estimate a k-order autoregressive parameter ϕ_k such that $RT_t = \phi_1 RT_{t-1} + \cdots + \phi_k RT_{t-k} + \varepsilon_t$. For the sake of simplicity, we will limit analysis in this study to first-order autoregressive vectors (also called at lag 1, when $k = 1$), estimating the direct effect of RT at time t-1 on RT at time t. Practically, the autoregressive parameters of order 1 estimated here indicate to what extent the RT at a given trial depends on the RT at the previous trial. As previously mentioned, a positive autoregressive parameter ϕ_k indicates a manifestation of coherence in response patterns across time (if one had a fast RT at trial 1, one would also tend to have, on average, a fast RT at trial 2), while a negative parameter reflects erraticism in responses (if one had a quite fast RT at trial 1, one would tend to have, on average, a rather slow RT at trial 2) (see [30,46]).

Autoregressive models are classically estimated separately for each individual time series. Here, this would imply estimating over 300 autoregressive models. A new approach allowing for the simultaneous estimation of multiple time series is called dynamic structural equation modeling (DSEM) and has recently been implemented in version 8 of Mplus software [81]. DSEM acknowledges the nested structure of the data by providing a multilevel extension of autoregressive models [70], in which trials (within-person, level 1) are nested within individuals (between-person, level 2), and allows for the inclusion of level-2 predictors and outcome variables in the model. In practice, these models can conjointly estimate both group effects and between-person variations in mean RT latency and net and time-structured IIV, while allowing these dimensions to predict other outcome variables such as accuracy or errors in the task. DSEM also has the advantage of taking into account missing values, which is typically not the case in most statistical software proposing time-series analyses. This feature is particularly important in the GNG task, as all correctly answered NoGo trials are followed by a missing RT (i.e., participants inhibit the prepotent motor response of pressing the J key when the number 3 appears). These models are implemented in a Bayesian framework such that parameter estimates are obtained from posterior distributions (based on noninformative priors following a normal distribution $N(0, 10^{10})$) and inferential conclusions are drawn based on the credible intervals (CIs) of these posterior distribution.

We follow Hamaker and colleagues [70,82,83] and Asparouhov and colleagues [84] to present DSEM. Conceptually, the model first decomposes a RT into within- and between-person components as follows:

$$RT_{it} = \mu_i + RT_{it}^*, \tag{1}$$

where μ_i is the time-invariant (between-person) mean RT for individual i, while RT_{it}^* represents the individual (within-person) deviations from μ_i at trial t.

The within-person component RT_{it}^* is decomposed as in the following equation:

$$RT_{it}^* = \phi_i RT_{i,t-1}^* + \zeta_{it}, \tag{2}$$

where ϕ_i is the first-order autoregressive parameter of individual i for RTs for two successive trials and ζ_{it} is the residual representing the variations in RT at trial t not explained by RT at trial t-1. These residuals are supposed to be normally distributed around zero with constant variance σ_ζ^2. Both the overall mean μ_i and the autoregressive parameter ϕ_i are allowed to vary across persons (hence the subscript i). That is, they both have random effects (v), as in

$$\begin{aligned} \mu_i &= \gamma_\mu + v_{\mu i}, \\ \phi_i &= \gamma_\phi + v_{\phi i}, \end{aligned} \tag{3}$$

where $v_{\mu i}$ and $v_{\phi i}$ are normally distributed, have constant variance σ_μ^2 and σ_ϕ^2, respectively, and are allowed to covary ($\sigma_{\mu \phi}$) with each other.

As is customary in multilevel modeling, we can combine Equations (1) to (3) to obtain

$$RT_{it} = \gamma_\mu + \gamma_\phi RT_{i,t-1}^* + v_{\mu i} + v_{\phi i} RT_{i,t-1}^* + \zeta_{it}, \tag{4}$$

where γ_μ and γ_ϕ are the fixed effects of the mean RT (i.e., mean RT averaged across participants) and the first-order autoregressive parameters (i.e., the mean autoregressive parameter on the whole sample), respectively. In turn, parameters $v_{\mu i}$ and $v_{\phi i}$ indicate the random effects of mean RT level and first-order autoregressive parameter, respectively (between-person variations in mean RT and autoregressive parameter at lag 1, respectively). To investigate the relationship between dimensions of IIV (amplitude of fluctuations and temporal dependency) and level of performance, we added $iSDs$ to the model and allowed it to correlate with ϕ_i and μ_i.

In the next step, we make full use of the strengths of DSEM by expanding the autoregressive model and considering additional between-person covariates. We therefore specify the overall traitlike mean μ_i, the autoregressive parameter ϕ_i, and the iSD_i to predict commission errors. Hence, level-2 outcome variables can be regressed on fixed effects as follows:

$$CE_i = \beta_0 + \beta_\mu \mu_i + \beta_\phi \phi_i + \beta_{iSD} iSD_i + v_{ei}, \tag{5}$$

where CE_i is the total number of commission errors during a block for individual i, β_0 is the intercept, β_μ, β_ϕ, and β_{iSD} are the regression weights of CE_i on mean level RT (μ_i) autoregressive parameter ϕ_i (estimated in Equation (3)), and amplitude of fluctuations (iSD_i), respectively. Finally, v_{ei} are the prediction residuals. We applied this model to each block of both task versions.

We computed successive DSEMs in order to test our hypothesis. First, single-block models were estimated to (a) assess the respective contributions of μ_i, iSD_i, and ϕ_i in RT decomposition in each block of CGNG and PGNG, respectively (models M1 to M4); and (b) regress inhibition errors on the fixed effects of these parameters (models M5 to M8). Second, a two-block model (model M9) was computed to (c) estimate relations between the respective μ_i, iSD_i, and ϕ_i from the second block of CGNG (CGNG2) and the first block of PGNG (PGNG1) and (d) regress prospective omissions in PGNG1 on μ_i, iSD_i, and ϕ_i and inhibition errors from CGNG2. Finally, given that PGNG had a higher cognitive load than CGNG, we estimated a last two-block model (model M10) to (e) rule out a possible confounded effect of general working memory resources (LNS score) in the prediction of PM errors by inhibition errors.

We fitted the same model (cf. Equations (1)–(4)) for each block of both versions of the tasks in models M1 to M4 and then included Equation (5) in models M5 to M8. In model M9, Equation (5) was estimated twice, to predict commission errors for CGNG2 and PGNG1. CE_i^{P1} (commission errors in PGNG1) was additionally regressed on CE_i^{C2} (commission errors in CGNG2), while PO_i^{P1} (prospective omissions in PGNG1) was regressed on μ_i^{P1}, ϕ_i^{P1}, iSD_i^{P1}, and CE_i^{P1}. Model M9 is represented in Figure 2. Finally, in model M10, CE_i^{C2}, CE_i^{P1}, and PO_i^{P1} were additionally regressed on the LNS score.

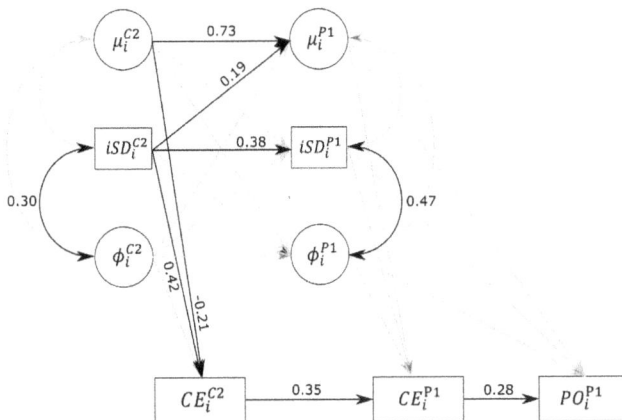

Figure 2. Path diagram for model M9 results. Variables represented in circles are parameters estimated within the dynamic structural equation modeling (DSEM) based on individual RTs, namely mean-level RT (μ_i) and the autoregressive parameter of order 1 (ϕ_i) in Classical Go/NoGo (CGNG)2 and Prospective Go/NoGo (PGNG)1. Variables represented in rectangles are the intraindividual amplitude of fluctuations (iSD_i), the total number of commission errors in CGNG2 and PGNG1 (CE_i^{C2} and CE_i^{P1}), and the total number of prospective omissions in PGNG1 (PO_i^{P1}). Parameters μ_i, iSD_i, and ϕ_i are regressed on one another across blocks and allowed to covariate within blocks. Finally, error variables are regressed on μ_i, iSD_i, and ϕ_i in their respective blocks. Single-headed arrows represent regression weights, double-headed arrows indicate covariances. Significant parameters and their corresponding standardized estimates are reported in black. Nonsignificant parameters are depicted in gray. Variances for each variable are not depicted but were nevertheless estimated and were all significant. $R^2_{\mu^{P1}} = 0.58$, $R^2_{iSD^{P1}} = 0.18$, $R^2_{\phi^{P1}} = 0.16$, $R^2_{CE^{C2}} = 0.25$, $R^2_{CE^{P1}} = 0.24$, $R^2_{PO^{P1}} = 0.13$.

3. Results

3.1. Stationarity

According to the ADF test, none of the time series for RT displayed a trend, indicating an absence of global speeding or fatigue effect across trials within each block. On the 368 time series, 363 were stationary across a constant nonzero mean, indicating fluctuations of RT around a within-person mean for each block. Surprisingly, five time series were found to be stationary around zero in PGNG, suggesting that the RTs in these time series vary around a mean not statistically different from zero, which is virtually impossible. Visual inspection of the time series revealed that these series presented extreme variations in RT, with a few abnormally short and long RTs across the block. We therefore excluded the five participants whose time series were stationary around zero from subsequent analysis.

3.2. Sample Characteristics and Descriptive Statistics

The final sample for analysis thus comprised 87 older adults (60.92% women). The average age of the participants was 72.44 years (SD = 5.01, range = 65–84). Participants had a relatively high number of years of education (M = 13.30, SD = 2.78), normal general cognitive performance (MMSE mean [M] = 27.77, SD = 1.86), and globally self-rated their health as good (M = 4.00, SD = 0.72, on a 5-point Likert scale from 1 = Very bad health to 5 = Very good health). The mean score for LNS was 9.41 (SD = 2.36).

3.3. Error Patterns

Commission errors and prospective omission rates in the respective blocks of CGNG and PGNG are displayed in Table 1. A Wilcoxon signed-ranks test indicated that summed commission errors were significantly higher in PGNG than in CGNG (Z = −7.52, p < 0.001). Pooled across blocks, participants failed to inhibit 8.5% of incorrect dominant responses in CGNG, which is comparable to what was reported in Rochat et al. for healthy older adults [62]. Inhibition failure increased to 23.4% in PGNG. Within CGNG, commission errors did not significantly differ between the two blocks (Z = −0.51, p = 1.00), while there were significantly more commission errors in PGNG1 than in PGNG2 (Z = −4.41, p < 0.001). Concerning PM, overall performance was extremely high, with a 91% mean accuracy pooled across blocks, and prospective omission errors were higher in PGNG1 than in PGNG2 (Z = −3.84, p < 0.001; p-values were multiplied by the number of tests to correct for type I error bias). Participants therefore had more trouble inhibiting a dominant response in PGNG than in CGNG and, furthermore, showed worse inhibition and prospective performance in the first block than in the second block of PGNG. This suggests some sort of learning effect, or calibration of performance, for the prospective version of the task.

Table 1. Means and standard deviations (M, SD) for commission errors and prospective omissions in blocks 1 and 2 of CGNG and PGNG.

Error Type	Block			
	CGNG1	CGNG2	PGNG1	PGNG2
Commission errors	1.18 (1.6)	1.03 (1.15)	3.61 (2.49)	2.48 (1.79)
Prospective omissions	na	na	1.53 (2.17)	0.75 (1.58)

Note: The maximum number of each type of error for each block is 13.

3.4. Estimation of DSEMs

Following Hamaker et al. [70,82,83], we estimated DSEMs with a Gibbs random walk sampler algorithm for the Markov chain Monte Carlo estimation running two parallel chains. Each model was estimated using 50,000 iterations and a thinning of 10, resulting in a 5000-iteration–based solution. All models satisfyingly converged according to potential scale reduction statistic values very close to 1.0 (highest value was 1.08 for model 5), indicating convergence of results for the two chains, and symmetric posterior distributions of all parameters, satisfying posterior parameter trace plots and rapidly decreasing to 0 autocorrelation plots for each parameter. Diagnostic plots were not initially satisfying for models 1, 9, and 10. For these, we increased the number of iterations to 250,000 and used a thinning of 50, still resulting in a 5000-iteration–based solution. All models presented satisfying diagnostic plots at the end, indicating stability of the final solutions.

3.4.1. Single-Block Models

Fixed and Random Effects

Fixed and random effects estimates for models M1 to M4, along with their 95% CIs, are reported in Table 2. As expected, fixed effects for both mean RT (γ_μ) and amplitude of fluctuations (γ_{iSD}) were consistently higher in PGNG (γ_μ^{P1} = 6.38 and γ_μ^{P2} = 6.36, corresponding to 589.93 ms and 561.16 ms, respectively, γ_{iSD}^{P1} = 0.20 and γ_{iSD}^{P2} = 0.18) than in CGNG (γ_μ^{C1} = 6.25 and γ_μ^{C2} = 6.22, corresponding to 518.01 ms and 502.70 ms, respectively, γ_{iSD}^{C1} = 0.15 and γ_{iSD}^{C2} = 0.14), as suggested by nonoverlapping 95% CIs. This strongly suggests that participants were overall slower and more variable in their RTs in PGNG than in CGNG. These results are consistent with previous findings from Ihle and colleagues indicating that adding a prospective task to the ongoing task comes with a cost, in terms of both mean RT and amplitude of fluctuations [64]. Estimates for the autoregressive parameter γ_ϕ were positive and significant in all models. They appeared higher in CGNG (γ_ϕ^{C1} = 0.30 and γ_ϕ^{C2} = 0.27 for blocks 1 and 2, respectively) than in PGNG (γ_ϕ^{P1} = 0.23 and γ_ϕ^{P2} = 0.14, respectively). Estimated means for ϕ suggest that RT patterns were less consistent in time in PGNG than in CGNG, and that there was even less consistency in the second block of the prospective version of the task.

Table 2. Posterior means (and 95% credible intervals) of fixed effects, random effect variances, and correlations between random effects estimated from models M1 to M4. Mean fixed effects and random variances are shown in raw metrics; correlations and regression weights are shown in within-level standardized metrics.

Parameter	Block (Model)			
	CGNG1 (M1)	CGNG2 (M2)	PGNG1 (M3)	PGNG2 (M4)
γ_μ	6.25 * (6.22 to 6.28)	6.22 * (6.19 to 6.25)	6.38 * (6.35 to 6.41)	6.33 * (6.30 to 6.36)
$v_{\mu i}$	0.02 * (0.01 to 0.02)	0.02 * (0.01 to 0.02)	0.01 * (0.01 to 0.02)	0.02 * (0.01 to 0.02)
γ_ϕ	0.30 * (0.26 to 0.33)	0.27 * (0.23 to 0.31)	0.23 * (0.19 to 0.21)	0.14 * (0.10 to 0.17)
$v_{\phi i}$	0.01 * (0.01 to 0.02)	0.02 * (0.01 to 0.03)	0.02 * (0.01 to 0.03)	0.01 * (0.01 to 0.02)
γ_{iSD}	0.15 * (0.14 to 0.16)	0.14 * (0.13 to 0.15)	0.20 * (0.19 to 0.21)	0.18 * (0.17 to 0.19)
v_{iSDi}	0.00 * (0.00 to 0.01)	0.00 * (0.00 to 0.01)	0.00 * (0.00 to 0.01)	0.00 * (0.00 to 0.01)
$r\left(v_{\mu i} - v_{\phi i}\right)$	0.22 (−0.10 to 0.47)	0.18 (−0.10 to 0.43)	−0.18 (−0.48 to 0.13)	0.09 (−0.25 to 0.39)
$r\left(v_{\mu i} - v_{iSDi}\right)$	0.11 (−0.12 to 0.31)	0.05 (−0.17 to 0.27)	0.11 (−0.12 to 0.33)	0.14 (−0.08 to 0.34)
$r\left(v_{\phi i} - v_{iSDi}\right)$	0.65 * (0.40 to 0.83)	0.29 * (0.03 to 0.52)	0.33 * (0.02 to 0.59)	−0.11 (−0.40 to 0.17)

Note: The parameters , γ_μ, γ_ϕ, γ_{iSD} are the fixed effects, while the parameters $v_{\mu i}$, $v_{\phi i}$, v_{iSDi} are the random variances of the within-person mean RT, the order-1 autoregressive parameter, and the intraindividual standard deviation, respectively. Correlations between random effects at level 2 are denoted by $r(v_{\mu i} - v_{\phi i})$, $r(v_{\mu i} - v_{iSDi})$, and $r(v_{\phi i} - v_{iSDi})$. * 95% CI does not include 0.

All random effects were significant, indicating that there were substantial between-person differences in mean RT, amplitude of fluctuations, and time dependency. Such nonzero random effects prompted the investigation of covariances among these parameters.

Correlation Estimates

Random effects were allowed to covary at level 2. We report standardized estimates of these covariations and interpret these effects as correlations between the random effects. Correlations between the random effects of mean RT, $v_{\mu i}$, and the autoregressive parameter, $v_{\phi i}$, as well as between mean RT and iSD, v_{iSDi}, did not significantly differ from 0. The latter reveals that net variability is independent from response latency in this study, which is in line with Bellgrove and co-workers' results [61]. This consistent independence of mean level of RT and amplitude of fluctuation in our data supports the claim that a linear relation between mean RT and iSD should not be arbitrarily assumed [85]. Instead, the two parameters need to be considered for their respective contribution to performance [59,86]. However, a positive correlation between the random effects of the autoregressive parameter and iSD was significant in both blocks of CGNG ($r\left(v_{\phi i} - v_{iSDi}\right)^{C1} = 0.65$ and $r\left(v_{\phi i} - v_{iSDi}\right)^{C2} = 0.29$) and the first block of PGNG ($r\left(v_{\phi i} - v_{iSDi}\right)^{P1} = 0.33$), but not in the second block of PGNG ($r\left(v_{\phi i} - v_{iSDi}\right)^{P2} = -0.11$). These positive correlations suggest that the participants with more variability were also more consistent in their pattern of RTs from one trial to the next, except in PGNG2. Hence, consistent response patterns across time seem to emerge in participants whose RTs vary more widely around a mean level. A somewhat rushed conclusion would be that amplitude of fluctuations and time-dependency components of IIV are collinear in these data.

Prediction of Commission Errors

Models M5 to M8 further included the prediction of commission (inhibition) errors CE_i on the previously mentioned fixed effects. This extension of the previous models allows testing whether indicators of level (μ) and IIV (iSD and ϕ) during performance of the task are related to the total number of commission errors. Estimates for the fixed and random effects of μ, iSD, and ϕ, as well as the covariances between these random effects, were virtually identical to those estimated in models M1 to M4. Thus, we only report estimates for the regression weights in Table 3 (the full version of the table, with all estimates, is available in Appendix A, Table A1). In all models, μ_i significantly and negatively predicted commission errors, which is consistent with the concept of speed/accuracy trade-off: the higher the RT, the fewer the errors, and the lower the RT, the more numerous the errors. Concerning net IIV, iSD_i was positively related to CE_i in CGNG1, CGNG2, and PGNG1. The effect just failed to reach significance in PGNG2 (95% credible interval (−0.00 to 0.40)). Hence, the faster and more variable the participant, the more likely inhibition errors were committed in both versions of the task, independent of the general response speed. These results replicate previous findings [59,61,62], and therefore corroborate the claim that increased amplitude of fluctuations in RT negatively impacts performance in a GNG task, reflecting fluctuations in controlled executive processes.

Table 3. Posterior means (and 95% CI) of intercepts and regression weights of CE_i, on μ_i, iSD_i, and ϕ_i, estimated for models 5 to 8. Estimates are shown in within-level standardized metrics.

Parameter	Block (Model)			
	CGNG1 (M5)	CGNG2 (M6)	PGNG1 (M7)	PGNG2 (M8)
β_0	11.15 * (1.74 to 19.51)	11.27 (−0.86 to 23.30)	14.94 * (2.78 to 26.53)	15.46 * (5.31 to 24.03)
β_μ	−0.27 *(−0.48 to −0.05)	−0.20 * (−0.40 to −0.00)	−0.27 * (−0.50 to −0.04)	−0.32 * (−0.51 to −0.10)
β_ϕ	−0.39 * (−0.93 to −0.00)	0.08 (−0.18 to 0.33)	−0.24 (−0.56 to 0.08)	0.16 (−0.15 to 0.45)
β_{iSD}	0.79 * (0.50 to 1.33)	0.42 * (0.21 to 0.59)	0.31 * (0.07 to 0.55)	0.20 (−0.00 to 0.40)
R^2_{CE}	0.45	0.25	0.16	0.17

Note: The parameters $\beta_0, \beta_\mu, \beta_\phi, \beta_{iSD}$ are the respective intercepts and regression weights of commission errors on μ_i, iSD_i, and ϕ_i, the order-1 autoregressive parameter. R^2_{CE} = between-level R^2 of commission errors. * 95% CI does not include 0. Full version of the table, including all estimates, is available in Table A1.

In turn, the autoregressive parameter ϕ negatively predicted CE_i in CGNG1 only, suggesting that in the first block of CGNG, participants with higher consistency in their RTs committed fewer errors. In this block, the three parameters together explained 45% of the variance of commission errors. Mean level RT, net IIV (iSD), and time-dependent IIV (ϕ), therefore substantially predicted almost half of the inhibition failure variance. This effect size estimate dropped to 25%, 16%, and 17% in models 6, 7, and 8, respectively.

3.4.2. Two-Block Models

Coherence of Fixed Effects across Both Versions of the Task

In model M9, all three PGNG1 parameters related to mean RT, amplitude of fluctuations, and time dependency were regressed on the analogous parameters of the CGNG2 block. This model allows testing whether performance (in terms of level and IIV components) during the classical version of the task predicts performance in the prospective version. Parameters within each block were allowed to correlate with each other and to predict commission errors in their respective block. Furthermore, the PGNG1 parameters were allowed to predict the prospective omission errors in the same block. Finally, commission errors in PGNG1 (CE^{P1}) were regressed on the same errors in CGNG2 (CE^{C2}), and prospective omissions (PO^{P1}) were regressed on commission errors in PGNG1. Significant standardized estimates for model M9 are reported in Figure 2. Results indicate that μ^{P1} was significantly predicted by μ^{C2} and iSD^{C2} (the respective regression weights are 0.73 (0.59 to 0.84) and 0.19 (0.02 to 0.34)), but not by ϕ^{C2} (−0.05 (−0.26 to 0.16)). This indicates a certain degree of traitlike stability of mean RT across the two versions of the tasks, and the more variability in CGNG2, the slower in PGNG1. iSD^{P1} was only significantly predicted by iSD^{C2} (0.38 (0.17 to 0.58)), indicating a moderate relationship between amplitude of fluctuations in CGNG2 and PGNG1. Finally, neither ϕ^{C2}, μ^{C2}, or iSD^{C2} significantly predicted ϕ^{P1}, indicating unrelated time-dependency parameters between the two versions of the task. In other words, the fact that one tends to deviate from one's mean level of RT for a long period of time in the last part of the CGNG does not necessarily imply that the same deviations will be observed when a prospective requirement is added to the task.

As seen previously in model M6, commission errors in CGNG2 (CE^{C2}) were still significantly predicted by μ^{C2} and iSD^{C2} (−0.21 (−0.41 to −0.01) and 0.42 (0.21 to 0.60), respectively; R^2 = 25%). In turn, CE^{C2} did positively predict CE^{P1} (0.35 (0.14 to 0.53), R^2 = 24%), while, unlike in model 7, μ^{P1} and iSD^{P1} effects just failed to reach significance after controlling for the effect of commission errors in the previous block (−0.18 (−0.40 to 0.04) and 0.18 (−0.07 to 0.42), respectively). In both blocks, even though there seemed to be a stable inhibition ability trait, three-quarters of the variance of inhibition errors in PGNG were not explained by the previous inhibition performance at a simpler version of the task. We interpret this unexplained variance at least partially in terms of ongoing task cost on the inhibition task.

Similarly to models M2, M3, M6, and M7, only the correlations between respective random effects of the iSD and the autoregressive parameter ϕ were significant (0.30 (0.03 to 0.53) and 0.47 (0.16 to 0.72) for CGNG2 and PGNG1, respectively).

Prospective Errors Prediction

As expected, CE^{P1} significantly predicted PO^{P1} (0.28 (0.06 to 0.49)), suggesting that the more inhibition failures, the more prospective failures as well. None of the effects of mean RT, amplitude of fluctuations, or autoregressive parameter further significantly predicted prospective omissions. As a whole, the model predicted 12.7% of the variance of PO^{P1}.

Controlling for Working Memory Performance

Finally, in model M10, we added three predictors to model M9. We included predictions from the total score at the LNS task onto CE^{C2}, CE^{P1}, and PO^{P1}. LNS score significantly predicted CE^{P1} (−0.20 (−0.38 to −0.00), R^2 = 29%), but failed to predict CE^{C2} and PO^{P1} (−0.14 (−0.32 to 0.06), R^2 = 28%, and −0.05 (−0.26 to 0.17), R^2 = 14%). This result confirms our expectation that PGNG is more taxing on cognitive resources than CGNG, and further suggests that inhibition performance suffers from limited working memory capacity while prospective performance does not. This is also in line with the claim that monitoring for prospective cues is taxing on working memory capacity, which is no longer available for successful completion of the ongoing task. Of importance, the regression weight from CE^{P1} to PO^{P1} remained significant (0.27 (0.03 to 0.49), R^2 = 14%), indicating that the relationship between inhibition and prospective failure is not due to a general confounded effect of working memory resources.

4. Discussion

In the present work, we considered healthy older adults' performance in both a classical and prospective version of a GNG task. Using DSEM [70,82,83], we gauged the respective contributions of mean level RT, net IIV, and time-structured IIV to inhibition and prospective performances. To our knowledge, this study is the first to use an inhibition task as an ongoing task for a PM task and to investigate time-structured IIV in inhibition and PM.

4.1. Inhibition, PM Performance, and Ongoing Task Costs

As hypothesized, inhibition performance in PGNG positively predicted PM performance in the same block. The better the inhibition performance, the higher the prospective accuracy. Importantly, recent work has suggested that age-related deficits in the GNG task could be attributed to impairments in the ability to maintain multiple task sets rather than actual prepotent inhibition impairments [53]. In our data, the link between prepotent inhibition and PM performance does not appear to be due to a confounded general lack of cognitive resources, because the effect was still significant when controlling for working memory performance (see also [54]). Therefore, this effect concurs with previous results from the PM literature indicating that prepotent response inhibition contributes to successful cue retrieval and intention initiation in PM [43,45,47,58]. The present relationship between inhibition and PM is not merely due to ongoing task costs in our data. Had it been the case, we would have observed a negative, instead of a positive, relationship between inhibition and PM errors.

Still, in line with the notion of competing resource allocation between ongoing and PM tasks, inhibition (commission) error rates increased in PGNG compared to CGNG, which indicates ongoing task costs in terms of accuracy on the inhibition (ongoing) task [87,88]. While ongoing task performance decreased in PGNG compared to CGNG, prospective performance was particularly high in the present study [88]. Therefore, error patterns suggest that, at least at the group level, participants prioritized the prospective task at the expense of the ongoing inhibition task. The ongoing task cost is further substantiated by increased mean-level RT and amplitude of fluctuations in PGNG compared to CGNG. Inasmuch as increased net IIV is often considered to reflect greater demand for executive control in exchange for maintained task performance [61,89], results confirm that PGNG is more taxing on executive resources than the classical version of the task [64,90].

4.2. Absence of Direct Link between PM Performance and IIV

In the present work, we extended the examination of IIV on inhibition and PM performance by taking into account both the amplitude of net IIV and its time structure, operationalized as the autoregressive parameter ϕ. Regarding PM performance, contrary to our expectations and to previous studies [36,64], neither mean-level RT or net or time-dependent IIV significantly predicted prospective omissions. We cannot tie this absence of effects to the fact that we controlled for the effect of commission errors. As a matter of fact, despite removing commission errors from the model, effects of mean-level RT and net and time-dependent IIV on prospective omission still failed to reach significance. We therefore discuss three nonmutually exclusive possible accounts for the absence of relations between IIV and PM performance.

First, as mentioned previously, PM performance was particularly good in this study (91% accuracy). Loft and colleagues, who did observe a relationship between IIV and PM performance, had accuracy ranges sensibly lower than that observed in our data [36]. We therefore may have failed to observe a link between PM performance and IIV in our data due to a restricted range in the number of prospective omissions. However, the fact that inhibition successfully predicted PM errors tends to invalidate this hypothesis. Indeed, there may be a narrow range of PM errors, but inhibition performance was able to successfully predict at least one part of its variance.

Second, and related to the first point, such high PM performance tends to suggest that our PM task is more demanding than the CGNG, but still not extremely demanding. Thus, the PM task would principally rely on automatic cognitive processes in both cue detection and intention execution. In effect, the multiprocess framework [31,91] states that demands in controlled monitoring processes vary according to certain characteristics of the PM task, among them target cue focality. In the present study, PGNG was designed as a nonfocal task, because the prospective cue, digit color, was irrelevant for the ongoing task. Such nonfocal tasks are expected to predominantly rely on controlled processes. However, the accuracy rate in our data is rather in line with those of studies in which prospective retrieval appeared to rely on spontaneous retrieval [90,92] rather than on controlled processes. Critically, albeit being nonfocal, our PM cue, color, was directly presented at the center of attention (i.e., on the number to be processed for ongoing task) and is a very basic feature to be processed [93]. Importantly, according to the multiprocess framework, such highly distinctive cues can trigger automatic recollection of the prospective intention without the need for strategical monitoring [91]. Hence, nonfocal tasks using highly distinctive PM cues can ultimately present the same pattern of results as focal tasks. Accordingly, the PM accuracy rate in our data is also more in line with the accuracy reported by Loft et al. for their focal task (85%) rather than their nonfocal task (60%). Of importance, effects of net IIV on PM performance were not observed for focal tasks in either Loft and colleagues or Ihle and colleagues [36,64]. Therefore, the absence of effects of both net and time-dependent IIV on PM performance in the present data eventually is in line with previous findings from these authors.

The third account for the absence of IIV effect on PM in the first block of PGNG performance revolves around interindividual differences in task-set prioritization and search for strategies. Participants may have differed in terms of which task they prioritized over the other. In that respect, IIV may, in the first block of PGNG, reflect different cognitive processes in different people, therefore blurring the relation between IIV and PM performance.

4.3. Adaptive and Nonadaptive Aspects of IIV and Inhibition Performance

In contrast to the absence of effects on PM, mean-level RT and IIV did predict inhibition performance. Faster RTs and higher *iSD*s consistently predicted increased inhibition errors, whereas higher autoregressive parameters ϕ predicted fewer errors in the first block of CGNG only. In this block, a higher autoregressive parameter was associated with fewer commission errors. Hence, the more coherent the RT pattern, the better the inhibition performance. Interestingly, although their respective influences on inhibition performance in the first block of CGNG went in opposite directions, net and time-dependent IIV correlated positively and strongly. That is, consistent response patterns across time seem to emerge in participants whose RTs vary more widely around a mean level. The more variable participants are, the more consistent their pattern of RT from one trial to the next, or the longer they tend to deviate from their mean RT. To disentangle respective effects of net IIV and time-dependent IIV, we additionally computed a model in which we excluded *iSD* as a predictor of inhibition failure (estimates for this additional model are reported in Appendix B, Table A2). In this model, ϕ did not significantly predict the number of errors. This suggests that higher consistency (as assessed with the autoregressive parameter ϕ) is beneficial to inhibition performance only when portioning out the confounded negative effects of net IIV.

While initially counterintuitive, these effects are compatible with the distinction made by Li and colleagues between adaptive and nonadaptive IIV [94]. In our opinion, this distinction is a key element to apprehend the meaning of IIV indices with regard to the global performance pattern in our data. Li and co-workers propose that detrimental random process fluctuations, indicating a lack of robustness in cognitive processes, are observed when participants arrive at an asymptotic level of functioning (i.e., when they are close to optimal performance). In contrast, adaptive types of IIV include functional diversity and adaptability. The former refers to variability reflecting adaptive exploratory behavior and search for strategies during acquisition of a novel task (i.e., before reaching an asymptotic level of functioning). An example of functional diversity was provided by Siegler [95], who showed, in his pioneering work, that increased IIV in children was associated with exploration of various strategies for successful problem-solving. Functional adaptability refers to the ability to alter functioning in response to perturbations, such as sudden fluctuations in processes or more cognitively demanding tasks, in order to restore optimal functioning. In line with this decomposition of IIV, Allaire and Marsiske reported that net IIV proved to be detrimental in tasks in which older adults already performed close to optimal performance, whereas net IIV appeared to be adaptive in more difficult tasks where exploration of various strategies enabled performance improvement along the task [96].

In our data, a higher autoregressive parameter (higher consistency in RT patterns) is beneficial to inhibition performance and can therefore be interpreted in terms of functional diversity. The fact that this effect only appeared in the first block of the task suggests that the autoregressive parameter here reflects exploration of speed/accuracy trade-off strategies in order to reach optimal performance (cf. [97] for a review of speed/accuracy trade-off). After reaching optimal equilibrium, the overall performance in CGNG, where participants have only one task to complete, is very high, and further exploration of strategies may not be beneficial anymore. In this context, the negative effect of *iSD* on inhibition performance can therefore be related to what Li et al. labeled as the detrimental effect of random process fluctuation [94]. This refers to the assumption that higher net IIV on a trial-to-trial basis reflects fluctuation in executive controlled processes underpinning successful completion of the task [14].

If a higher autoregressive parameter (higher consistency in RT patterns) reflects exploration of strategies in order to master the task, as indicated by results in the first block of CGNG, we would have expected a similar pattern in the first block of PGNG, when the prospective task was added to the GNG. Results indicate that the autoregressive parameter's effect on inhibition performance just failed to reach significance in PGNG1. A possible explanation is that after two blocks of CGNG, participants were quite familiar with the task, and adjustment to the additional task in PGNG would probably not require an entire block of trials. To test this hypothesis, we split PGNG1 into two time series (trials 1–58 and 59–107) and applied the same model (model 7) to each half-block (results are presented in Appendix B, Table A3). As expected, the autoregressive parameter ϕ was sensibly higher in the first half of the first block of PGNG than in the second half, and also significantly predicted fewer inhibition errors, which was no longer the case in the second half of PGNG1. Similar to what was observed for CGNG1, a higher autoregressive parameter predicted less inhibition failure, whereas increased amplitude of fluctuations predicted more inhibition errors. These results reinforce our proposition that a high autoregressive parameter at the beginning of a task reflects strategy exploration and learning of the task, which we can also interpret as functional adaptability.

Indeed, in PGNG, executive demands of the task increase and participants have to balance the two task sets. Increased variability may become useful when trying to juggle both tasks' requirements. In the first block of PGNG, participants may try to continue using the same, now counterproductive, response strategy they used in CGNG, which results in more errors of both types. Because participants now have to monitor for both the NoGo cue (digit 3) and the prospective cue (color blue), a more successful strategy is to attend to NoGo trials and prospective cues more accurately on a trial-by-trial basis and respond independently to each item. This item-specific focus ultimately results in a decreased autoregressive parameter ϕ. This latter strategy seems to be implemented by participants in the second block of PGNG (and already in the second half of the first block of PGNG), as indicated by a higher amplitude of fluctuations and a lower autoregressive parameter value compared to the first PGNG block.

In PGNG, increased net IIV may thus result from two separate processes. First, as in CGNG, one part of net IIV in PGNG may reflect random process fluctuation. Second, the remaining part of increased net IIV might represent functional adaptability to the newly imposed requirements in PGNG. In addition, we see a change in performance pattern between the first and second block of PGNG. First, both inhibition and prospective errors decreased in the second block, indicating there was space for performance improvement in the first block. Second, while the amplitude of fluctuations remained stable across blocks, the autoregressive parameter was quite high in the first half of the first block of PGNG and decreased at the end of the block and in the second block, indicating less coherence in response pattern despite similar net IIV. Taken together, this confirms our expectation that at least some aspects of variability may be beneficial to performance in PGNG.

To summarize our interpretation of the two IIV components in these data, we suggest that a high autoregressive parameter ϕ in CGNG1 and in the first half of PGNG1 indicates exploration of best possible strategies during early phases of task acquisition, while net-IIV, as indicated by iSD, reflects detrimental random processes in the classical version of GNG. In turn, increased net IIV in both blocks of PGNG and decreased time-dependent autoregressive ϕ parameter in the second block both reflect a beneficial functional adaptability. In sum, these results confirm that mean level and net and time-dependent IIV in RTs provide different and complementary information in respect to task performance.

Our interpretations are coherent with the results from Loft and colleagues and Ihle and colleagues [36,64]. Because accuracy in the PM task used by Loft and colleagues was rather low and net IIV had a positive effect on PM performance, net IIV appears to reflect functional diversity and/or functional adaptability in their data. In contrast, PM performance in Ihle and colleagues was very close to optimal and net IIV had a detrimental effect on PM performance, reflecting random process fluctuations. In the end, these results illustrate the complexity and multiple aspects of IIV effects on cognitive processes and performance.

4.4. Limitations and Perspectives

First, it is not clear whether the divergent effects of random process fluctuations or functional adaptability in PGNG occur within the same individual, reflecting competing parallel processes, or across different individuals, reflecting interindividual differences in prioritizing one task over the other. Further studies are therefore needed to clarify under which circumstances net and time-dependent IIV appear to be adaptive strategies, and systematically examine how random process fluctuation and functional adaptability can simultaneously co-occur in the same task. If both effects add up in the same individual, methodological and statistical tools to disentangle their respective effects on iSD need to be further studied. From a methodological standpoint, manipulating instructions in order to clearly tell participants which task to prioritize over the other might help to clarify the effect of iSD on performance. From a statistical perspective, the conjoint combination of iSD and ϕ patterns appears to be a promising tool in that regard. We would predict that high iSD coupled with low ϕ would indicate nonadaptive RT strategies in simple tasks, but beneficial strategies in more complex or dual tasks. An additional lead would also be to classify participants into high versus low performers and to test for differential effects of iSD and ϕ in both groups.

Second, given that involvement of executive functions in PM seems to be exacerbated in older adults in comparison to younger adults [47], the present study could be extended to younger adults in order to clarify whether these results generalize to other age groups.

Third, the present study analyzed IIV in time series for RT only. Results could be extended to IIV in accuracy using an autoregressive model for binary data (e.g., [98]). These models would provide valuable complementary information in terms of regularity in response correctness, and potentially help to disentangle respective effects of net and time-structured IIV.

Fourth, we used raw IIV indices in this study. Ihle and colleagues analyzed costs to IIV and RT [64], and this methodological approach may provide leads to clarify which task participants might prioritize over the other. This could also help disentangle opposite effects of IIV on PM performance. We would predict that participants whose ϕ parameter decreased more between blocks 1 and 2 of PGNG would have better performance in the latter than the former.

Fifth, as previously proposed, the absence of a predictive effect of IIV on PM performance may result from the fact that automatic processes for cue detection might be sufficient for successful performance in PGNG. Indeed, despite requiring more cognitive control than CGNG, it appears that PGNG is not particularly taxing on executive resources, as shown by the particularly high PM accuracy rate. Because PGNG has the advantage of presenting a relatively simple design as compared to most PM tasks, this task was well suited for a first application of DSEM analysis. However, given that IIV appears to reflect controlled processes, PGNG might not be the most adequate task to reveal effects of IIV on PM performance. We therefore propose some methodological modifications to the task in order to increase controlled process task requirements. A first possibility is to use a less distinctive prospective cue, such as a particular color of frame in the periphery of the screen or a change in background pattern. Furthermore, because participants have to press an additional key for the prospective trials (space bar), in addition to the usual key-press for the ongoing task (J key) in PGNG, prepotent response inhibitory control is not directly required during the intention execution phase in PGNG. Critically, Bisiacchi and colleagues showed that prepotent inhibition response is particularly involved in PM performance when inhibitory control is directly required in intention execution (i.e., when participants have to inhibit the usual ongoing task response in order to press an alternative key for the prospective trials) [99] (see also [42]). We therefore expect the relationship between prepotent response inhibition and PM performance to be stronger in a paradigm where participants have to refrain from pressing the usual ongoing task response and instead press another response key for prospective trials only. As also suggested by Verbruggen and Logan, GNG itself might not be the best paradigm to measure controlled processes in prepotent response inhibition [100]. Because there is a consistent mapping between stimuli and response (Go or NoGo trials), with time, successful inhibition of the motor response in NoGo trials can rely on automatic processes too. The authors therefore recommend using a stop-signal paradigm, a task in which the stimulus-response mapping is inconsistent, instead of GNG, or reversing stimulus-response mapping between blocks (i.e., not always associating NoGo trials with the digit 3, but changing cue digits across blocks). However, we note that the stop-signal task, as the GNG task used here, might imply a strong motor component, which may diminish generalization to other PM tasks with inferior motor components. To conclude, using PGNG, we were able to underscore a predictive effect of inhibition on PM performance, but we expect this relation to be stronger and to strengthen the effect of IIV on PM performance with some task modifications aimed at increasing task requirements for controlled processes.

Sixth, the main indices we used to address our hypothesis are potentially quite different with respect to their reliability. As pointed out by past work (e.g., [85,101,102]), it is generally the case that in RT data the intraindividual mean is more reliable than the *iSD*. Indeed, the correlation between the indices estimated across the two blocks of the same tasks were r = 0.83, 0.68, and 0.41 for μ, *iSD*, and ϕ in CGNG, and 0.78, 0.65, and 0.45 in PGNG. This may point to a decreasing level of reliability going from μ to the *iSD* and ϕ, as was similarly obtained by Ghisletta and colleagues [16]. Yet, simulation work (e.g., [101,103]) has shown that with over 100 trials, one can reliably estimate *iSD* and ϕ. Given that here we worked with blocks of 117 trials, we suppose that our *iSD* estimates were reliable enough for inclusion in the extended DSEM models. As a matter of fact, *iSD* and ϕ were found to be significant predictors of commission errors in multiple blocks. In sum, while we recognize that the indices do vary with respect to measurement reliability, we do not think this feature alone explains our results.

Finally, we relied on DSEM to assess the respective contributions of mean level of RT as well as both net and time-structured aspects of IIV in within-task cognitive performance. This modeling framework lacks reliable goodness-of-fit indices, in both absolute and relative terms. In particular, at present the deviance information criterion (DIC) cannot be used to compare models directly, as is usually done in SEM [70]. We are sure that in the near future, model comparison will become possible also for DSEM.

5. Conclusions

Results of the present study indicate that higher RT latency and increased net variability are consistently associated with increased inhibition failure, while coherence in RT pattern predicts inhibition performance only when the task is novel. In turn, inhibition failure significantly predicts PM errors therein, corroborating the current PM literature on the involvement of prepotent response inhibition in successful PM processes. However, we did not find any effect of IIV on PM performance. In conclusion, the present work allowed us to highlight the multiple facets of IIV, in both its adaptive and detrimental aspects, in a classical inhibition task and in its prospective version. Our results further suggest that IIV should be considered not solely as reflecting inefficient sustained cognitive processes, but also as efficiently exploring strategies to attain and restore optimal performance [95]. In that regard, examining time-dependent aspects of IIV besides amplitude proved insightful. We encourage future developmental cognitive researchers to model time-dependent IIV as a window to deepening their understanding of dynamic cognitive processes and possible trade-off processes between competing tasks.

Acknowledgments: This project was supported by the Swiss National Science Foundation grant FNS—100019_159359/1. We thank Elisa Gallerne for her help in data collection and global contribution to the whole research project. We additionally thank Nicola Ballhausen, Alexandra Hering and Sascha Zuber for their most helpful comments and suggestions regarding task design and data interpretation.

Author Contributions: Emilie Joly-Burra, Martial Van der Linden, and Paolo Ghisletta conceived and designed the experiments; Emilie Joly-Burra performed the experiments; Emilie Joly-Burra and Paolo Ghisletta analyzed the data; Emilie Joly-Burra, Paolo Ghisletta, and Martial Van der Linden wrote the paper.

Conflicts of Interest: The authors declare no conflict of interest. The founding sponsors had no role in the design of the study; in the collection, analyses, or interpretation of data; in the writing of the manuscript, and in the decision to publish the results

Appendix A

Table A1. Posterior means (and 95% credible intervals) of fixed effects, random effect variances, correlations between random effects, intercepts and regression weights of CE_i on μ_i, iSD_i and ϕ_i estimated for models 5 to 8. Mean fixed effects and random variances are shown in raw metrics while correlations and regression weights are shown in within-level standardized metrics.

Parameter	Block (Model)			
	CGNG1 (M5)	CGNG2 (M6)	PGNG1 (M7)	PGNG2 (M8)
γ_μ	6.25 * (6.22 to 6.28)	6.22 * (6.19 to 6.25)	6.38 * (6.35 to 6.41)	6.33 * (6.30 to 6.36)
$v_{\mu i}$	0.02 * (0.01 to 0.04)	0.02 * (0.01 to 0.02)	0.01 * (0.01 to 0.02)	0.02 * (0.01 to 0.03)
γ_ϕ	0.29 * (0.25 to 0.33)	0.27 * (0.23 to 0.31)	0.23 * (0.20 to 0.27)	0.14 * (0.10 to 0.17)
$v_{\phi i}$	0.01 * (0.01 to 0.19)	0.02 * (0.01 to 0.03)	0.02 * (0.01 to 0.02)	0.01 * (0.01 to 0.02)
γ_{iSD}	0.15 * (0.14 to 0.16)	0.14 * (0.13 to 0.15)	0.20 * (0.19 to 0.21)	0.18 * (0.17 to 0.19)
v_{iSDi}	0.00 * (0.00 to 0.01)	0.00 * (0.00 to 0.01)	0.00 * (0.00 to 0.01)	0.00 * (0.00 to 0.01)
$r\left(v_{\mu i} - v_{\phi i}\right)$	0.23 (−0.07 to 0.72)	0.17 (−0.11 to 0.43)	−0.18 (−0.47 to 0.15)	0.09 (−0.24 to 0.39)
$r\left(v_{\mu i} - v_{iSDi}\right)$	0.13 (−0.11 to 0.64)	0.05 (−0.17 to 0.26)	0.11 (−0.11 to 0.32)	0.13 (−0.10 to 0.35)
$r\left(v_{\phi i} - v_{iSDi}\right)$	0.68 * (0.42 to 0.91)	0.30 * (0.02 to 0.53)	0.34 * (0.06 to 0.60)	−0.11 (−0.40 to 0.19)
β_0	11.15 * (1.74 to 19.51)	11.27 (−0.86 to 23.30)	14.94 * (2.78 to 26.53)	15.46 * (5.31 to 24.03)
β_μ	−0.27 * (−0.48 to −0.05)	−0.20 * (−0.40 to −0.00)	−0.27 * (−0.50 to −0.04)	−0.32 * (−0.51 to −0.10)
β_ϕ	−0.39 * (−0.93 to −0.00)	0.08 (−0.18 to 0.33)	−0.24 (−0.56 to 0.08)	0.16 (−0.15 to 0.45)
β_{iSD}	0.79 * (0.50 to 1.33)	0.42 * (0.21 to 0.59)	0.31 * (0.07 to 0.55)	0.20 (−0.00 to 0.40)
R^2_{CE}	0.45	0.25	0.16	0.17

Note: The parameters γ_μ, γ_ϕ, γ_{iSD} are the fixed effects, while the parameters $v_{\mu i}$, $v_{\phi i}$, v_{iSDi} are the random variances of the within-person mean RT, the order-1 autoregressive parameter, and the intraindividual standard deviation, respectively. Correlations between random effects at level 2 are denoted by $r\left(v_{\mu i} - v_{\phi i}\right)$, $r\left(v_{\mu i} - v_{iSDi}\right)$, and $r\left(v_{\phi i} - v_{iSDi}\right)$. β_0, β_μ, β_ϕ, β_{iSD} are the respective intercepts and regression weights of commission errors on μ_i, iSD_i, and ϕ_i. R^2_{CE} = between-level R^2 of commission errors. * 95% CI does not include 0.

Appendix B

Table A2. Posterior means (and 95% credible intervals) of fixed effects, random effect variances, correlations between random effects, and regression weights of CE_i on μ_i and ϕ_i estimated for models 5bis. Mean fixed effects and random variances are shown in raw metrics, while correlations and regression weights are shown in within-level standardized metrics.

Parameter	CGNG1 (M5bis)
γ_μ	6.25 * (6.23–6.28)
$\upsilon_{\mu i}$	0.02 * (0.01–0.03)
γ_ϕ	0.31 * (0.28–0.34)
$\upsilon_{\phi i}$	0.01 * (0.01–0.02)
$r\left(\upsilon_{\mu i} - \upsilon_{\phi i}\right)$	0.27 (−0.06 to 0.56)
β_μ	−0.28 * (−0.49 to −0.05)
β_ϕ	0.11 (−0.19 to 0.38)
R^2_{CE}	0.09

Note: The parameters γ_μ and γ_ϕ are the fixed effects, while the parameters $\upsilon_{\mu i}$ and $\upsilon_{\phi i}$ are the random variances of the within-person mean RT and the order-1 autoregressive parameter, respectively. Correlation between random effects at level 2 is denoted by $r\left(\upsilon_{\mu i} - \upsilon_{\phi i}\right)$. β_μ and β_ϕ are the respective regression weights of commission errors on μ_i and ϕ_i. R^2_{CE} = between-level R^2 of commission errors. * 95% CI does not include 0.

Table A3. Posterior means (and 95% credible intervals) of fixed effects, random effect variances, correlations between random effects, intercepts, and regression weights of CE_i on μ_i, iSD_i, and ϕ_i estimated for the first and second half of PGNG1 trials. Mean fixed effects and random variances are shown in raw metrics, while correlations and regression weights are shown in within-level standardized metrics.

Parameter	Block	
	PGNG1—First Half of Block	PGNG1—Second Half of Block
γ_μ	6.40 * (6.37 to 6.43)	6.33 * (6.30 to 6.36)
$\upsilon_{\mu i}$	0.01 * (0.01 to 0.02)	0.02 * (0.01 to 0.02)
γ_ϕ	0.24 * (0.20 to 0.29)	0.14 * (0.10 to 0.17)
$\upsilon_{\phi i}$	0.02 * (0.01 to 0.03)	0.01 * (0.00 to 0.02)
γ_{iSD}	0.21 * (0.20 to 0.22)	0.18 * (0.17 to 0.19)
υ_{iSDi}	0.00 * (0.00 to 0.01)	0.00 * (0.00 to 0.01)
$r\left(\upsilon_{\mu i} - \upsilon_{\phi i}\right)$	−0.03 (−0.41 to 0.35)	−0.16 (−0.56 to 0.30)
$r\left(\upsilon_{\mu i} - \upsilon_{iSDi}\right)$	0.25 * (0.02 to 0.46)	0.01 (−0.22 to 0.23)
$r\left(\upsilon_{\phi i} - \upsilon_{iSDi}\right)$	0.48 * (0.13 to 0.77)	0.08 (−0.32 to 0.49)
β_0	12.46 (−2.38 to 30.40)	15.46 * (5.31 to 24.03)
β_μ	−0.22 (−0.57 to 0.06)	−0.20 (−0.43 to 0.09)
β_ϕ	−0.48 * (−1.06 to −0.07)	0.31 (−0.05 to 0.76)
β_{iSD}	0.41 * (0.10 to 0.97)	0.33 * (0.07 to 0.54)
R^2_{CE}	0.23	0.30

Note: The parameters γ_μ, γ_ϕ, γ_{iSD} are the fixed effects, while the parameters $\upsilon_{\mu i}$, $\upsilon_{\phi i}$, υ_{iSDi} are the random variances of the within-person mean RT, the order-1 autoregressive parameter, and the intraindividual standard deviation, respectively. Correlations between random effects at level 2 are denoted by $r\left(\upsilon_{\mu i} - \upsilon_{\phi i}\right)$, $r\left(\upsilon_{\mu i} - \upsilon_{iSDi}\right)$, and $r\left(\upsilon_{\phi i} - \upsilon_{iSDi}\right)$. β_0, β_μ, β_ϕ, β_{iSD} are the respective intercepts and regression weights of commission errors on μ_i, iSD_i, and ϕ_i. R^2_{CE} = between-level R^2 of commission errors. * 95% CI does not include 0.

References

1. Harada, C.N.; Love, M.C.N.; Triebel, K.L. Normal Cognitive Aging. *Clin. Geriatr. Med.* **2013**, *29*, 737–752. [CrossRef] [PubMed]
2. Molenaar, P.C.M. A Manifesto on Psychology as Idiographic Science: Bringing the Person Back into Scientific Psychology, This Time Forever. *Meas. Interdiscip. Res. Perspect.* **2004**, *2*, 201–218. [CrossRef]

3. Fiske, D.W.; Rice, L. Intra-individual response variability. *Psychol. Bull.* **1955**, *52*, 217–250. [CrossRef] [PubMed]

4. Hultsch, D.F.; MacDonald, S.W. Intraindividual variability in performance as a theoretical window onto cognitive aging. In *New Frontiers in Cognitive Aging*; Dixon, A., Bäckman, L., Nilsson, L.-G., Eds.; Oxford University Press: New York, NY, USA, 2004; pp. 65–88, ISBN 978-0198525691.

5. Nesselroade, J.R. The warp and the woof of the developmental fabric. In *Visions of Aesthetics, the Environment & Development: The Legacy of Joachim F. Wohlwill*; Downs, R.M., Liben, L.S., Palermo, D.S., Eds.; Lawrence Erlbaum Associates: Hillsdale, NJ, USA, 1991; pp. 213–240, ISBN 978-1138873292.

6. Nesselroade, J.R.; Molenaar, P.C.M. Some Behaviorial Science Measurement Concerns and Proposals. *Multivar. Behav. Res.* **2016**, *51*, 396–412. [CrossRef] [PubMed]

7. Shammi, P.; Bosman, E.; Stuss, D.T. Aging and Variability in Performance. *Aging Neuropsychol. Cogn.* **1998**, *5*, 1–13. [CrossRef]

8. Anstey, K.J. Sensorimotor Variables and Forced Expiratory Volume as Correlates of Speed, Accuracy, and Variability in Reaction Time Performance in Late Adulthood. *Aging Neuropsychol. Cogn.* **1999**, *6*, 84–95. [CrossRef]

9. Hultsch, D.F.; MacDonald, S.W.S.; Dixon, R.A. Variability in reaction time performance of younger and older adults. *J. Gerontol. B Psychol. Sci. Soc. Sci.* **2002**, *57*, 101–115. [CrossRef]

10. MacDonald, S.W.S.; Hultsch, D.F.; Dixon, R.A. Performance variability is related to change in cognition: Evidence from the Victoria Longitudinal Study. *Psychol. Aging* **2003**, *18*, 510–523. [CrossRef] [PubMed]

11. Stuss, D.T.; Murphy, K.J.; Binns, M.A.; Alexander, M.P. Staying on the job: The frontal lobes control individual performance variability. *Brain* **2003**, *126*, 2363–2380. [CrossRef] [PubMed]

12. Anstey, K.J.; Mack, H.A.; Christensen, H.; Li, S.-C.; Reglade-Meslin, C.; Maller, J.; Kumar, R.; Dear, K.; Easteal, S.; Sachdev, P. Corpus callosum size, reaction time speed and variability in mild cognitive disorders and in a normative sample. *Neuropsychologia* **2007**, *45*, 1911–1920. [CrossRef] [PubMed]

13. Hultsch, D.F.; MacDonald, S.W.; Hunter, M.A.; Levy-Bencheton, J.; Strauss, E. Intraindividual variability in cognitive performance in older adults: Comparison of adults with mild dementia, adults with arthritis, and healthy adults. *Neuropsychology* **2000**, *14*, 588–598. [CrossRef] [PubMed]

14. West, R.; Murphy, K.J.; Armilio, M.L.; Craik, F.I.M.; Stuss, D.T. Lapses of Intention and Performance Variability Reveal Age-Related Increases in Fluctuations of Executive Control. *Brain Cogn.* **2002**, *49*, 402–419. [CrossRef] [PubMed]

15. Bunce, D.; MacDonald, S.W.S.; Hultsch, D.F. Inconsistency in serial choice decision and motor reaction times dissociate in younger and older adults. *Brain Cogn.* **2004**, *56*, 320–327. [CrossRef] [PubMed]

16. Ghisletta, P.; Fagot, D.; Lecerf, T.; de Ribaupierre, A. Amplitude of Fluctuations and Temporal Dependency in Intraindividual Variability. *GeroPsych* **2013**, *26*, 141–151. [CrossRef]

17. Lövdén, M.; Li, S.-C.; Shing, Y.L.; Lindenberger, U. Within-person trial-to-trial variability precedes and predicts cognitive decline in old and very old age: Longitudinal data from the Berlin Aging Study. *Neuropsychologia* **2007**, *45*, 2827–2838. [CrossRef] [PubMed]

18. Burton, C.L.; Strauss, E.; Hultsch, D.F.; Hunter, M.A. Cognitive Functioning and Everyday Problem Solving in Older Adults. *Clin. Neuropsychol.* **2006**, *20*, 432–452. [CrossRef] [PubMed]

19. MacDonald, S.W.S.; Nyberg, L.; Bäckman, L. Intra-individual variability in behavior: Links to brain structure, neurotransmission and neuronal activity. *Trends Neurosci.* **2006**, *29*, 474–480. [CrossRef] [PubMed]

20. Ghisletta, P.; Nesselroade, J.R.; Featherman, D.L.; Rowe, J.W. Structure and predictive power of intraindividual variability in health and activity measures. *Swiss J. Psychol.* **2002**, *61*, 73–83. [CrossRef]

21. Kochan, N.A.; Bunce, D.; Pont, S.; Crawford, J.D.; Brodaty, H.; Sachdev, P.S. Is intraindividual reaction time variability an independent cognitive predictor of mortality in old age? Findings from the Sydney Memory and Ageing Study. *PLoS ONE* **2017**, *12*, e0181719. [CrossRef] [PubMed]

22. Bielak, A.A.M.; Cherbuin, N.; Bunce, D.; Anstey, K.J. Intraindividual variability is a fundamental phenomenon of aging: Evidence from an 8-year longitudinal study across young, middle, and older adulthood. *Dev. Psychol.* **2014**, *50*, 143–151. [CrossRef] [PubMed]

23. Ellis, J.A.; Freeman, J.E. Ten years on: Realizing delayed intentions. In *Prospective Memory: Cognitive, Neuroscience, Developmental, and Applied Perspectives*; Kliegel, M., McDaniel, M.A., Einstein, G.O., Eds.; Psychology Press: Hove, UK, 2008; pp. 1–28, ISBN 978-0-8058-5858-7.

24. Kliegel, M.; Jäger, T.; Phillips, L.H. Adult age differences in event-based prospective memory: A meta-analysis on the role of focal versus nonfocal cues. *Psychol. Aging* **2008**, *23*, 203–208. [CrossRef] [PubMed]

25. Uttl, B. Transparent Meta-Analysis of Prospective Memory and Aging. *PLoS ONE* **2008**, *3*, e1568. [CrossRef] [PubMed]

26. Uttl, B. Transparent meta-analysis: Does aging spare prospective memory with focal vs. non-focal cues? *PLoS ONE* **2011**, *6*, e16618. [CrossRef] [PubMed]

27. Kliegel, M.; McDaniel, M.A.; Einstein, G.O. Plan formation, retention, and execution in prospective memory: A new approach and age-related effects. *Mem. Cogn.* **2000**, *28*, 1041–1049. [CrossRef]

28. Burgess, P.W.; Veitch, E.; de Lacy Costello, A.; Shallice, T. The cognitive and neuroanatomical correlates of multitasking. *Neuropsychologia* **2000**, *38*, 848–863. [CrossRef]

29. Kvavilashvili, L.; Ellis, J. Varieties of intention: Some distinctions and classifications. In *Prospective Memory: Theory and Applications*; Brandimonte, M., Einstein, G.O., McDaniel, M.A., Eds.; Lawrence Erlbaum Associates: Mahway, NJ, USA, 1996; pp. 23–52, ISBN 978-1-317-78068-7.

30. Einstein, G.O.; McDaniel, M.A. Retrieval processes in prospective memory: Theoretical approaches and some new empirical findings. In *Prospective Memory: Theory and Applications*; Brandimonte, M., Einstein, G.O., McDaniel, M.A., Eds.; Lawrence Erlbaum Associates: Mahway, NJ, USA, 1996; pp. 115–141, ISBN 978-1-317-78068-7.

31. McDaniel, M.A.; Einstein, G.O. Strategic and automatic processes in prospective memory retrieval: A multiprocess framework. *Appl. Cogn. Psychol.* **2000**, *14*, 127–144. [CrossRef]

32. Smith, R.E. The cost of remembering to remember in event-based prospective memory: Investigating the capacity demands of delayed intention performance. *J. Exp. Psychol. Learn. Mem. Cogn.* **2003**, *29*, 347–361. [CrossRef] [PubMed]

33. Guynn, M.J. Theory of monitoring in prospective memory: Instantiating a retrieval mode and periodic target checking. In *Prospective Memory: Cognitive, Neuroscience, Developmental, and Applied Perspectives*; Kliegel, M., McDaniel, M.A., Einstein, G.O., Eds.; Taylor & Francis Group/Lawrence Erlbaum Associates: New York, NY, USA, 2008; pp. 53–76, ISBN 978-0-8058-5858-7.

34. Smith, R.E.; Bayen, U.J. The effects of working memory resource availability on prospective memory: A formal modeling approach. *Exp. Psychol.* **2005**, *52*, 243–256. [CrossRef] [PubMed]

35. Burgess, P.W.; Quayle, A.; Frith, C.D. Brain regions involved in prospective memory as determined by positron emission tomography. *Neuropsychologia* **2001**, *39*, 545–555. [CrossRef]

36. Loft, S.; Bowden, V.K.; Ball, B.H.; Brewer, G.A. Fitting an ex-Gaussian function to examine costs in event-based prospective memory: Evidence for a continuous monitoring profile. *Acta Psychol.* **2014**, *152*, 177–182. [CrossRef] [PubMed]

37. Collette, F.; Germain, S.; Hogge, M.; Van der Linden, M. Inhibitory control of memory in normal ageing: Dissociation between impaired intentional and preserved unintentional processes. *Memory* **2009**, *17*, 104–122. [CrossRef] [PubMed]

38. Hay, J.F.; Jacoby, L.L. Separating habit and recollection in young and older adults: Effects of elaborative processing and distinctiveness. *Psychol. Aging* **1999**, *14*, 122–134. [CrossRef] [PubMed]

39. Andrés, P.; Guerrini, C.; Phillips, L.H.; Perfect, T.J. Differential effects of aging on executive and automatic inhibition. *Dev. Neuropsychol.* **2008**, *33*, 101–123. [CrossRef] [PubMed]

40. Braver, T.S.; West, R. Working memory, executive control, and aging. In *The Handbook of Aging and Cognition*; Craik, F.I., Salthouse, T.A., Eds.; Psychology Press: New York, NY, USA, 2008; pp. 311–372, ISBN 0-8058-5990-X.

41. West, R.L. An application of prefrontal cortex function theory to cognitive aging. *Psychol. Bull.* **1996**, *120*, 272–292. [CrossRef] [PubMed]

42. Ihle, A.; Hering, A.; Mahy, C.E.V.; Bisiacchi, P.S.; Kliegel, M. Adult age differences, response management, and cue focality in event-based prospective memory: A meta-analysis on the role of task order specificity. *Psychol. Aging* **2013**, *28*, 714–720. [CrossRef] [PubMed]

43. Schnitzspahn, K.M.; Stahl, C.; Zeintl, M.; Kaller, C.P.; Kliegel, M. The role of shifting, updating, and inhibition in prospective memory performance in young and older adults. *Dev. Psychol.* **2013**, *49*, 1544–1553. [CrossRef] [PubMed]

44. Einstein, G.O.; Smith, R.E.; McDaniel, M.A.; Shaw, P. Aging and prospective memory: The influence of increased task demands at encoding and retrieval. *Psychol. Aging* **1997**, *12*, 479–488. [CrossRef] [PubMed]

45. Zuber, S.; Kliegel, M.; Ihle, A. An individual difference perspective on focal versus nonfocal prospective memory. *Mem. Cogn.* **2016**, *44*, 1192–1203. [CrossRef] [PubMed]

46. Craik, F.I.; Govoni, R.; Naveh-Benjamin, M.; Anderson, N.D. The effects of divided attention on encoding and retrieval processes in human memory. *J. Exp. Psychol. Gen.* **1996**, *125*, 159–180. [CrossRef] [PubMed]

47. Martin, M.; Kliegel, M.; McDaniel, M.A. The involvement of executive functions in prospective memory performance of adults. *Int. J. Psychol.* **2003**, *38*, 195–206. [CrossRef]

48. McDaniel, M.A.; Glisky, E.L.; Rubin, S.R.; Guynn, M.J.; Routhieaux, B.C. Prospective memory: A neuropsychological study. *Neuropsychology* **1999**, *13*, 103–110. [CrossRef] [PubMed]

49. Miyake, A.; Friedman, N.P.; Emerson, M.J.; Witzki, A.H.; Howerter, A.; Wager, T.D. The unity and diversity of executive functions and their contributions to complex "Frontal Lobe" tasks: A latent variable analysis. *Cogn. Psychol.* **2000**, *41*, 49–100. [CrossRef] [PubMed]

50. Friedman, N.P.; Miyake, A. The relations among inhibition and interference control functions: A latent-variable analysis. *J. Exp. Psychol. Gen.* **2004**, *133*, 101–135. [CrossRef] [PubMed]

51. West, R.; Craik, F.I. Influences on the efficiency of prospective memory in younger and older adults. *Psychol. Aging* **2001**, *16*, 682–696. [CrossRef] [PubMed]

52. Hasher, L.; Zacks, R.T. Working Memory, Comprehension, and Aging: A Review and a New View. In *Psychology of Learning and Motivation*; Bower, G.H., Ed.; Academic Press: Cambridge, MA, USA, 1988; Volume 22, pp. 193–225, ISBN 0-12-543322-0.

53. Rey-Mermet, A.; Gade, M. Inhibition in aging: What is preserved? What declines? A meta-analysis. *Psychon. Bull. Rev.* **2017**, 1–22. [CrossRef] [PubMed]

54. Wasylyshyn, C.; Verhaeghen, P.; Sliwinski, M.J. Aging and task switching: A meta-analysis. *Psychol. Aging* **2011**, *26*, 15–20. [CrossRef] [PubMed]

55. Rose, N.S.; Rendell, P.G.; McDaniel, M.A.; Aberle, I.; Kliegel, M. Age and Individual Differences in Prospective Memory during a "Virtual Week": The Roles of Working Memory, Vigilance, Task Regularity, and Cue Focality. *Psychol. Aging* **2010**, *25*, 595–605. [CrossRef] [PubMed]

56. Maylor, E.A. Age-related impairment in an event-based prospective-memory task. *Psychol. Aging* **1996**, *11*, 74–78. [CrossRef] [PubMed]

57. West, R.; Scolaro, A.J.; Bailey, K. When goals collide: The interaction between prospective memory and task switching. *Can. J. Exp. Psychol. Rev. Can. Psychol. Exp.* **2011**, *65*, 38–47. [CrossRef] [PubMed]

58. Kliegel, M.; Mackinlay, R.; Jäger, T. Complex prospective memory: Development across the lifespan and the role of task interruption. *Dev. Psychol.* **2008**, *44*, 612–617. [CrossRef] [PubMed]

59. Manly, T.; Davison, B.; Heutink, J.; Galloway, M.; Robertson, I. Not enough time or not enough attention: Speed, error and self-maintained control in the Sustained Attention to Response Test (SART). *Clin. Neuropsychol. Assess.* **2000**, *3*, 167–177.

60. MacLeod, C.M. The concept of inhibition in cognition. In *Inhibition in Cognition*; Gorfein, D.S., MacLeod, C.M., Eds.; American Psychological Association: Washington, DC, USA, 2007; pp. 3–23, ISBN 978-1-59147-930-7.

61. Bellgrove, M.A.; Hester, R.; Garavan, H. The functional neuroanatomical correlates of response variability: Evidence from a response inhibition task. *Neuropsychologia* **2004**, *42*, 1910–1916. [CrossRef] [PubMed]

62. Rochat, L.; Billieux, J.; Juillerat Van der Linden, A.-C.; Annoni, J.-M.; Zekry, D.; Gold, G.; Van der Linden, M. A multidimensional approach to impulsivity changes in mild Alzheimer's disease and control participants: Cognitive correlates. *Cortex J. Devoted Study Nerv. Syst. Behav.* **2013**, *49*, 90–100. [CrossRef] [PubMed]

63. Haynes, B.I.; Kliegel, M.; Zimprich, D.; Bunce, D. Intraindividual reaction time variability predicts prospective memory failures in older adults. *Neuropsychol. Dev. Cogn. B Aging Neuropsychol. Cogn.* **2016**, 1–14. [CrossRef] [PubMed]

64. Ihle, A.; Ghisletta, P.; Kliegel, M. Prospective memory and intraindividual variability in ongoing task response times in an adult lifespan sample: The role of cue focality. *Memory* **2017**, *25*, 370–376. [CrossRef] [PubMed]

65. Molenaar, P.C.M. A dynamic factor model for the analysis of multivariate time series. *Psychometrika* **1985**, *50*, 181–202. [CrossRef]

66. Ram, N.; Gerstorf, D. Time-Structured and Net Intraindividual Variability: Tools for Examining the Development of Dynamic Characteristics and Processes. *Psychol. Aging* **2009**, *24*, 778–791. [CrossRef] [PubMed]

67. Gilden, D.L. Cognitive emissions of 1/f noise. *Psychol. Rev.* **2001**, *108*, 33–56. [CrossRef] [PubMed]

68. Wang, L.P.; Hamaker, E.; Bergeman, C.S. Investigating inter-individual differences in short-term intra-individual variability. *Psychol. Methods* **2012**, *17*, 567–581. [CrossRef] [PubMed]

69. Kuppens, P.; Allen, N.B.; Sheeber, L.B. Emotional inertia and psychological maladjustment. *Psychol. Sci.* **2010**, *21*, 984–991. [CrossRef] [PubMed]

70. Hamaker, E.; Asparouhov, T.; Brose, A.; Schmiedek, F.; Muthén, B.O. At the frontiers of modeling intensive longitudinal data: Dynamic structural equation models for the affective measurements from the COGITO study. *Multivar. Behav. Res.* **2017**, in press.

71. Kliegel, M.; Altgassen, M.; Hering, A.; Rose, N.S. A process-model based approach to prospective memory impairment in Parkinson's disease. *Neuropsychologia* **2011**, *49*, 2166–2177. [CrossRef] [PubMed]

72. Folstein, M.F.; Folstein, S.E.; McHugh, P.R. "Mini-mental state". A practical method for grading the cognitive state of patients for the clinician. *J. Psychiatr. Res.* **1975**, *12*, 189–198. [CrossRef]

73. Wechsler, D. *Wechsler Memory Scale*; Psychological Corporation: San Antonio, TX, USA, 1945.

74. Esposito, F.; Rochat, L.; Juillerat Van der Linden, A.-C.; Lekeu, F.; Charnallet, A.; Van der Linden, M. Apathy in aging: Are lack of interest and lack of initiative dissociable? *Arch. Gerontol. Geriatr.* **2014**, *58*, 43–50. [CrossRef] [PubMed]

75. Fuhrer, R.; Rouillon, F. La version française de l'échelle CES-D (Center for Epidemiologic Studies-Depression Scale). Description et traduction de l'échelle d'autoévaluation [The French version of the CES-D (Center for Epidemiologic Studies-Depression Scale)]. *Psychiatr. Psychobiol.* **1989**, *4*, 163–166.

76. Einstein, G.O.; McDaniel, M.A. Prospective Memory: Multiple Retrieval Processes. *Curr. Dir. Psychol. Sci.* **2005**, *14*, 286–290. [CrossRef]

77. Der, G.; Deary, I.J. Age and sex differences in reaction time in adulthood: Results from the United Kingdom Health and Lifestyle Survey. *Psychol. Aging* **2006**, *21*, 62–73. [CrossRef] [PubMed]

78. Dykiert, D.; Hall, D.; van Gemeren, N.; Benson, R.; Der, G.; Starr, J.M.; Deary, I.J. The effects of high altitude on choice reaction time mean and intra-individual variability: Results of the Edinburgh Altitude Research Expedition of 2008. *Neuropsychology* **2010**, *24*, 391–401. [CrossRef] [PubMed]

79. Ghisletta, P.; Renaud, O.; Fagot, D.; Lecerf, T.; Ribaupierre, A. De Age and sex differences in intra-individual variability in a simple reaction time task. *Int. J. Behav. Dev.* **2017**. [CrossRef]

80. Dickey, D.A.; Fuller, W.A. Distribution of the Estimators for Autoregressive Time Series with a Unit Root. *J. Am. Stat. Assoc.* **1979**, *74*, 427–431. [CrossRef]

81. Muthén, L.K.; Muthén, B.O. *Mplus, Version 8*; Muthen & Muthen: Los Angeles, CA, USA, 2017; ISBN 0-9829983-2-5.

82. Hamaker, E.; Asparouhov, T.; Muthén, B.O. Dynamic Structural Equation Modeling of Intensive Longitudinal Data Using Mplus Version 8. Available online: https://www.statmodel.com/download/HamakerDSEMforPSMG.pdf (accessed on 20 October 2017).

83. Hamaker, E. PSMG: Dynamic Structural Equation Modeling of Intensive Longitudinal Data Using Mplus Version 8: Part 1. Available online: https://vimeo.com/230220417 (accessed on 20 October 2017).

84. Asparouhov, T.; Hamaker, E.L.; Muthén, B. Dynamic Structural Equation Models. *Struct. Equ. Model. Multidiscip. J.* **2017**. [CrossRef]

85. Schmiedek, F.; Lövdén, M.; Lindenberger, U. On the relation of mean reaction time and intraindividual reaction time variability. *Psychol. Aging* **2009**, *24*, 841–857. [CrossRef] [PubMed]

86. De Ribaupierre, A.; Borella, E. Differential aging of cognition. In *Encyclopedia of Adulthood and Aging*; Whitbourne, S.K., Ed.; Wiley-Blackwell: Oxford, UK, 2016; ISBN 978-1-118-52892-1.

87. Guynn, M.J. A two-process model of strategic monitoring in event-based prospective memory: Activation/retrieval mode and checking. *Int. J. Psychol.* **2003**, *38*, 245–256. [CrossRef]

88. Smith, R.E.; Loft, S. Investigating the Cost to Ongoing Tasks Not Associated with Prospective Memory Task Requirements. *Conscious. Cogn.* **2014**, *27*, 1–13. [CrossRef] [PubMed]

89. Hultsch, D.F.; Strauss, E.; Hunter, M.A.; MacDonald, W.S. Intraindividual variability, cognition and aging. In *The Handbook of Aging and Cognition*; Craik, F.I., Salthouse, T.A., Eds.; Psychology Press: New York, NY, USA, 2008; pp. 491–556, ISBN 0-8058-5990-X.

90. Marsh, R.L.; Hicks, J.; Cook, G.; Hansen, J.S.; Pallos, A.L. Interference to Ongoing Activities Covaries with the Characteristics of an Event-Based Intention. *J. Exp. Psychol. Learn. Mem. Cogn.* **2003**, *29*, 861–870. [CrossRef] [PubMed]

91. McDaniel, M.; Einstein, G. *Prospective Memory: An Overview and Synthesis of an Emerging Field*; Sage Publications: Thousand Oaks, CA, USA, 2007; ISBN 1-4129-2469-3.

92. Einstein, G.O.; McDaniel, M.A.; Thomas, R.; Mayfield, S.; Shank, H.; Morrisette, N.; Breneiser, J. Multiple processes in prospective memory retrieval: Factors determining monitoring versus spontaneous retrieval. *J. Exp. Psychol. Gen.* **2005**, *134*, 327–342. [CrossRef] [PubMed]

93. Treisman, A.M.; Gelade, G. A feature-integration theory of attention. *Cogn. Psychol.* **1980**, *12*, 97–136. [CrossRef]

94. Li, S.-C.; Huxhold, O.; Schmiedek, F. Aging and attenuated processing robustness. Evidence from cognitive and sensorimotor functioning. *Gerontology* **2004**, *50*, 28–34. [CrossRef] [PubMed]

95. Siegler, R.S. Cognitive Variability: A Key to Understanding Cognitive Development. *Curr. Dir. Psychol. Sci.* **1994**, *3*, 1–5. [CrossRef]

96. Allaire, J.C.; Marsiske, M. Intraindividual variability may not always indicate vulnerability in elders' cognitive performance. *Psychol. Aging* **2005**, *20*, 390–401. [CrossRef] [PubMed]

97. Heitz, R.P. The speed-accuracy tradeoff: History, physiology, methodology, and behavior. *Front. Neurosci.* **2014**, *8*, 150. [CrossRef] [PubMed]

98. Albert, P.S.; Follmann, D.A.; Wang, S.A.; Suh, E.B. A Latent Autoregressive Model for Longitudinal Binary Data Subject to Informative Missingness. *Biometrics* **2002**, *58*, 631–642. [CrossRef] [PubMed]

99. Bisiacchi, P.S.; Schiff, S.; Ciccola, A.; Kliegel, M. The role of dual-task and task-switch in prospective memory: Behavioural data and neural correlates. *Neuropsychologia* **2009**, *47*, 1362–1373. [CrossRef] [PubMed]

100. Verbruggen, F.; Logan, G.D. Automatic and controlled response inhibition: Associative learning in the go/no-go and stop-signal paradigms. *J. Exp. Psychol. Gen.* **2008**, *137*, 649–672. [CrossRef] [PubMed]

101. Estabrook, R.; Grimm, K.J.; Bowles, R.P. A Monte Carlo simulation study of the reliability of intraindividual variability. *Psychol. Aging* **2012**, *27*, 560–576. [CrossRef] [PubMed]

102. Wang, L.; Grimm, K.J. Investigating Reliabilities of Intraindividual Variability Indicators. *Multivar. Behav. Res.* **2012**, *47*, 771–802. [CrossRef] [PubMed]

103. Cowpertwait, P.S.P. *Introductory Time Series with R*; Springer-Verlag: New York, NY, USA, 2009; ISBN 978-0-387-88698-5.

Journal of
Intelligence

MDPI

Article

Intraindividual Variability across Neuropsychological Tests: Dispersion and Disengaged Lifestyle Increase Risk for Alzheimer's Disease

Drew W. R. Halliday [1,2,*], Robert S. Stawski [3], Eric S. Cerino [3], Correne A. DeCarlo [1,2], Karl Grewal [1] and Stuart W. S. MacDonald [1,2]

1   Department of Psychology, University of Victoria, Victoria, BC V8P 5C2, Canada; decarloc@uvic.ca (C.A.D.); kgrewal@uvic.ca (K.G.); smacd@uvic.ca (S.W.S.M.)
2   Institute on Aging and Lifelong Health, University of Victoria, Victoria, BC V8P 5C2, Canada
3   School of Social and Behavioral Health Sciences, Oregon State University, Corvallis, OR 97331, USA; Robert.Stawski@oregonstate.edu (R.S.S.); cerinoe@oregonstate.edu (E.S.C.)
*   Correspondence: drewh@uvic.ca

Received: 15 November 2017; Accepted: 27 February 2018; Published: 1 March 2018

Abstract: *Objective*: Increased intraindividual variability (IIV) in function has been linked to various age-related outcomes including cognitive decline and dementia. Most studies have operationalized IIV as fluctuations across trials (e.g., response latencies) for a single task, with comparatively few studies examining variability across multiple tasks for a given individual. In the present study, we derive a multivariable operationalization of dispersion across a broad profile of neuropsychological measures and use this index along with degree of engaged lifestyle to predict risk of cognitive impairment. *Participants and Methods*: Participants (n = 60) were community-dwelling older adults aged 65+ years (M = 74.1, SD = 6.5) participating in a cross-sectional investigation of risk factors for amnestic mild cognitive impairment (a-MCI) and probable Alzheimer's Disease (AD). Participants were classified into three subgroups based on test performance and clinical judgement. Healthy controls (n = 30) scored better than −1 SD relative to existing norms on all classification measures, in the absence of memory complaints or functional impairments. The a-MCI group (n = 23) had self- or informant-reported memory complaints and scored 1 SD or more below the mean for at least one memory task while scoring better than 1 SD below the mean for all other cognitive domains, in the absence of functional impairments. The AD group (n = 7) scored at least 2 SD below the mean for two cognitive domains (including memory) with impairments in functioning. Measures spanned a range of cognitive domains (episodic memory, executive function, language), with the derived dispersion estimates reflecting variability across an individual's neuropsychological profile relative to the group average. Further, an Activities Lifestyle Questionnaire, indexing social, cognitive, and physical behaviors, was administered to assess the protective benefits of engaged lifestyle. *Results*: Multinomial logistic regression models examined the risk of being classified as a-MCI or AD as a function of increased dispersion, (dis)engaged lifestyle, and their interaction. Greater dispersion was associated with an increased likelihood of being classified with AD, with protective engaged-lifestyle benefits apparent for a-MCI individuals only. *Conclusion*: As a measure of IIV, dispersion across neuropsychological profiles holds promise for the detection of cognitive impairment.

Keywords: intraindividual variability; dispersion; cognitive impairment; mild cognitive impairment; Alzheimer's Disease; neuropsychological assessment

1. Introduction

Intraindividual variability (IIV) is increasingly employed as a metric of functioning across behavioral (e.g., response time) [1], physical (e.g., gait) [2], physiological (e.g., heart rate) [3], and neurophysiological (e.g., blood-oxygen-level-dependent signal) functioning [4]. Research has shown that IIV often confers information that is independent to that of central tendency metrics and that in some cases, IIV is more sensitive to deleterious health outcomes and pathophysiological processes [5,6]. Most commonly, IIV refers to inconsistency in function (e.g., behavioral performance) within-persons and across time, and can be indexed across broader (e.g., week-to-week) or narrower (e.g., trial-to-trial performance) time scales. Greater IIV in trial-to-trial behavioral performance has been associated with risk for decline in cognitive status, including Mild Cognitive Impairment and dementia [7–9]. Evidence for the mechanisms driving increased behavioral inconsistency has pointed to compromised neural integrity at anatomical, functional, neuromodulatory and genetic levels [10], further implicating the potential utility of IIV for detecting early cognitive decline.

Although inconsistency in behavioral performance (i.e., IIV over time) has elucidated several insights in terms of late-life developmental and health-related outcomes, less is understood about IIV in terms of performance across different tasks within individuals. Dispersion refers to IIV across multiple different indicators within-persons; most typically, across cognitive and neuropsychological tasks [11,12] and may reflect similar underlying processes (e.g., age related changes in neurological integrity) to those identified for inconsistency [12]. Like inconsistency, dispersion is sensitive to age differences in late-life, with old-old adults (75–92 years) demonstrating higher levels of dispersion relative to young-old adults (65–74 years) [13]. Differences in dispersion have also been observed across broader segments of the lifespan. A recent investigation demonstrated that dispersion across working memory and RT tasks may reflect different developmental phenomena, with greater dispersion in RT tasks observed during childhood and older adulthood and greater dispersion in working memory observed during young adulthood [14].

In addition to developmental phenomena, dispersion has been examined in the context of acquired and neurodegenerative conditions impacting cognitive performance. While some studies have found distinct and meaningful profiles of dispersion [13,15], others have focused on the relative magnitude of overall dispersion between groups with cross sectional [14,16] and longitudinal designs [11,17,18]. Rabinowitz and Arnett [16] found that greater dispersion was associated with post-concussive cognitive dysfunction in a sample of college athletes across a battery of computerized and paper-pencil neuropsychological tasks, suggesting that such disparate profiles across a broad range of tasks may be sensitive to mild neurological trauma. Similarly, greater dispersion in neuropsychological test performance predicted incident dementia, independent of performance on each individual test, in a population-based longitudinal study of older adults [17]. This finding was replicated in a larger sample of older women, such that greater baseline dispersion subsequently predicted probable dementia; however, the effect was attenuated in individuals with higher verbal episodic memory scores [18]. Previous investigations of conversion from cognitively-impaired-not-demented to dementia status using cluster analyses also suggest that memory and verbal dysfunction are most predictive of conversion to dementia [15]. Independent of more nuanced cognitive profiles, greater dispersion has also been associated with poorer activities of daily living (ADLs) in older adults [11]. In this study, dispersion was not associated with age, level of education or lifestyle activity levels. Notably, however, lifestyle activity levels were coarsely indexed, with only a marginal distinction observed between different types of activities (e.g., social, physical, cognitive) and for a relatively restricted response range.

Lifestyle, including engagement in cognitive, physical, and social activities, plays a critical role in psychosocial well-being and maintaining neurological integrity [19]. For example, higher lifetime cognitive activity and current level of physical activity in older adults is associated with the presence of fewer white matter lesions, which are in turn associated with greater neural integrity and global cognitive functioning [20]. Cognitive reserve-enhancing factors, including late-life engagement in cognitive, physical, and social activity, were recently demonstrated to reduce the relative risk of dementia in older adults [21]. In older adulthood, engagement in protective lifestyle activities may both contribute to and be facilitated by healthy cognitive functioning [22]. Recent longitudinal evidence using latent growth curve modelling suggests that engagement in cognitive, social, and physical activity is associated with less cognitive decline in late-life [23], affirming a long line of assertions implicating engaged lifestyle as a target for preventive efforts.

As markers of cognitive decline and dementia risk, an index of dispersion across a comprehensive battery of cognitive performance measures as well as a psychometrically well-validated measure of lifestyle activities have yet to be thoroughly examined both individually and simultaneously. The present study sought to examine two primary research questions. First, can previous findings linking dispersion to cognitive subgroup differences be replicated and extended to demonstrate the sensitivity of dispersion across a broad neuropsychological-assessment profile to amnestic-MCI (a-MCI) and probable Alzheimer's disease (AD)? Although dispersion has been regularly observed in relatively impaired individuals, the sensitivity of dispersion for predicting a-MCI or for AD (in contrast to all-cause dementia) is less clear. Second, does living an engaged lifestyle, characterized by relatively high frequency of participation in social, physical, and cognitive activities and indexed employing a psychometrically well-validated measure, confer protective benefits independent of neuropsychological dispersion? Given the association between cognitive status and engaged lifestyle, engagement in activity may serve as an avenue to decrease cognitive dispersion and promote greater well-being overall.

2. Method

2.1. Participants

Participants were community-dwelling older adults from Victoria, BC, Canada participating in The PREVENT Study; a cross-sectional multi-factorial (e.g., biological, physiological, environmental) investigation of risk factors for a-MCI and probable AD. Participants were recruited through descriptions of the study in various news outlets and presentations to community groups; individuals aged 65 years and older were sought in an effort to target late-onset pathology. Exclusionary criteria for participation focused on factors that could directly result in cognitive deficits or impairment not reflective of emerging neurodegenerative conditions consistent with AD or its prodrome. These included (a) newly diagnosed psychiatric disturbance within the past year (i.e., Major Depressive Disorder); (b) history of a chronic neurological condition (i.e., Parkinson's disease, brain tumor); (c) episode(s) of cardio- and/or cerebro-vascular disease (i.e., heart attack, stroke, heart surgery) within the past year; and (d) other factors that could contribute to changes in cognitive functioning (i.e., head injury, vitamin deficiency). Severe sensory and/or motor impairment (i.e., unable to read newspaper-sized print with glasses, difficulty writing or pressing keys on a keyboard, or unable to hear a normal spoken conversation adequately with the use of a hearing aid) were also used as exclusionary criteria, given the nature of participation.

2.2. Cognitive Status Classification

Participants were classified as either healthy control (HC, $n = 30$), a-MCI ($n = 23$) or AD ($n = 7$), based on a standard and objective classification system involving both neuropsychological test scores (based on 7 classification measures yielding 8 different scores) and clinical judgement. To meet criteria for the HC group, participants were required to (a) score better than 1.0 SD below the mean for all cognitive domains, and (b) report no subjective memory complaints or impairment in social, occupational, or daily functioning during interview. To meet criteria for the a-MCI group [24–26], participants were required to (a) score at least 1.0 SD below the mean in the memory domain; (b) score better than 1.0 SD below the mean in all other cognitive domains; (c) report at least one subjective complaint associated with memory during interview; and (d) report an absence of impairment in social, occupational or daily functioning during interview. To meet criteria for the probable AD group, consistent with DSM-IV-TR guidelines [27], participants were required to (a) score at least 2.0 SD below the mean for memory and in one other cognitive domain; (b) have subjective or collateral-reported significant declines from previous levels of functioning in both domains that were gradual and progressive (i.e., versus acute declines that are more likely to be associated with cerebrovascular events or other pathophysiological changes not associated with AD), with (c) these deficits resulting in impairments in social, occupational and/or daily life functioning. These latter two criteria were assessed during interview. Table 1 depicts select demographic characteristics for each group.

Table 1. Demographic characteristics by group.

Characteristics	HC	a-MCI	AD
n	30	23	7
Sex	23 females; 7 males	9 females; 14 males	3 females; 4 males
Age	73.57 (6.40)	73.95 (6.79)	77.00 (5.68)
Years of Education	15.05 (2.56)	15.39 (3.97)	13.29 (2.98)
Self-reported memory	7.41 (1.28)	5.81 (2.13)	6.00 (2.24)

There were no significant differences between-groups in terms of chronological age ($F(2,57) = 0.807$, $p = 0.45$), or years of education ($F(2,57) = 1.164$, $p = 0.32$). Significant between-group differences were found in terms of self-reported memory function in the 30 days prior to the screening interview ($F(2,54) = 5.757$, $p < 0.005$, $\eta^2 = 0.18$), with the HC group ($m = 7.41$, $SD = 1.28$) reporting greater memory function relative to the a-MCI ($m = 5.81$, $SD = 2.13$) group. No differences were observed between the a-MCI and AD ($m = 6.00$, $SD = 2.24$) groups, or between the AD and HC groups (based on post-hoc comparison using Tukey's HSD)[1].

3. Measures

3.1. Test Battery

The test battery included measures spanning the following cognitive domains, as outlined in Table 2; global cognitive functioning (Modified Mini-Mental State Test (3MS)), auditory attention (WAIS-R Digit Span (Total score)), auditory working memory (WAIS-R Digit Span Backwards), visual memory (Benton Visual Retention Task-BVRT), auditory immediate and delayed memory (Rey Auditory Verbal Learning Task (RAVLT; A1-5 Total, A6 (short delay interference), A7 (long delay), d' (recognition)), executive functioning (WAIS-R Similarities, Trail Making Test B-TMT-B, Mental Alternation Test-MAT), language (Controlled Oral Word Associations Test-COWAT, Animal Naming, North American Adult Reading Test-NAART), visuospatial ability (WAIS-R Block Design), and processing speed (Trail Making Test A-TMT-A, WAIS-R Digit Symbol, Serial Response Time-SRT, Lexical Decision Task (accuracy and RT)). Normative data from the Canadian Study of Health and Aging (CSHA) were used to derive T-scores for the WAIS-R short-form subtests, RAVLT interference (A6) and long-delay (A7), BVRT, COWAT (using CFL) and Animal Naming [28]. Normative data from the Mayo's Older Americans Normative Studies (MOANS) were used to derive T-scores for TMT-A, TMT-B [29], and the immediate recall trials of RAVLT (A1-5) [30], due to the lack of available normative data for these tests in the CSHA study. Individuals over the age of 90 ($n = 1$; age 93, a-MCI group) were compared to 90-year-olds in the CSHA reference sample. In addition to the neuropsychological tests administered, a structured interview with the participant and/or their family member was conducted to obtain self-report or collateral-report information pertaining to the participant's social, occupational, or daily life functioning. During the screening interview, participants were asked to rate their level of memory functioning on a scale of 1–10 (1 = worst, 10 = best) over the past 30 days. As noted in the table and as described further in Section 4.1, select measures were reserved for classification purposes

---

[1] The lack of observed group differences between the AD and HC groups may be due to the presence of anosognosia in the AD individuals with respect to their memory functioning.

solely, with additional independent measures employed for deriving estimates of dispersion. Group comparisons across each of the cognitive measures is available in the Supplementary Materials online.

Table 2. List of Neuropsychological and Cognitive tasks.

Cognitive Domain	Test	Scores
Global Cognition	3MS	Total
Attention	WAIS-R Digit Span Forwards	Total
Working Memory	WAIS-R Digit Span Backwards	Total
Memory	Benton Visual Retention Task (BVRT) Rey Auditory Verbal Learning Task (RAVLT)	BVRT—Total * RAVLT—A1-5 * total, A6, A7, d'
Executive Function	WAIS-R Similarities Trail Making Test B (TMT-B) Mental Alternation Test (MAT)	Similarities—Total * TMT-B—Total * MAT—1, 2, 3 totals
Visuo-construction	WAIS-R Block Design	Total *
Language	Controlled Oral Word Association Test (COWAT) Animal Naming North American Adult Reading Test (NAART)	COWAT—Total * Animal—Total * NAART—Total
Processing Speed	WAIS-R Digit Symbol (DS) Trail Making Test A (TMT-A) Serial Response Time (SRT) Lexical Decision Task (LDT)	DS—Total TMT-A—Total SRT—Average RT LDT—average accuracy, average RT

* Measures used for classification and therefore not employed in the dispersion computation.

3.2. Lifestyle Activities

The revised Activity Lifestyle Questionnaire (ALQ) [31], a self-report activity questionnaire of adult leisure activities, was initially developed and administered for the Victoria Longitudinal Study (VLS) [32]. The revised version of the VLS-ALQ employed in this study enhanced the content validity of the scale by including supplemental items on physical and social activities. The structure of this revised ALQ was validated using confirmatory factor analyses in independent samples. Good psychometric properties (reliability, convergent and discriminant validity) for the ALQ support the use of its subscales as indicators of leisure activities across the lifespan [31]. For each of the items, individuals self-reported the frequency of participation for a given activity within the past year on a 9-point scale (0 = never, 1 = less than once a year, 2 = about once a year, 3 = 2 or 3 times a year, 4 = about once a month, 5 = 2 or 3 times a month, 6 = about once a week, 7 = 2 or 3 times a week, 8 = daily). An aggregate score of *lifestyle engagement* was computed as the total score summing across each of the subscales. The confirmatory factor validation of the revised ALQ [31] yielded a well-fitting higher-order general activity factor in two independent samples, thereby supporting the use of a single lifestyle engagement score in the present investigation. The 11 first-order activity factors approximate social, physical, and cognitive pursuits, briefly summarized in the following sections.

3.3. Physical Activities

The physical activities included in the lifestyle engagement aggregate score were derived from a subset of 10 items from the revised VLS-ALQ. These 10 individual items indexed various physical activities including select exercises (e.g., swimming, cycling), outdoor activities (e.g., sailing, fishing), sports (e.g., tennis, bowling, golf), aerobics (e.g., cardiovascular workouts), flexibility training (e.g., yoga, tai chi), walking, dancing, and resistance training (e.g., weight lifting, strength training).

3.4. Social Activities

Similarly, the social activities in the lifestyle engagement score were based upon a subset of 15 items from the revised VLS-ALQ. These 15 items indexed various socially-engaging activities including visiting friends/relatives, dining out at restaurants, hosting dinner parties, attending church, attending club meetings, volunteering, as well as attending public events or lectures.

3.5. Cognitive Activities

Cognitive activities in the aggregate score were based upon a subset of 27 items from the revised VLS-ALQ. These individual items reflected leisure activities that are cognitively stimulating such as playing a musical instrument, photography, computer use, tax preparation, engaging in business activity, reconciling a financial statement, mathematical calculations (with and without a calculator), creative writing, reading, taking continuing education courses, studying a second language, crosswords and playing games (e.g., chess, checkers, knowledge games, word games, jigsaw puzzles).

4. Results

4.1. Dispersion Index

Dispersion is a measure of intraindividual variability that is computed as an intraindividual standard deviation (ISD), reflecting performance fluctuations across a profile of cognitive measures within an individual. Dispersion profiles were derived using a regression technique, which computes ISD scores from standardized test scores [11,12]. Test scores of interest (MAT, Digit Span Forward and Backward, 3MS, NAART, TMT-A, RAVLT A6, A7 and recognition, Digit Symbol, SRT, Lexical Decision) were initially regressed on linear and quadratic age trends to control for group differences in mean performance, given that greater variance tends to be associated with greater means [33,34] and that mean-level performance is likely to differ across age bands present in the current sample. The resulting residuals from these models were standardized as T-scores (M = 50, SD = 10), with ISDs subsequently computed across these residualized test scores. The resulting dispersion estimate, indexed on a common metric, reflects the amount of variability across an individual's neuropsychological profile relative to the group average level of performance; higher values reflect greater IIV in cognitive function. Dispersion was computed across all test scores in the battery that were not used for cognitive classification (*n* = 15). Across the entire sample, the average dispersion score was 8.69 (*SD* = 4.15) T-score units. Figure 1 depicts the magnitude of dispersion within each cognitive status subgroup.

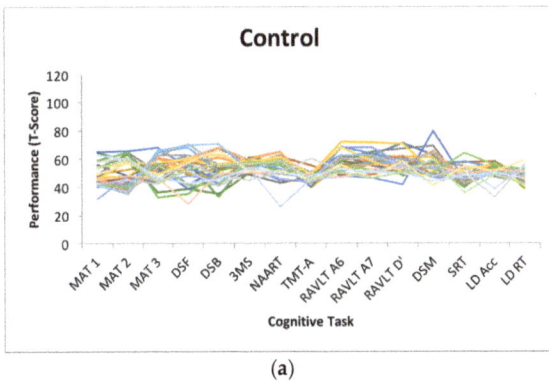

(a)

Figure 1. *Cont.*

(b)

(c)

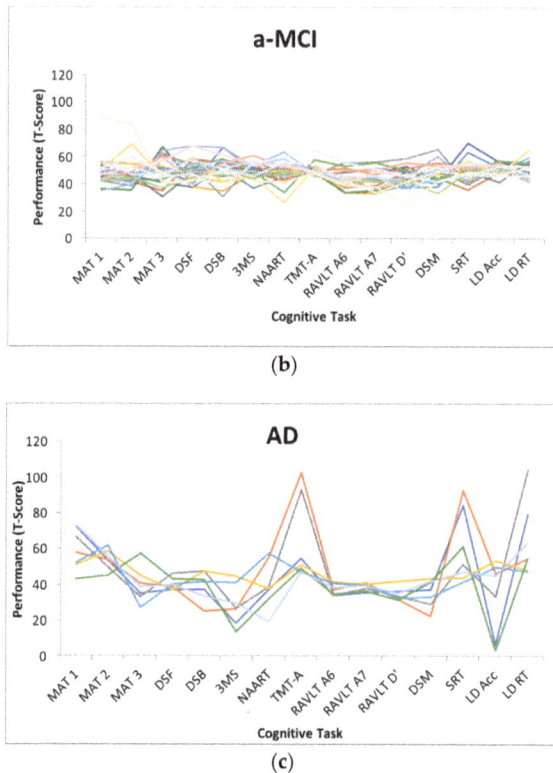

Figure 1. Dispersion profiles for each group of participants, classified as (**a**) healthy control (HC), amnestic (**b**) Mild Cognitive Impairment (a-MCI) and (**c**) Alzheimer's disease (AD).

4.2. Between-Group Differences in Dispersion and Lifestyle

Employing analysis of variance, between-group differences were observed on average amount of dispersion ($F(2,57) = 25.326$, $p < 0.001$, $\eta^2 = 0.47$), with the AD group ($m = 16.42$, $SD = 7.26$) scoring higher than the a-MCI ($m = 7.39$, $SD = 2.69$) and HC ($m = 7.87$, $SD = 1.45$) groups, who did not differ based on post-hoc comparisons using Tukey's HSD. Between-group differences were also observed in terms of overall engaged lifestyle summary score, based on the ALQ ($F(2, 56) = 7.564$, $p < 0.001$, $\eta^2 = 0.21$), with post hoc comparisons indicating that the HC group ($m = 154.86$, $SD = 28.35$) reported more engagement relative to the AD group ($m = 102.71$, $SD = 52.72$), but not the a-MCI group ($m = 132.91$, $SD = 33.60$).

4.3. Risk of Cognitive Impairment

Multinomial logistic regression models were used to examine the likelihood of being classified as a-MCI or AD, relative to HC, using dispersion, lifestyle engagement (total ALQ score) as well as demographic covariates (age and education) as predictors. Independent of age and education, increased dispersion was associated with a greater likelihood of being classified as AD (OR = 1.20, CI = 1.04, 1.38, $p < 0.05$), $\chi^2(6) = 24.223$ $p < 0.001$, Nagelkerke's R-squared = 0.39. For every T-score unit increase in dispersion (approximately 1/10 of a standard deviation), the likelihood of being classified as AD increased by 20%. Dispersion was not, however, associated with a greater likelihood of being classified as a-MCI. Similarly, a more engaged lifestyle was associated with a reduced likelihood of being classified as either a-MCI (OR = 0.92, CI = 0.85, 0.99, $p < 0.05$) or AD (OR = 0.84, CI = 0.74, 0.94, $p < 0.005$), independent of age and education, $\chi^2(6) = 18.454$ $p < 0.005$, Nagelkerke's R-squared = 0.31. For every T-score unit increase in the engaged-lifestyle score, the likelihood of being classified as a-MCI or AD was reduced by 8% and 16, respectively.

With both the dispersion and engaged lifestyle scores entered simultaneously in a multinomial logistic regression model, engaged lifestyle remained protective against a-MCI (OR = 0.90, CI = 0.83, 0.98, $p < 0.05$), but not AD (OR = 0.88, CI = 0.73, 1.05, $p > 0.05$), $\chi^2(8) = 32.508$ $p < 0.001$, Nagelkerke's R-squared = 0.50. Conversely, dispersion remained predictive of AD (OR = 1.23, CI = 1.02, 1.47, $p < 0.05$), but not a-MCI risk (OR = 0.97, CI = 0.85, 1.10, $p > 0.05$). Independently, cognitive dispersion was predictive of cognitive impairment for more substantial (AD) degrees of impairment only, while lifestyle engagement was predictive of cognitive impairment risk for moderate (a-MCI) and substantial (AD) impairment; however, when examined simultaneously, lifestyle engagement was sensitive only to moderate impairment (a-MCI), while dispersion was sensitive only to the most impaired cognitive status (AD). Lastly, we computed a model specifying both main effects (dispersion and total ALQ) as well as the interaction between dispersion and total ALQ to evaluate the potential modulating influence of engaged lifestyle on the neuropsychological dispersion-cognitive impairment association. No significant dispersion-engaged lifestyle interactions were observed ($p > 0.05$) for risk of either a-MCI or AD, $\chi^2(10) = 33.190$ $p < 0.001$, Nagelkerke's R-squared = 0.50.

5. Discussion

As a measure of intraindividual variability that is sensitive to developmental phenomena and to deleterious health outcomes in late-life, dispersion (i.e., intraindividual variability across a profile of tests) has received less attention relative to the more commonly employed measure of inconsistency (i.e., intraindividual variability in performance across time). Like inconsistency, dispersion has shown sensitivity to acquired [16] and neurodegenerative conditions [9,11,13,15,17,18], including MCI and dementia classification. In this context, greater dispersion observed for individuals not yet presenting with additional symptomatology (e.g., functional impairment, subjective memory complaints) may stem from early declines in neural integrity reflective of the dementia prodrome (e.g., medial temporal lobe atrophy). Further, engagement in lifestyle activities play a known protective factor in late-life [19–23] and is important for maintaining healthy cognitive functioning. Although previous investigations of dispersion have found that greater dispersion was related to poorer ADLs, but not to overall activity levels [11], the relationship between activity levels and dispersion in late-life has not been examined using psychometrically-validated measures of lifestyle activities in a sample of rigorously classified older adults.

The present study sought to replicate previous findings linking dispersion to cognitive subgroups and to examine whether lifestyle activity was protective against risk for cognitive decline, given recent findings demonstrating the sensitivity of engaged lifestyle in predicting dementia risk [21]. Relative to previous investigations examining dispersion-cognitive impairment links, a particular strength of the present study concerns the rigor of the screening criteria for indexing AD. We observed group differences in dispersion, computed across a battery of 15 cognitive and neuropsychological tests, such that the AD group showed greater dispersion relative to the HC group and those classified as a-MCI. Considerable variance in dispersion was also observed within the HC group. Greater dispersion emerged as a significant predictor in examining the risk of AD classification relative to HC. Interestingly, dispersion did not emerge as a significant predictor of a-MCI classification, relative to HC. Among the potential reasons, this finding may be due to the well-known heterogeneity between-individuals for even the most rigorously-screened MCI groups [35]. The lack of differentiation may also be due to the nature of the tasks included in the broad profile dispersion computation. Given the nature of a-MCI and the circumscribed memory impairments that represent a hallmark of the condition, a-MCI individuals may only demonstrate greater dispersion with the inclusion of sufficient short-term and episodic memory measures in the battery. As the condition progresses towards AD pathology, inconsistent cognitive performance in domains that are initially more robust may become more apparent. As most of the memory tests included in the present battery were used for cognitive classification, they were necessarily excluded from the dispersion computation.

In addition to demonstrating lower levels of dispersion, the HC group reported greater engagement in physical, cognitive, and social lifestyle activities on a comprehensive and psychometrically-validated measure of adult lifestyle activities [31]. Independent of the effects of dispersion, engaged lifestyle was protective against a-MCI, but not AD classification. This finding is consistent with the documented importance of an engaged lifestyle for maintaining cognitive function and mitigating cognitive impairment [19,23]. As central nervous system (CNS) impairment becomes more progressive and pronounced, engagement in lifestyle activities may no longer be as protective against cognitive impairment. This may be especially the case for well-characterized AD individuals who are also demonstrating greater inconsistency across cognitive areas. Further, our findings are consistent with claims that dispersion, as a marker of CNS integrity, may be particularly sensitive for detecting individuals with progressive neuropathology [12,17]. Notably, regarding detection of AD risk in particular, dispersion (i.e., inconsistency across tasks) can be computed using both speed and accuracy measures, which is important as some of the most extensively researched and validated standardized measures used in clinical practice to assess neuropsychological functioning yield accuracy scores only. As researchers attempt to better understand the relationship between enrichment effects on cognitive development, including lifestyle engagement, such validated measures that predict success in more complex day-to-day behaviors may afford greater ecological validity. This is especially the case as intervention efforts shift away from cognitive training in isolation to cognitive training in a more applied context to facilitate greater far transfer and generalization of the intervention [19].

Limitations and Future Directions

Several limitations and future directions are noted. As is common for clinical neuropsychology studies, the present study contained only a small sample of individuals diagnosed as probable-AD, which limited statistical power and precluded an examination of more nuanced associations between dispersion and lifestyle activities that share theoretical underpinnings (e.g., executive functioning and engagement in cognitively demanding lifestyle activities). Future studies may consider examining the association between dispersion within a particular cognitive domain and more specific lifestyle activities (e.g., a physically-engaged lifestyle) to help further elucidate the potential utility of dispersion to inform intervention strategies (e.g., to target an area of lifestyle activity that draws upon cognitive processes showing early decline). Contrasting specific profiles of dispersion may also be useful in determining which cognitive domains show greater and lesser variability within-persons of a given cognitive status [13,15], given that isolated impairments in some clinical populations will result in fairly stable scores within a domain (e.g., consistently low memory performance in an AD sample). Further, examining the comparative utility of different operationalizations of IIV (e.g., dispersion and response time inconsistency) remains an important avenue for future research. Future investigations employing dispersion should be mindful of how the nature of the tasks selected for the computation will affect results. For example, across a broader profile of tasks spanning crystallized to fluid abilities, we might expect greater dispersion profiles (intact performance on some measures, impaired on others) for the cognitively impaired group vs. controls. Examining the comparative protective benefit across subtypes of lifestyle engagement also remains an important topic for further investigation.

Given the comparatively greater number of empirical studies examining IIV across trials (e.g., inconsistency) in other areas of functioning (e.g., heart rate, neural activity, gait), future dispersion studies may also consider examining dispersion across multiple domains of functioning, especially to the extent that increased dispersion may be driven by common underlying systems. Motoric Cognitive Risk Syndrome (MCR) is characterized by cognitive and gait dysfunction and is both highly prevalent in older adults [36] and sensitive to risk for dementia [37]. MCR represents an opportunity for future investigation of multi-domain dispersion (i.e., gait and cognition) that may yield useful insights into the etiology of the condition and the potential predictive utility of dispersion, beyond single-domain dispersion in isolation.

6. Conclusions

The results of this study replicate previous findings suggesting that dispersion across cognitive tests is sensitive to cognitive status in late-life, particularly when individuals are relatively impaired. Individuals who are disengaged from cognitive, physical, and social lifestyle activities are more likely to be classified as having a-MCI as the stability of their cognitive processes decreases, relative to those who are more engaged. Notably, this relationship may be viewed both ways; that is, disengaged lifestyle may lead to atrophy of cognitive and neurological systems that may otherwise be stimulated through activity engagement. Conversely, cognitive impairment may preclude engagement in certain activities that rely on cognitive processes that have become compromised. Regardless, individuals at risk may be better identified through an assessment of both dispersion and lifestyle activities. Further, interventions for those at risk may consider targeting activity engagement, while monitoring cognitive dispersion as a marker of stability and risk for deleterious health outcomes.

Supplementary Materials: The following are available online at www.mdpi.com/2079-3200/6/1/12/s1, Group differences on neuropsychological tests between the health control (HC), amnestic Mild Cognitive Impairment (a-MCI) and Alzheimer's Disease (AD) groups. Standard deviations are presented in parentheses. Post-hoc comparisons are based on Tukey's HSD.

Acknowledgments: This research was supported by a Canada Graduate Scholarship from the Canadian Institutes of Health Research to D.W.R. Halliday, and by grants to S.W.S. MacDonald and R.S. Stawski from the National Institute on Aging at the National Institutes of Health (R21 AG045575), the Natural Sciences and Engineering Research Council of Canada, and the Michael Smith Foundation for Health Research. S.W.S. MacDonald also gratefully acknowledges support by the Royal Society of Canada's College of New Scholars, Artists and Scientists. Further information about the PREVENT Study may be obtained by contacting S.W.S. MacDonald at smacd@uvic.ca.

Author Contributions: Stuart W. S. MacDonald, Correne A. DeCarlo and Drew W. R. Halliday conceived and designed the experiments; Drew W. R. Halliday and Correne A. DeCarlo performed the experiments; Drew W. R. Halliday, Stuart W. S. MacDonald, Robert S. Stawski, Eric S. Cerino and Karl Grewal analyzed the data; Karl Grewal contributed data visualization tools; Drew W. R. Halliday, Stuart W. S. MacDonald and Robert S. Stawski wrote the paper.

Conflicts of Interest: The authors declare no conflict of interest.

References

1. Grand, J.H.G.; Stawski, R.S.; MacDonald, S.W.S. Comparing individual differences in inconsistency and plasticity as predictors of cognitive function in older adults. *J. Clin. Exp. Neuropsychol.* **2016**, *38*, 534–550. [CrossRef] [PubMed]
2. Rosano, C.; Brach, J.; Studenski, S.; Longstreth, W.T., Jr.; Newman, A.B. Gait variability is associated with subclinical brain vascular abnormalities in high-functioning older adults. *Neuroepidemiology* **2007**, *29*, 193–200. [CrossRef] [PubMed]
3. Jennings, R.J.; Allen, B.; Gianaros, P.J.; Thayer, J.F.; Manuck, S.B. Focusing neurovisceral integration: Cognition, heart rate variability, and cerebral blood flow. *Psychophysiology* **2015**, *52*, 214–224. [CrossRef] [PubMed]
4. Armbruster-Genç, D.J.N.; Ueltzhöffer, K.; Fiebach, C.J. Brain signal variability differentially affects cognitive flexibility and cognitive stability. *J. Neurosci.* **2016**, *36*, 3978–3987. [CrossRef] [PubMed]
5. Garrett, D.G.; Samanez-Larkin, G.R.; MacDonald, S.W.S.; Lindenberger, U.; McIntosh, A.R.; Grady, C.L. Moment-to-moment brain signal variability: A next frontier in human brain mapping? *Neurosci. Biobehav. Rev.* **2013**, *37*, 610–624. [CrossRef] [PubMed]
6. MacDonald, S.W.S.; Stawski, R.S. Intraindividual Variability—An Indicator of Vulnerability or Resilience in Adult Development and Aging? In *Handbook of Intraindividual Variability across the Life Span*; Diehl, M., Hooker, K., Sliwinski, M., Eds.; Routledge: New York, NY, USA, 2015; pp. 231–257.

7. Dixon, R.A.; Garrett, D.G.; Lentz, T.L.; MacDonald, S.W.S.; Strauss, E.; Hultsch, D.F. Neurocognitive markers of cognitive impairment: Exploring the roles of speed and inconsistency. *Neuropsychology* **2007**, *21*, 381–399. [CrossRef] [PubMed]

8. Duchek, J.M.; Balota, D.A.; Tse, C.S.; Holtzman, D.M.; Fagan, A.M.; Goate, A.M. The utility of intraindividual variability in selective attention tasks as an early marker for Alzheimer's disease. *Neuropsychology* **2009**, *23*, 746–758. [CrossRef] [PubMed]

9. Hultsch, D.F.; MacDonald, S.W.S.; Hunter, M.A.; Levy-Bencheton, J.; Strauss, E. Intraindividual variability in cognitive performance in older adults: Comparison of adults with mild dementia, adults with arthritis, and health adults. *Neuropsychology* **2000**, *14*, 588–598. [CrossRef] [PubMed]

10. MacDonald, S.W.S.; Li, S.-C.; Bäckman, L. Neural underpinnings of within-person variability in cognitive functioning. *Psychol. Aging* **2009**, *24*, 792–808. [CrossRef] [PubMed]

11. Christensen, H.; Mackinnon, A.J.; Korten, A.E.; Jorm, A.F.; Henderson, A.S.; Jacomb, P. Dispersion in cognitive ability as a function of age: A longitudinal study of an elderly community sample. *Aging Neuropsychol. Cogn.* **1999**, *6*, 214–228. [CrossRef]

12. Hultsch, D.F.; MacDonald, S.W.S.; Dixon, R.A. Variability in reaction time performance of younger and older adults. *J. Gerontol. Psychol. Sci.* **2002**, *57B*, 101–115. [CrossRef]

13. Hilborn, J.V.; Strauss, E.; Hultsch, D.F.; Hunter, M.A. Intraindividual variability across cognitive domains: Investigation of dispersion levels and performance profiles in older adults. *J. Clin. Exp. Neuropsychol.* **2009**, *31*, 412–424. [CrossRef] [PubMed]

14. Mella, N.; Fagot, D.; de Ribaupierre, A. Dispersion in cognitive functioning: Age differences of the lifespan. *J. Clin. Exp. Neuropsychol.* **2016**, *38*, 111–126. [CrossRef] [PubMed]

15. Peters, K.R.; Graf, P.; Hayden, S.; Feldman, H. Neuropsychological subgroups of cognitively-impaired-not-demented (CIND) individuals: Delineation, reliability, and predictive validity. *J. Clin. Exp. Neuropsychol.* **2005**, *27*, 164–188. [CrossRef] [PubMed]

16. Rabinowitz, A.R.; Arnett, P.A. Intraindividual cognitive variability before and after sports-related concussion. *Neuropsychology* **2013**, *27*, 481–490. [CrossRef] [PubMed]

17. Holtzer, R.; Verghese, J.; Wang, C.; Hall, C.B.; Lipton, R. Within-person across-neuropsychological test variability and incident dementia. *JAMA* **2008**, *300*, 823–830. [CrossRef] [PubMed]

18. Vaughan, L.; Leng, I.; Dagenbach, D.; Resnick, S.M.; Rapp, S.R.; Jennings, J.M.; Espeland, M.A. Intraindividual variability in domain-specific cognition and risk of mild cognitive impairment and dementia. *Curr. Gerontol. Geriatr. Res.* **2013**. [CrossRef] [PubMed]

19. Hertzog, C.; Kramer, A.F.; Wilson, R.S.; Lindenberger, U. Enrichment effects on adult cognitive development. *Psychol. Sci.* **2009**, *9*, 1–65. [CrossRef] [PubMed]

20. Wirth, M.; Haase, C.M.; Villeneuve, S.; Vogel, J.; Jagust, W.J. Neuroprotective pathways: Lifestyle activity, brain pathology, and cognition in cognitively normal older adults. *Neurobiol. Aging* **2014**, *35*, 1873–1882. [CrossRef] [PubMed]

21. Wang, H.-X.; MacDonald, S.W.S.; Dekhtyar, S.; Fratiglioni, L. Association of lifelong exposure to cognitive reserve-enhancing factors with dementia risk: A community-based cohort study. *PLoS Med.* **2017**, *14*. [CrossRef] [PubMed]

22. Salthouse, T.A. Mental exercise and mental aging. *Perspect. Psychol. Sci.* **2006**, *1*, 68–87. [CrossRef] [PubMed]

23. Gow, A.J.; Pattie, A.; Deary, I.J. Lifecourse activity participation from early, mid, and later adulthood as determinants of cognitive aging: The Lotian Birth Cohort 1921. *J. Gerontol. Psychol. Sci.* **2017**, *72*, 25–37. [CrossRef] [PubMed]

24. Petersen, R.C.; Smith, G.E.; Waring, S.C.; Ivnik, R.J.; Tangalos, E.G.; Kokmen, E. Mild cognitive impairment: Clinical characterization and outcome. *Arch. Neurol.* **1999**, *56*, 303–308. [CrossRef] [PubMed]

25. Petersen, R.C.; Roberts, R.O.; Knopman, D.S.; Boeve, B.F.; Geda, Y.E.; Ivnik, R.J.; Jack, C.R., Jr. Mild cognitive impairment: Ten years later. *Arch. Neurol.* **2009**, *66*, 1447–1455. [CrossRef] [PubMed]

26. Petersen, R.C. Mild cognitive impairment as a diagnostic entity. *J. Int. Med.* **2004**, *256*, 183–194. [CrossRef] [PubMed]

27. American Psychiatric Association. *Diagnostic and Statistical Manual of Mental Disorders: DSM-IV-TR*; American Psychiatric Association: Washington, DC, USA, 2000.

28. Tuokko, H.; Woodward, T.S. Development and validation of a demographic correction system for neuropsychological measures used in the Canadian study of health and aging. *J. Clin. Exp. Neuropsychol.* **1996**, *18*, 479–616. [CrossRef] [PubMed]

29. Ivnik, R.J.; Malec, J.F.; Smith, G.E.; Tangalos, E.G.; Petersen, R.C. Neuropsychologists tests' norms above age 55: COWAT, BNT, MAE token, WRAT-R reading, AMNART, STROOP, TMT, and JLO. *Clin. Neuropsychol.* **1996**, *10*, 262–278. [CrossRef]

30. Steinberg, B.A.; Bieliauskas, L.A.; Smith, G.E.; Ivnik, R.J.; Malec, J.F. Mayo's older American normative studies: Age- and IQ-adjusted norms for the auditory verbal learning test and the visual spatial learning test. *Clin. Neuropsychol.* **2005**, *19*, 464–523. [CrossRef] [PubMed]

31. Jopp, D.S.; Hertzog, C. Assessing adult leisure activities: An extension of a self-report activity questionnaire. *Psychol. Assess.* **2010**, *22*, 108–120. [CrossRef] [PubMed]

32. Dixon, R.A.; de Frias, C.M. The Victoria Longitudinal Study: From characterizing cognitive aging to illustrating changes in memory compensation. *Aging Neuropsychol. Cogn.* **2004**, *11*, 346–376. [CrossRef]

33. Hale, S.; Myerson, J.; Smith, G.A.; Poon, L.W. Age, variability, and speed: Between-subjects diversity. *Psychol. Aging* **1998**, *3*, 407–410. [CrossRef]

34. Stawski, R.S.; MacDonald, S.W.S.; Brewster, P.H.; Munoz, E.; Cerino, E.S.; Halliday, D.R.W. A comprehensive comparison of quantifications of intraindividual variability in response times: A measurement burst approach. *J. Gerontol. B Psychol. Sci. Soc. Sci.* **2017**. [CrossRef] [PubMed]

35. Palmer, K.; Wang, H.-X.; Bäckman, L.; Winblad, B.; Fratiglioni, L. Differential evolution of cognitive impairment in nondemented older persons: Results from the Kungsholmen project. *Am. J. Psychiatry* **2002**, *159*, 436–442. [CrossRef] [PubMed]

36. Verghese, J.; Ayers, E.; Barzilai, N.; Bennett, D.A.; Buchman, A.S.; Holtzer, R.; Wang, C. Motoric cognitive risk syndrome: Multicenter incidence study. *Neurology* **2014**, *83*, 2278–2284. [CrossRef] [PubMed]

37. Verghese, J.; Wang, C.; Lipton, R.B.; Holtzer, R. Motoric cognitive risk syndrome and the risk of dementia. *J. Gerontol. Med. Sci.* **2013**, *68*, 412–418. [CrossRef] [PubMed]

Journal of
Intelligence

MDPI

Article

Intra-Individual Variability from a Lifespan Perspective: A Comparison of Latency and Accuracy Measures

Delphine Fagot [1,2,*], Nathalie Mella [3], Erika Borella [4], Paolo Ghisletta [2,5,6], Thierry Lecerf [5,6,7] and Anik De Ribaupierre [1,5]

1   Center for the Interdisciplinary Study of Gerontology and Vulnerability (CIGEV), University of Geneva, 1211 Geneva, Switzerland; Anik.deRibaupierre@unige.ch
2   Swiss National Centre of Competence in Research LIVES–Overcoming Vulnerability, Life Course Perspectives, University of Geneva, 1211 Geneva, Switzerland; Paolo.Ghisletta@unige.ch
3   Cognitive Aging Lab, University of Geneva, 1211 Geneva, Switzerland; Nathalie.Mella-Barraco@unige.ch
4   Department of General Psychology, University of Padova, 35122 Padova, Italy; erika.borella@unipd.it
5   Faculty of Psychology and Educational Sciences, University of Geneva, 1211 Geneva, Switzerland; Thierry.Lecerf@unige.ch
6   Swiss Distance Learning University, 3900 Brig, Switzerland
7   Faculty of Social and Political Sciences, University of Lausanne, 1015 Lausanne, Switzerland
*   Correspondence: Delphine.Fagot@unige.ch; Tel.: +41-22-379-37-81

Received: 7 December 2017; Accepted: 9 March 2018; Published: 14 March 2018

Abstract: Within-task variability across trials (intra-individual variability (IIV)) has been mainly studied using latency measures but rarely with accuracy measures. The aim of the Geneva Variability Study was to examine IIV in both latency and accuracy measures of cognitive performance across the lifespan, administering the same tasks to children, younger adults, and older adults. Six processing speed tasks (Response Time (RT) tasks, 8 conditions) and two working memory tasks scored in terms of the number of correct responses (Working Memory (WM)—verbal and visuo-spatial, 6 conditions), as well as control tasks, were administered to over 500 individuals distributed across the three age periods. The main questions were whether age differences in IIV would vary throughout the lifespan according (i) to the type of measure used (RTs vs. accuracy); and (ii) to task complexity. The objective of this paper was to present the general experimental design and to provide an essentially descriptive picture of the results. For all experimental tasks, IIV was estimated using intra-individual standard deviation (iSDr), controlling for the individual level (mean) of performance and for potential practice effects. As concerns RTs, and in conformity with a majority of the literature, younger adults were less variable than both children and older adults, and the young children were often the most variable. In contrast, IIV in the WM accuracy scores pointed to different age trends—age effects were either not observed or, when found, they indicated that younger adults were the more variable group. Overall, the findings suggest that IIV provides complementary information to that based on a mean performance, and that the relation of IIV to cognitive development depends on the type of measure used.

Keywords: intra-individual variability; working memory; life-span; reaction time

1. Introduction

Almost all research in cognitive psychology, including cognitive developmental psychology, has focused on mean performance. Yet, individual variability should not be neglected, whether inter- or intra-individual. Many authors have proposed to consider that individual variability should be taken into consideration when proposing general laws of behavior (e.g., Reference [1]). That is, general psychology should be able to integrate the bulk of individual variability, just as much as differential psychology should also lean on experimental manipulations (e.g., Reference [2]). Several types of individual variabilities should be distinguished (e.g., Reference [3]). Inter-individual variability has been often acknowledged, for instance when comparing groups or individuals from an applied perspective, or when standard deviations are reported. Note, however, that standard deviations only provide information about quantitative differences among individuals, as if they differed solely in how distant from their group mean they are; they do not provide any indication on qualitative differences.

Intra-individual variability (IIV) can be further distinguished as a function of the time period considered: across long-term periods (developmental change), across trials within tasks (inconsistency), and across tasks at a given point in time (dispersion). The present study focused on short-term within-task intra-individual variability, that is, on inconsistency or fluctuations across trials [4–6], and examined whether age differences (i) are observed throughout the lifespan; and (ii) vary across tasks. It has been argued already years ago that within-task variability might represent better the entire performance than a measure of central tendency alone [3,7–9]. A new gain in interest has recently emerged again, backed up by empirical data. The interest for a change in amplitude of IIV with age has primarily been demonstrated in the cognitive aging domain [4,10] and is now also burgeoning in cognitive developmental research in children [6,11–14].

Note that the label "inconsistency", the focus of the present study, attached to within-task intra-individual variability shows that IIV usually bears a negative connotation, as a cursory review of literature attests. IIV has indeed been shown to be a predictor of cognitive dysfunction. A first set of studies by Hultsch and collaborators [15] has compared three groups of older adults (mildly demented, physically ill with arthritis, and healthy adults) and observed that the demented persons presented a much larger IIV in latency and accuracy of cognitive performance. Moreover, IIV was uniquely predictive of neurological status, independent of the level of performance. IIV is also presented as a useful marker of cognitive functioning in children with learning disabilities, such as children with attention-deficit hyperactivity disorder (ADHD), as compared to children with typical development [11,12].

With respect to age, IIV has been observed to be larger in children and older adults [4,16–27]. Cross-sectional studies showed a developmental trend across the lifespan similar to that of the mean level of performance: A typical U-shaped curve with a decrease in IIV in response time (RT) from childhood to young adulthood followed by an increase throughout adulthood relatively early on [6,22,28–30]. Older adults were found to be more inconsistent than younger ones on RT measures in simple tasks, and baseline differences in IIV were shown to be associated with the level of performance. A few aging studies were longitudinal, having followed the same individuals across several years [19,27]. They showed an increase in IIV from adulthood to late adulthood with an acceleration beyond the age of 70 [24]. There are, however, some discrepancies in the literature, some studies reporting no age effect in IIV [31,32].

IIV is thus considered as an important source of information in addition to the mean performance in both aging and child development [33,34]. Yet, although steadily increasing, the empirical evidence is still far from sufficient to demonstrate the usefulness of adding a measure of variability to that of the mean level, and its specificity. Moreover, a number of methodological and theoretical issues and questions are pending, some of which will be examined in the present paper. First, it is not always the case that IIV is larger in older adults, or in children, once the mean RT is controlled for (e.g., Reference [35]). Intra-individual standard deviations are often used to study IIV; however it is known that, even though means and standard deviations are considered to be statistically independent, they tend to vary together [36]. Larger mean reaction times, as observed in children and older adults for instance, will therefore tend to be associated with larger standard deviations. Hence, it is important to control for the level of performance when estimating IIV. Second, although a similar (and inverse) trend has been observed in childhood and older adulthood as concerns mean performance, few studies have analyzed IIV across the entire lifespan, from childhood to advanced old age, using the same tasks in the different age groups (but see [6,22,30]). Third, nearly all studies on IIV have relied on RT tasks, while few studies have focused on correct responses (accuracy performance scores). Yet, a number of cognitive processes, and thus tasks, need to be assessed taking into account both level of accuracy and correct responses. This is the case of memory tasks, including complex working memory (WM) span tasks, in which accuracy scores (such as span scores) are more generally considered. The use of other scores and non RT tasks might explain why some authors did not observe age differences in IIV (e.g., Reference [31,32]).

Furthermore, the meaning of a large IIV is not very clear from a theoretical point of view. Larger IIV is often associated with vulnerability or impairment, as mentioned above with respect to the use of the term inconsistency. However, in the child developmental domain, IIV is not specifically linked to learning disabilities, but simply with younger age; young children show larger IIV than older children [6,12]. It is noteworthy to add that IIV has also been addressed from a different perspective as concerns development in children. Siegler [13] or van Geert and van Dijk [37] often emphasized a larger variability in younger children, and considered it to index the development of multiple strategies or/and to reflect the upcoming of a stage transition. Not only can IIV be considered as a "prominent feature in child development," but also it "is an important characteristic of self-organization in development" as viewed already by dynamic systems theorists in the early 1990's ([38], p. 53). In this case, IIV would thus reflect a developmental progress.

The question of whether large IIV is dysfunctional or adaptive (pointing to resilience) is still being presently discussed in the aging domain [39,40]. Also, and in spite of the quantitative similarity in IIV trends in childhood and in aging, different processes probably account for IIV changes [41,42]. During childhood, among several factors, the maturation of white matter such as myelination [43] has been suggested to be linked to the decrease in IIV. For older adults, IIV might reflect structural and functional changes in frontal lobe functions, as well as in dopaminergic neuromodulation [44], in the quality/integrity of white matter [43,45–48] or in neuromodulatory efficiency [19,22]. In particular, the quality of white matter seems to present a stronger relation with IIV than with the mean level of performance, a result that has been interpreted as reflecting a less stable communication between cerebral regions [45,47,49].

The present study pursued the following objectives: (i) Examine age trends in inconsistency throughout the lifespan by administering the same tasks to children, younger adults and older adults; (ii) Compare IIV in both RT and in working memory (WM) tasks assessing accuracy; (iii) Compare tasks of varying complexity, to determine whether IIV would be larger in more complex tasks and assessing for possible interactions of age and complexity.

Several tasks were administered to all individuals: six RT tasks varying in complexity, from a simple RT task to Choice RT tasks (Lines comparison, Cross-square), complex processing speed tasks (Digit Symbol and Comparison of letters), an interference task (Stroop), as well as two WM span tasks (Reading Span and Visuo-spatial WM) also varying in complexity. All the tasks were administered in an identical manner to children, younger adults and older ones. IIV was examined in each task, using an intra-individual standard deviation, residualized for the individual level of performance (iSDr, see method). The use of residualized scores before computing an iSD is in line with the suggestion by Hultsch and coll. (e.g., Reference [50]).

Our expectation, based on the extant literature, was that both children and older adults would exhibit larger IIV than younger adults in the RT tasks [6,10,23,51–53]. We expected also more variability in the more difficult condition (complex RT tasks), and an interaction with age, the difference being larger in children and older adults. The question of whether the same trend would be observed for IIV in the two WM tasks was left open. There are several reasons why the age trend of IIV might differ between the two types of tasks, such as the discordant results obtained with the two types of scores [31], the range of possible responses—smaller for the WM tasks than the RT tasks [54]—and the different implications of a larger IIV. In RT tasks, larger IIV has been observed in those individuals considered to present a lower performance, that is, those with longer RTs. In the case of a WM task, it is known that children and older adults present lower scores than younger adults. If IIV was indeed indicative of lower cognitive functioning, it should be associated with lower scores in contrast with what is observed in RT tasks.

2. Materials and Methods

2.1. Participants

Two hundred and one children (age range = 9–12 years, tested within 2 months of their birthday), 137 younger adults (age range = 19–33), and 219 older adults (age range = 59–89) participated in the study[1]. Children were recruited from primary schools in the city of Geneva. The younger adults were undergraduate students at the University of Geneva participating for course credit. The older adults were volunteers recruited from the community, either from the University of the Third Age of Geneva, or through newspaper and association advertisements for pensioners. None of the older adults, as shown by a large battery of tasks administered (e.g., Reference [55]), presented an incipient dementia. Only participants who spoke French either as their first language or fluently were included.

The French version of the Mill-Hill vocabulary scale [56] was administered to the younger and older adults. A one-way ANOVA on vocabulary scores in the two adult groups indicated a main effect of age, $F(1, 351) = 45.489$, $p < 0.001$, $\eta_p^2 = 0.12$; as frequently observed in aging studies for abilities related to crystallized intelligence (e.g., Reference [57]), younger adults had a lower vocabulary score than older adults ($p < 0.05$). Additionally, the Raven's Progressive matrices task (Raven, 1938) was administered to all participants. A one-way ANOVA on correct responses indicated a main effect of age, $F(2, 552) = 197.33$, $p < 0.001$, $\eta_p^2 = 0.42$; younger adults had better performances than children and older adults ($p < 0.001$). Children and older adults did not differ significantly.

Descriptive statistics for the demographic variables of the participants are provided in Table 1 (see also Table A1 in Appendix A).

Table 1. Participants' Characteristics by Age Group.

	Age Groups					
	Children		Young Adults		Older Adults	
N	201		137		219	
female	92		117		165	
	M	SD	M	SD	M	SD
Age	10.50	1.12	21.71	2.53	70.10	6.78
Vocabulary Score	—	—	34.67	3.25	37.73	4.64
Raven	36.84	8.21	52.15	4.91	36.47	9.12

Note: M: Group's mean; SD: Group's standard deviations.

2.2. Materials and Procedure

All participants were administered the same tasks, in a quiet room either at school for children or in our laboratory for adults, during two or three sessions, at most one week apart. All tasks were individually administered on a Dell computer using E-Prime [58] in the same order for all participants.

Latency scores. Six tasks (9 experimental conditions) were used to assess reaction times (RTs): one simple reaction time task (SRT), two choice reaction time tasks (line comparison—LI, and cross-square—CS), two processing speed tasks (digit symbol—DI, and letter comparison—LC,

---

[1] For the Reading span task, a memory score was computed only when the participants responded correctly for at least 85% of the sentences. This precaution was adopted to insure that participants did process the sentence while retaining the last word, that is, that the task was a dual one. The participants who made more errors when judging the sentence were attributed a missing score. Note that the sentences were simple. Overall, forty-one participants (essentially children) were discarded from the analyses because they did not reach the 85% accuracy criterion on the judgment task.

2 conditions, 6 vs. 9 letters) and one interference task[2] (Stroop color-word, 2 conditions, neutral vs. incongruent).

Accuracy scores. Two working memory (WM) tasks were used. In an adaptive version of the Reading span task [59,60], participants had to judge series of sentences while memorizing the last word; at the end of a series, they had to retrieve all the words. In the Matrices task, a grid of 5×5 cells was presented on a touch screen, with either a certain number of cells colored (spatial condition) or words contained in certain cells (spatio-verbal condition); participants had to point at the previously colored cells onto an empty matrix (Position score), or orally retrieve the word and simultaneously indicate its position onto the screen (Word-position score). For these two tasks, increasing series of sentences or number of positions (position or word-position) were first presented in a preliminary phase to assess the span level of each individual[3]. In order to make it possible to compute an intra-individual standard deviation, ten trials were then presented for each of two complexity conditions: at the individual's span level, and at span + 1 level[4]. Scores consisted of the number of correctly recalled items for each condition.

Brief descriptions of all these tasks are provided in Table 2; for more details on the procedure see [1]. For all tasks, only the correct responses contributed to the score.

Table 2. Descriptions and characteristics of tasks used in this study.

	Category	Task	Instructions	Condition	Trial
Latency score	Simple reaction Time	SRT	To detect as quickly as possible when a stimulus appeared on the screen	-	120
	Choice reaction time	LI	To detect on which of two sides the longest of two lines was located	-	120
		CS	To detect on which of two sides one of the six crosses changed into a square	-	120
	Processing speed	LC	to decide whether two series of letters were identical or not	6 or 9 letters	60
		DI	to determine whether a number–symbol pair was similar to a reference matrix	-	144
	Interference	ST	To name the color in which words or signs were written	Neutral Congruent Incongruent	144 144 144
Accuracy score	Working memory task	Rspan	To memorize and recall words	Span level Span + 1 level	20 20
		Matrices	To memorize and recall positions	Span level Span + 1 level	10 10
			To memorize and recall word-positions associations	Span + 1 level Span + 2 level	10 10

Note: SRT: Simple reaction time task. LI: Line comparison task; CS: Cross-square task; LC: Letter comparison task; DI: Digit symbol task; ST: Stroop task; Rspan: Reading span task.

Note: For the Stroop task, the three conditions were randomly distributed within each block. Only the conditions Neutral (colored geometrical signs) and Incongruent (colored word colored in a different color, e.g., red colored in blue) were used in the analyses. The Reading span was administered twice, with 10 trials per condition; the two sessions were pooled in the present analyses.

---

[2] The Stroop task was administered twice, at one week intervals, to split the task because it had a large number of items (432 in total). The correlations were high so that analyses were conducted on the total number of trials.

[3] The Reading span task was administered twice, at one week intervals, to test for possible retest effects. Performance was very similar; consequently, scores were computed on 20 items by condition.

[4] In these analyses, we analyzed the number of correctly recalled words/position by trial and not the percentage of success on the task (often used as an accuracy score). This allows the computing of a standard deviation across trials (20 trials by condition for reading span and 10 trials by condition for matrices task), but is of course computed on a range that is smaller in low span individuals. Note also that the errors in recall were, for the most part, omissions.

2.3. Statistical Analyses

Analyses were conducted on latency scores in the RT tasks and on the accuracy scores of the WM tasks. For all tasks, we conducted analyses on the mean performance (iM) and on the intra-individual standard deviation (iSDr)[5]. For the latter, scores were first residualized (standardized residual scores) for the mean level of the individual (iM), as well as for the order of trials and blocks, to control for possible practice effects. In the WM tasks, analyses were conducted on the number of correctly recalled items for each trial (words in the Reading span tasks, positions, and words/position[6] in the Matrices conditions). Then, intra-individual standard deviation (iSDr) were computed on those scores residualized for iM, order of trials and of blocks.

3. Results

3.1. Reaction Times Tasks

Descriptive statistics for the different RT tasks used are presented in Table 3; Table A2 reports the statistics for the five age groups. The data were submitted to one-way ANOVAs, comparing the age groups, by condition. Thresholds of significance were corrected for multiple comparisons (Bonferroni correction for a threshold of 0.05; $p < 0.004$).

Table 3. Reaction time tasks: Means (iM) and intra-individual standard deviation of residual scores (iSDr) by Age group.

			Age Groups					
			Children		Young Adults		Older Adults	
			M	SD	M	SD	M	SD
iM	SRT		360.03	68.78	272.89	39.16	333.50	73.41
	LI		565.38	101.31	372.38	43.52	457.66	70.46
	CS		495.57	105.41	325.69	39.26	431.16	76.75
	DI		1737.32	447.94	1040.56	221.47	1668.96	352.86
	LC	6 letters	3626.06	1236.06	1838.17	423.31	2971.24	799.48
		9 letters	5092.16	1550.37	2798.36	654.47	4316.61	1114.48
	ST	Neutral	842.21	146.76	594.77	75.85	724.31	110.05
		Incongruent	1019.96	184.77	720.89	102.30	927.75	166.67
iSDr	SRT		11.38	3.04	7.17	2.15	9.23	2.75
	LI		12.24	3.48	6.42	1.98	8.58	2.72
	CS		12.27	3.94	5.93	1.78	8.86	2.50
	DI		12.04	3.55	5.69	1.91	9.23	2.35
	LC	6 letters	12.56	5.22	5.03	1.67	8.17	2.86
		9 letters	12.64	4.11	5.83	1.81	8.88	2.56
	ST	Neutral	12.97	3.85	6.16	1.91	7.71	2.81
		Incongruent	12.40	2.95	7.16	1.92	8.83	2.55

Note: SRT: Simple reaction time task; LI: Line comparison task; CS: Cross-square task; LC: Letter comparison task; DI: Digit symbol task; ST: Stroop task; iM: intra-individual mean; iSDr: standard deviation of residual scores; M: Group's mean; SD: Group's standard deviations.

---

[5] Analyses on the coefficient of variation (CV) have also been conducted, the results on the reaction times (RTs) score are substantially the same as those obtained with the standard deviations. However, the use of CV has often been criticized, on the basis of our ignorance of its distribution. More importantly, we did not use CV because we wanted to use the same indices on both types of measures, namely, RTs and accuracy. Indeed, Golay, Fagot & Lecerf (2013) showed that the CV cannot be used, or at least generates problems, on accuracy data. Contrary to RTs, accuracy data have a lower and an upper bound, whereas RTs have only a lower bound. Moreover, these authors also showed that the CV is influenced by the number of items which is an issue when dealing with missing data. Therefore the intra-individual standard deviations seemed more appropriate than CVs.

[6] Remember that the WM tasks were not strictly identical for all participants, as they were adapted to their individual span (see Table A2). This is an optimal solution given the range of age and individual differences in the sample: If the task had been strictly identical for all, it would have been much too difficult for children (or too easy for younger adults), and would have tapped a very different capability while also yielding discouragement in the participants. This was not a problem for the RT tasks, as most of them are very simple. Consequently, age differences in the mean level of WM tasks might reflect both the level of the task and the participant's WM capacity. Using a percentage score (e.g., ratio of the correctly remembered words on the mean difficulty presented) would not provide much relevant information because it would simply reflect how well the task is adapted to the individuals' capacity.

3.1.1. Intra-Individual Mean (iM)

- Simple RT task. The main effect of age was significant, $F(2, 554) = 74.78$, $p < 0.001$, $\eta^2 = 0.21$. Children were significantly slower than older adults ($p < 0.001$), themselves being significantly slower than younger adults ($p < 0.001$). Furthermore, children were significantly slower than younger adults ($p < 0.001$).

- Choice RT tasks. For the LI and CC tasks, the main effect of age was significant, $F(2, 554) = 257.23$, $p < 0.001$, $\eta^2 = 0.48$ and $F(2, 554) = 175.42$, $p < 0.001$, $\eta^2 = 0.39$ respectively. For both tasks, children were significantly slower than older adults ($p < 0.001$), themselves being significantly slower than younger adults ($p < 0.001$). Furthermore, children were significantly slower than younger adults ($p < 0.001$).

- Processing speed tasks. For the DI task, the main effect of age was significant, $F(2, 554) = 170.97$, $p < 0.001$, $\eta^2 = 0.38$. Children were significantly slower than younger adults ($p < 0.001$), themselves significantly faster than older adults ($p < 0.001$). Children did not differ significantly from older adults. For the LC task, the main effect of age was significant, $F(2, 552) = 161.99$, $p < 0.001$, $\eta^2 = 0.37$. Children were significantly slower than older adults ($p < 0.001$), the latter being significantly slower than younger adults ($p < 0.001$). Furthermore, children were significantly slower than younger adults ($p < 0.001$). A main effect of condition was also observed, $F(1, 552) = 2067.01$, $p < 0.001$, $\eta^2 = 0.79$. Participants were significantly faster in the 6 letters condition than in the 9 letters condition. Finally, the age group x condition interaction was significant, $F(2, 552) = 26.54$, $p < 0.001$, $\eta^2 = 0.09$. Post-hoc comparisons revealed that the age group effect was significant for all conditions (all $ps < 0.001$). Moreover, the main effect of condition was significant for all age groups (all $ps < 0.001$); the interaction reflects a more pronounced effect for children and older adults than for younger adults.

- Stroop task. The main effect of age was significant, $F(2, 548) = 164.56$, $p < 0.001$, $\eta^2 = 0.38$. Children were significantly slower than older adults ($p < 0.001$), themselves being significantly slower than younger adults ($p < 0.001$). Furthermore, children were significantly slower than younger adults ($p < 0.001$). A main effect of condition was also observed $F(1, 548) = 2721.60$, $p < 0.001$, $\eta^2 = 0.83$. Participants were significantly faster in the neutral condition compared to incongruent condition. Finally, the age group x condition interaction was significant, $F(2, 548) = 44.96$, $p < 0.001$, $\eta^2 = 0.14$. Post-hoc comparisons revealed that the age group effect was significant for all conditions (all $ps < 0.001$). The main effect of condition was significant for all age groups (all $ps < 0.001$); this effect seemed more pronounced for children and older adults than for the younger adults, as shown by a significant interaction effect.

In sum, in all RT tasks, children and older adults were slower than the younger adults; children were also slower than older adults except in DI (see also footnote 7).

3.1.2. Intra-Individual Standard Deviation of Residual Scores (iSDr)

- Simple RT task. The main effect of age was significant $F(2, 554) = 99.18$, $p < 0.001$, $\eta^2 = 0.26$. Children were significantly more variable than older adults ($p < 0.001$), who were significantly more variable than younger adults ($p < 0.001$). Furthermore, children were significantly more variable than younger adults ($p < 0.001$).

- Choice RT tasks. For the LI and CC task, the main effect of age was significant, $F(2, 554) = 180.83$, $p < 0.001$, $\eta^2 = 0.40$ and $F(2, 554) = 190.26$, $p < 0.001$, $\eta^2 = 0.41$ respectively. Children were significantly more variable than older adults ($p < 0.001$), themselves being significantly more variable than younger adults ($p < 0.001$). Furthermore, children were significantly more variable than younger adults ($p < 0.001$).

- Processing speed tasks. For the DI task, the main effect of age was significant, $F(2, 554) = 215.70$, $p < 0.001$, $\eta^2 = 0.44$. Children were significantly more variable than older adults ($p < 0.001$), themselves being significantly more variable than younger adults ($p < 0.001$). Furthermore, children were significantly more variable than younger adults ($p < 0.001$). For the LC task, the main effect of age was significant, $F(2, 552) = 211.35$, $p < 0.001$, $\eta^2 = 0.43$. Children were significantly more variable than older adults ($p < 0.001$), themselves being significantly more variable than younger adults ($p < 0.001$). Furthermore, children were significantly more variable than younger adults ($p < 0.001$). A main effect of condition was also obtained, $F(1, 552) = 29.06$, $p < 0.001$, $\eta^2 = 0.05$. Participants were significantly less variable in the 6 letters condition than in the 9 letters condition. Finally, the age group x condition interaction was significant, $F(2, 552) = 5.42$, $p < 0.005$, $\eta^2 = 0.02$. Post-hoc comparisons revealed that the age group effect was significant for all conditions (all $ps < 0.001$). Moreover the main effect of condition was significant for younger adults and older adults (all $ps < 0.001$), but not for children.

- Stroop task. The main effect of age was significant, $F(2, 548) = 251.85$, $p < 0.001$, $\eta^2 = 0.48$. Children were significantly more variable than older adults ($p < 0.001$), themselves significantly more variable than younger adults ($p < 0.001$). Furthermore, children were significantly more variable than younger adults ($p < 0.001$). A main effect of condition was also significant, $F(1, 548) = 32.23$, $p < 0.001$, $\eta^2 = 0.06$. Participants were significantly less variable in the neutral condition than in the incongruent condition. Finally, the age group x condition interaction was significant, $F(2, 548) = 32.23$, $p < 0.001$, $\eta^2 = 0.06$. Post-hoc comparisons revealed that the age group effect was significant for all conditions (all $ps < 0.001$). Moreover, the main effect of condition was significant for all age groups (all $ps < 0.001$), this effect seemed more pronounced for older adults, leading to a significant age group x condition interaction.

To sum up[7], whichever the task, children were slower and more variable than older adults; the latter were slower and more variable than younger adults. It should be noted that for the DI task, children and older adults did not differ significantly in their intra-individual means (iM). Also, a condition effect showed, leading to larger RTs and increased variability: Participants were slower and more variable in the 9-letter LC condition than in the 6-letter one, as well as in the ST Interference condition compared to the Neutral one. Note, however, that children were not more variable in the 9-letter condition than in the 6-letter one.

3.2. Working Memory Tasks

Descriptive statistics for the different scores used are presented in Table 4. Table A2 provides descriptive data for the initial phases of the WM tasks (assessment of span level). The data of each task were submitted to 3 × 2 repeated-measures ANOVAs with age group (children, younger adults, older adults) as between-subject factor and list length (n and $n + 1$) as within-subject factor. The decision criterion was adapted using the Bonferroni procedure ($p < 0.004$ corresponding to a 0.05 threshold).

---

[7] Additional analyses were conducted on RTs, by refining the age group comparisons (see Table A1). First, these analyses showed that whichever the task, young children (9–10 years) were slower and more variable than older children (11–12 years). Second, for SRT, LI, CC and DI tasks, no difference between young-old adults (<70 years) and old-old adults (≥70 years) was obtained on iM. For LC and ST tasks, young-old adults were faster than old-old adults. As concerns the iSDr analyses, except for the LC task, young-old adults were less variable than old-old adults (see Table A3 for more details).

Table 4. Accuracy tasks: Means (iM) and intra-individual standard deviation of residual scores (iSDr) by Age group.

			Age Groups					
			Children		Young Adults		Older Adults	
			M	SD	M	SD	M	SD
iM	Reading span	List length n	2.08	0.54	2.83	0.76	2.46	0.76
		List length $n + 1$	2.35	0.58	3.27	0.69	2.82	0.77
	Matrices tasks— Positions	List length n	3.35	1.33	5.32	1.41	3.30	1.09
		List length $n + 1$	4.03	1.48	6.14	1.53	3.82	1.10
	Matrices tasks— associations	List length $n + 1$	2.25	0.68	3.24	0.63	2.51	0.65
		List length $n + 2$	2.25	0.70	3.29	0.75	2.37	0.73
iSDr	Reading span	List length n	8.43	3.31	9.20	4.84	9.84	4.56
		List length $n + 1$	9.59	2.23	10.14	2.90	10.08	2.75
	Matrices tasks— Positions	List length n	9.70	4.76	8.49	6.03	9.12	4.98
		List length $n + 1$	9.38	3.72	8.92	5.03	10.23	4.31
	Matrices tasks— associations	List length $n + 1$	9.50	2.65	11.28	4.40	9.77	3.34
		List length $n + 2$	9.35	2.51	11.49	3.42	9.98	2.66

Note: iM: intra-individual mean; iSDr: standard deviation of residual scores; M: Group's mean; SD: Group's standard deviations.

3.2.1. Intra-Individual Mean (iM)

- Reading span task. The analysis of the mean number of correctly recalled words indicated a main effect of age group, $F(2, 511) = 57.31$, $p < 0.001$, $\eta_p^2 = 0.18$. Children recalled significantly fewer words than older adults ($p < 0.001$), themselves recalling significantly fewer words than younger adults ($p < 0.001$). Furthermore, children recalled significantly less words than younger adults ($p < 0.001$). A main effect of list length was also found, $F(1, 511) = 504.61$, $p < 0.001$, $\eta_p^2 = 0.50$. Participants recalled significantly fewer words for the n list than for the $n + 1$ list. Finally, the age group x list length interaction was significant, $F(2, 511) = 9.23$, $p < 0.001$, $\eta_p^2 = 0.04$. Post-hoc comparisons revealed that the age effect was significant for both n and $n + 1$ lists ($p < 0.001$). Moreover, the list length effect was significant for all age groups ($p < 0.001$); this effect seemed more pronounced for younger adults than for children and older adults, leading to a significant age group x list length interaction.

- Matrices task—Simple positions. The main effect of age group was significant, $F(2, 550) = 138.53$, $p < 0.001$, $\eta_p^2 = 0.34$. Children recalled significantly fewer positions than younger adults ($p < 0.001$). Older adults recalled significantly fewer positions than younger adults ($p < 0.001$). Children did not differ significantly from older adults. A main effect of list length was also obtained, $F(1, 550) = 992.25$, $p < 0.001$, $\eta_p^2 = 0.64$. Participants recalled significantly fewer positions for the n list than for the $n + 1$ list. Finally, the age group x list length interaction was significant, $F(2, 550) = 15.31$, $p < 0.001$, $\eta_p^2 = 0.05$. Post-hoc comparisons revealed that the main age effect was significant for both n and $n + 1$ lists. Children recalled significantly fewer positions than younger adults and older adults recalled significantly fewer positions than younger adults; $p < 0.001$. Moreover, the list length effect was significant for all age groups ($p < 0.001$); this effect seemed more pronounced for younger adults (cf. significant age x condition interaction).

- Matrices task—word-position associations. Results indicated only a main effect of age, $F(2, 548) = 121.68$, $p < 0.000$, $\eta_p^2 = 0.31$. Children recalled significantly fewer associations than older adults ($p < 0.006$), themselves recalling significantly fewer associations than younger adults ($p < 0.000$). Furthermore, children recalled significantly fewer associations than younger adults ($p < 0.000$). The effects of list length and its interaction with age were not significant.

To sum up, in all tasks, children and older adults recalled fewer items (words in the Reading span task, positions and word-position associations in the Matrices task) than younger adults. Children recalled fewer words and fewer word-positions associations than older adults. Interestingly, both groups did not differ in the number of positions retrieved, except as concerns positions in the Matrices task.

3.2.2. Intra-Individual Standard Deviation of Residual Scores (iSDr)

- Reading span task. Results indicated only a main effect of list length, $F(1, 511) = 23.57$, $p < 0.001$, $\eta_p^2 = 0.04$. Participants were significantly less variable for the n list than for the $n + 1$ list. Neither the effects of age group nor its interaction with list length were significant.
- Matrices task—Simple positions. Neither effects of age and list length nor their interactions were significant.
- Matrices Task—word-position associations. Results indicated only a main effect of age, $F(2, 548) = 29.47$, $p < 0.001$, $\eta_p^2 = 0.10$. Children were significantly less variable than younger adults ($p < 0.001$). Older adults were significantly less variable than younger adults ($p < 0.001$). Children did not differ significantly from older adults.

To sum up[8], as concerns iSDr, only word-position associations in the matrices task showed an age effect, with younger adults being more variable than children and older adults.

4. Discussion

As discussed in the introduction, intra-individual variability (IIV) can provide crucial information, at least when RTs are examined, on both normative development/aging and processing impairment, beyond the information associated with the mean level (e.g., Reference [61]). The novelty of the present study was to examine IIV across the lifespan, in particular within-task fluctuations (inconsistency), in both latencies, -RTs-, and in accuracy -WM- tasks that varied with complexity. An additional contribution was to use the same tasks in all the age groups. We analyzed six RT tasks (8 conditions) using response times, and two WM tasks (6 conditions) to children, younger and older adults using an accuracy score based on the number of items recalled by trial. We were also interested in determining whether IIV would vary with complexity. The RT tasks ranged from a simple RT task in which one had simply to detect a target (SRT), to simple choice RT tasks (LI and CS), to more difficult processing speed tasks (DI and LC) in which two longer series of items had to be compared. A Stroop task was used, comparing a neutral and an incongruent condition, considered as more difficult. Finally, two WM tasks were used, which differed from the RT tasks not only because an accuracy score was used, but also because they are altogether much more complex tasks to process; moreover, two levels of complexity were presented for each task. It was expected that IIV would increase with complexity, in the two groups of tasks.

As expected, and in line with previous studies, results for both groups of tasks showed age-related differences in the mean level of performance between children, as well as between younger adults and older adults, replicating observations made in development [41], or in aging [62–64] or in studies conducted across the lifespan [6,22,30,65]. Younger adults had shorter RTs (they processed information faster) and recalled a larger number of correct items in the WM tasks than children, on the one hand, and than older adults, on the other hand. Such a pattern of results confirms that (i) processing speed increases in efficiency from childhood to adulthood and then decreases again in older adults; older adults were nevertheless still faster than children; (ii) WM performance increases from children to younger adults and then decreases again in older adults. Age differences were, however, less marked in the WM tasks, depending on the condition; this was particularly the case when age groups were

---

8 Additional analyses, refining the age group comparisons, were conducted on accuracy scores. First, the analyses of iM showed that whichever the task, young children (9–10 years) recalled fewer items than older children (11–12 years). No significant difference between these two groups was obtained for iSDr in all tasks. Second, young-old adults recalled more items than old-old adults only for Matrices task word-position associations. No significant difference between young-old and old-old adults was obtained for iSDr in any task (see Table A4 for more details).

analyzed more finely (distinguishing younger and older children, on the one hand, and young-old and old-old adults, on the other hand—see Footnotes 6 and 7). Taken together, these results are consistent with the well-known mean age trends across the lifespan.

When intra-individual standard deviations (iSDrs) were considered, once the individual mean performance controlled for, age differences varied depending on the measure considered (RTs vs. accuracies). In line with a majority of previous studies [6,21,62], the picture remained more or less similar as concerns the RTs: Younger adults were the least variable and children were the most variable. The additional analyses in finer age groups showed that younger (9–10 years of age) and older children (11–12 years of age) also differed significantly; a difference was also observed between the young-old and old-old adults, the latter being more variable in all the tasks, except in LC. IIV in the WM tasks presented a very different pattern with respect to age differences. Even though most differences were not significant, the highest iSDrs were obtained in younger and older adults, and the lowest in children. The only significant age effect was obtained in the Matrices task, for the word-positions associations, that is, when the information to be retrieved is rather complex. In that condition, children and older adults did not differ, but younger adults differed from both age groups. The additional analyses in five age groups showed no further age difference between the two children groups, or between the two older adults groups. Overall, one can thus conclude that there was no age effect in most conditions of the WM tasks, and when one was observed, it pointed to a larger variability in younger adults than in the other groups.

The results obtained in the RT tasks are compatible with the hypothesis often adopted in the literature [35] that IIV reflects reflect failures in attentional control or attentional lapses in children and older adults. Furthermore, these results were obtained independently from the IIV index used (raw intra-individual standard deviation—iSD-, or iSDr computed on the RTs residualized for age group as presented here). IIV in WM accuracy scores offered a different picture. Very interestingly, the age differences tended to be reversed, although not significantly so in all conditions. Younger adults were not less variable than the two other age groups; they were even significantly more variable in the most complex condition of the Matrices task (word-position associations for both span levels). The iSDrs in younger children were the smallest, for all conditions, even if not significantly so. Thus, results clearly showed that children and older adults were not more variable than younger adults. We mentioned in the introduction that other studies using an accuracy score and analyzing IIV also failed to support a larger IIV in memory [15] or in WM performance [31] not only in older adults but also in children.

If this was the case that IIV in general relates to attentional control and to brain development, the age differences in WM accuracy performance would be similar to those obtained in RTs, all the more so as WM is supposed to call for more attentional or executive processes than speed measures. IIV in accuracy might also reflect attentional lapses (i.e., irregularities in attentional control) like IIV in RTs, but it might just as well point to a greater diversity in the strategies used; it is known that the repertoire of strategies increases with development as Siegler [13] observed in children learning arithmetical skills. On this basis, one would indeed expect that young adults be more variable. One could also adopt a slightly different perspective, and consider that IIV increases with the proximity to a developmental transition [38]. We will come back later to the possible role of strategies.

The failure to observe a larger IIV in WM performance in children and older adults could find a number of other explanations, among which essentially the task characteristics. First, the number of trials, which is typically low in WM tasks, might not be sufficient to obtain a reliable score. In contrast to simple RT tasks, it is indeed difficult to administer a WM task with a very large number of complex trials, in particular because trials should preferably not be repeated, but also in order not to fatigue participants and make the task too complex to be completed, leading to discouragement. Therefore, tasks focusing on accuracy often do not use a sufficient number of trials to provide a reliable indicator of IIV. In the present study, iSDr was computed across ten or twenty trials by condition for the WM tasks; this is certainly sufficient, but nevertheless less than in the RT tasks (from 60 to 144 trials by condition). Second, a factor that could play a role in explaining the present results might be the task complexity: It is possible that IIV in accuracy of WM performance is more sensitive to the task complexity (e.g., larger in $n + 1$ than in n trials-rather than to age differences per se). Yet, as expected, complexity also played a role in RT tasks: iSDrs were larger in the more difficult speed tasks and this difference was significant in all groups when it could be tested, that is, in the LC and the Stroop tasks. Thus, complexity might be relevant but is not sufficient to account for the difference between IIV in RT and WM tasks. Third, accuracy scores might lack sensitivity. The grain of variation is, indeed, coarser. In WM tasks, scores typically range from zero to six or seven as a maximum (the mean performance of younger adults was around 3, except for the Matrices-Positions score which was around 6); one item more or one less to be memorized represents therefore a large difference. Moreover, the difficulty of the task was adapted to the individual's span, probably leading to fewer fluctuations. In contrast, there is a continuous and large range of potential variations in RT tasks (i.e., mean of around 300–400 ms in young adults in the simpler RT tasks, and greater than 1000 ms in the more complex conditions). Fourth, in RT tasks, the range of possible responses has only a lower bound but not really an upper bound. Therefore, considering the relationship between the individual mean performance and IIV [54], the longer the RTs, the larger the magnitude of the variability may be. In accuracy tasks, the entire interval of responses is delimited, between 0 and the upper limit of the WM trial administered. Consequently, the variability is not "observable" when the scores are too low (floor effect) or too high (ceiling effect). This is incidentally one of the reasons why the length of the series administered was adapted to the individual's span.

It could finally be argued that the difference between the two types of tasks is linked to a speed-accuracy trade-off, taking place essentially in the RT tasks but probably not in the WM ones. Older adults might be more concerned than younger adults by maintaining accuracy rather than speed, and control their response to the expense of a heightened variability in speed. However, there were no age differences in the number of errors in the RT tasks and the number of errors was very small (somewhat higher in the Interference condition of the Stroop task). Also, this speed-accuracy trade-off hypothesis is rather unlikely, as it would lead to a same conclusion as regards children. Although, at least to our knowledge, there are no empirical studies on this topic, it does not seem plausible that children would deliberately slow down in some trials in order to maintain a high rate of accuracy, and more so than younger adults.

A different, and more global, argument could be of a more statistical nature: Variability might simply be higher when mean scores are higher. Therefore young adults would show less intra-individual variability in the RT tasks, and more variability in the WM tasks, as in the present study. This is precisely why we relied on residualized intra-individual standard deviations, controlling for mean score. Perhaps this correction is not sufficient. Note, however, that this argument applies to both types of tasks, and that, usually, authors working on intra-individual variability in RT tasks attribute a psychological rather than a statistical meaning to a larger variability in older adults. Moreover, this argument would not in turn account for the fact that the age group has much less effect in the WM tasks even though the mean scores are clearly sensitive to age. Results clearly are not symmetrical between the two types of tasks: They clearly show that the tasks differ but not that intra-individual variability is significantly larger in the young adults. We therefore still need an additional explanation to account for the difference.

From a behavioral point of view, and as concerns age differences, it may be that IIV in performance in WM tasks is less informative than IIV in RTs or more interestingly that it points to different underlying processes. For instance, as we discussed above, IIV could reflect a change in the strategies used, more so in the WM tasks where they are more useful. Examples of strategies are attempting to chunk the last words in the Reading span task, or finding a mnemonic to associate word and position in the Matrices task. Of course, strategies can also be used in the RT tasks (for instance memorizing the reference matrix in the DI task, or comparing subgroups of letters in the LC task); they are useful for responding faster but not necessarily for achieving higher accuracy in a task that remains relatively easy to process. Strategies are probably more numerous in adults, but might differ in their applicability across items; moreover, switching strategy might contribute to maintaining a higher performance in the case of a temporary failure in other processes; in both cases, their use would lead to larger intra-individual variability. Variability might therefore prove more adaptive in WM tasks than in RT tasks and reflect the underlying dynamics [39]. It is not possible, however to test this hypothesis in the present version of our WM tasks because we did not question the participants on how they maintained and retrieved items. It is also possible that different brain mechanisms underlie IIV in RT tasks, on the one hand, and IIV in accuracy in complex WM tasks, on the other hand. As mentioned in the introduction, a larger IIV in RTs has been shown to be associated with structural and functional brain changes; however, to date, there is very little evidence of an association between IIV in WM and brain processes. In a recent study on older adults using Diffusion Tensor Imaging, IIV in RTs was shown to be correlated with fractional anisotropy, and more strongly so than the mean RT score; no such correlation was observed for IIV in verbal WM IIV [46]. A final argument supporting an essential difference between RT and WM tasks has been brought by another study focusing this time on dispersion in the same sample, that is on intra-individual variability across tasks rather than across trials [66]. In this study, young adults were less variable in their mean level across the RT tasks than both children and older adults; they were, however, more variable across the conditions of the WM tasks (the same two tasks as in the present study).

To clarify those issues further, future studies should make the effort to replicate the present results also by (i) using different tasks while also combining RT and accuracy scores; and (ii) analyze within a same WM task accuracy and RTs (note that response time is not really relevant in a complex WM task such as the Reading span task). Perhaps, also, it would be worthwhile to examine more contiguous age groups than we did in the present study.

5. Conclusions

To conclude, our results suggest that inconsistency—IIV across trials—is informative of age-related differences across the lifespan when RTs are considered but less so when performance in WM task is examined. This issue does not preclude the interest to study IIV in WM accuracy scores, to assess first whether it varies across different tasks, and second whether it remains a predictor of individual differences (beyond age differences) in cognitive functioning. The present study clearly demonstrates that IIV does not behave similarly in these two types of tasks, even though they were administered to the same individuals. Future studies should pursue the question raised here of whether different processes are involved in IIV, depending on the type of task and of score used.

Acknowledgments: This work was supported by the Swiss National Science Foundation (SNSF grant 100011107764, principal investigator: Anik de Ribaupierre, co-investigators: Thierry Lecerf and Paolo Ghisletta). The authors would like to thank their colleagues in the group of Developmental and Differential Psychology at the University of Geneva for their help with data collection and for fruitful discussions, and the participants for their patience and willingness to sit for several hours through a rather heavy experimental protocol.

Author Contributions: Anik de Ribaupierre, Thierry Lecerf and Paolo Ghisletta conceived and designed the experiments; Delphine Fagot, Nathalie Mella and Erika Borella performed the experiments; Delphine Fagot and Nathalie Mella analyzed the data; Anik de Ribaupierre, Delphine Fagot and Erika Borella wrote the paper.

Conflicts of Interest: The authors declare no conflict of interest.

Appendix A

Table A1. Participants' Characteristics by Age Group.

	Age Groups									
	Children				Adults					
	Young		Old		Young		Young-Old		Old-Old	
N	100		101		137		117		102	
Female	38		54		117		90		75	
	M	SD	M	SD	M	SD	M	SD	M	SD
Age	9.5	0.50	11.50	0.50	21.71	2.53	64.82	2.68	76.15	4.65
Vocabulary Score	-	-	-	-	34.67	3.25	38.04	4.38	37.37	4.91
Raven	34.14	8.39	39.51	7.11	52.15	4.91	39.53	7.54	32.90	9.54

Note: M: Group's mean; SD: Group's standard deviations.

Table A2. Participants' span level (preliminary phase) by Task and by Age Group.

		Children	Young Adults	Older Adults
Rspan task Span level	Min	2	2	2
	Max	5	6	6
	M	2.39	3.15	2.85
	SD	0.63	0.90	0.90
Matrices task Span level	Min	2	2	2
	Max	7	7	7
	M	3.4	5.71	3.91
	SD	1.45	1.45	1.23

Note: Min: Minimum; Max: Maximum; M: Group's mean; SD: Group's standard deviations.

Table A3. Reaction time tasks: Means (iM) and intra-individual standard deviation of residual scores (iSDr) by Age group (five groups).

			Age Groups									
			Children				Adults					
			Young		Old		Young		Young-Old		Old-Old	
			M	SD	M	SD	M	SD	M	SD	M	SD
iM	SRT		381.92	74.88	338.35	54.38	272.89	39.16	324.42	76.48	343.91	72.95
	LI		605.34	97.71	525.81	88.85	372.38	43.53	446.26	64.32	470.75	75.10
	CC		536.80	106.33	454.75	87.46	325.69	39.26	417.52	68.44	446.66	82.86
	DI		1924.67	396.48	1551.83	419.32	1040.56	221.47	1569.50	302.43	1783.05	372.95
	LC	6 letters	4038.80	1323.61	3213.18	385.40	1838.17	423.31	2771.18	624.07	3200.73	912.54
		9 letters	5493.01	1646.70	4687.25	1336.96	2798.36	654.47	4029.01	950.60	4646.51	1198.88
	ST	Neutral	885.56	147.50	799.29	133.41	594.78	75.85	694.66	93.16	758.45	118.29
		Incongruent	1074.46	188.02	965.99	165.44	720.89	102.31	875.75	137.56	987.62	177.51
iSDr	SRT		12.18	2.94	10.60	2.94	7.16	2.15	8.64	2.31	9.90	3.06
	LI		13.23	3.59	11.27	3.10	6.42	1.98	7.97	2.11	9.29	3.15
	CC		13.58	3.91	10398	3.54	5.93	1.78	8.25	2.27	9.56	2.57
	DI		13.42	3.08	10.68	3.47	5.69	1.91	8.74	2.39	9.82	2.18
	LC	6 letters	14.38	5.29	10.71	4.47	5.03	1.67	7.70	2.64	8.72	3.01
		9 letters	14.01	3.93	11.25	3.84	5.83	1.81	8.38	2.30	9.44	2.72
	ST	Neutral	14.03	3.61	11.91	3.80	6.16	1.91	7.03	2.26	8.49	3.17
		Incongruent	13.22	2.95	11.59	2.73	7.16	1.92	8.24	2.33	9.52	2.62

Note: SRT: Simple reaction time task, LI: Line comparison task; CS: Cross-square task; LC: Letter comparison task; DI: Digit symbol task; ST: Stroop task; iM: intra-individual mean; iSDr: standard deviation of residual scores; M: Group's mean; SD: Group's standard deviations.

Table A4. Accuracy tasks: Means (iM) and intra-individual standard deviation of residual scores (iSDr) by Age group (five groups).

			Age Groups								
			Children				Adults				
			Young		Old		Young		Young-Old		Old-Old	
			M	SD	M	SD	M	SD	M	SD	M	SD
iM	Reading span	n	1.92	0.41	2.22	0.59	2.83	0.76	2.59	0.82	2.31	0.67
		$n+1$	2.12	0.47	2.52	0.61	3.27	0.69	2.95	0.81	2.68	0.69
	Matrices tasks—	n	3.04	1.19	3.66	1.40	5.32	1.41	3.41	1.17	3.16	0.97
	Positions	$n+1$	3.66	1.28	4.40	1.57	6.14	1.53	3.98	1.17	3.64	0.97
	Matrices tasks—	$n+1$	1.98	0.70	2.52	0.54	3.24	0.63	2.65	0.66	2.33	0.59
	Associations	$n+2$	1.98	0.65	2.53	0.64	3.30	0.75	2.50	0.77	2.21	0.63
iSDr	Reading span	n	8.09	2.66	8.70	3.75	9.20	4.84	9.71	4.71	9.98	4.40
		$n+1$	9.26	2.00	9.85	2.38	10.14	2.90	10.18	2.81	9.96	2.69
	Matrices tasks—	n	9.32	4.53	10.0	4.97	8.49	6.03	9.28	4.98	8.94	4.99
	Positions	$n+1$	9.67	3.62	9.08	3.80	8.92	5.02	10.34	4.57	10.1	4.0
	Matrices tasks—	$n+1$	9.01	2.58	9.97	2.64	11.28	3.40	9.73	3.59	9.82	3.03
	Associations	$n+2$	8.93	2.49	9.77	2.47	11.49	3.42	10.08	2.80	9.87	2.49

Note: iM: intra-individual mean; iSDr: standard deviation of residual scores; M: Group's mean; SD: Group's standard deviations.

References

1. Reuchlin, M. Apports de la méthode différentielle à la psychologie générale. *J. Psychol.* **1981**, *4*, 377–395.
2. Cronbach, L.J. The two disciplines of scientific psychology. *Am. Psychol.* **1957**, *12*, 671–684. [CrossRef]
3. Nesselroade, J.R. The Warp and Woof of the Developmental Fabric. In *Visions of Development, the Environment, and Aesthetics: The Legacy of Joachim F. Wohlwill*; Downs, R., Liben, L., Palermo, D., Eds.; Erlbaum: Hillsdale, NJ, USA, 1991; pp. 213–240.
4. Hultsch, D.F.; MacDonald, S.W. Intra-individual variability in performance as a theoretical window onto cognitive aging. In *New Frontiers in Cognitive Aging*; Oxford University Press: Oxford, UK, 2004; pp. 65–88.
5. Walhovd, K.B.; Fjell, A.M. White matter volume predicts reaction time instability. *Neuropsychologia* **2007**, *45*, 2277–2284. [CrossRef] [PubMed]
6. Williams, B.R.; Hultsch, D.F.; Strauss, E.H.; Hunter, M.A.; Tannock, R. Inconsistency in Reaction Time Across the Life Span. *Neuropsychology* **2005**, *19*, 88–96. [CrossRef] [PubMed]
7. Jensen, A.R. *Clocking the Mind: Mental Chronometry and Individual Differences*; Elsevier: Oxford, UK, 2006; ISBN 978-0-08-046372-8.
8. De Ribaupierre, A. Why Should Cognitive Developmental Psychology Remember that Individuals Are Different? *Res. Hum. Dev.* **2015**, *12*, 237–245. [CrossRef]
9. Van Der Maas, H.L.J.; Dolan, C.V.; Grasman, R.P.P.P.; Wicherts, J.M.; Huizenga, H.M.; Raijmakers, M.E.J. A dynamical model of general intelligence: The positive manifold of intelligence by mutualism. *Psychol. Rev.* **2006**, *113*, 842–861. [CrossRef] [PubMed]
10. Hultsch, D.F.; Strauss, E.; Hunter, M.A.; MacDonald, S.W.S. Intra-individual variability, cognition, and aging. In *The Handbook of Aging and Cognition*; Craik, F.I.M., Salthouse, T.A., Eds.; Psychology Press: New York, NY, USA, 2008; pp. 491–556.
11. Borella, E.; de Ribaupierre, A.; Cornoldi, C.; Chicherio, C. Beyond interference control impairment in ADHD: Evidence from increased intra-individual variability in the color-stroop test. *Child Neuropsychol. J. Norm. Abnorm. Dev. Child. Adolesc.* **2013**, *19*, 495–515. [CrossRef] [PubMed]
12. Leth-Steensen, C.; Elbaz, Z.K.; Douglas, V.I. Mean response times, variability, and skew in the responding of ADHD children: A response time distributional approach. *Acta Psychol.* **2000**, *104*, 167–190. [CrossRef]
13. Siegler, R.S. Cognitive Variability: A Key to Understanding Cognitive Development. *Curr. Dir. Psychol. Sci.* **1994**, *3*, 1–5. [CrossRef]
14. Van Geert, P. Variability and fluctuation: A dynamic view. In The Jean Piaget symposium series. In *Change and Development: Issues of Theory, Method, and Application*; Amsel, E., Renninger, K.A., Eds.; Lawrence Erlbaum Associates: Mahwah, NJ, USA, 1997; pp. 193–212.

15. Hultsch, D.F.; MacDonald, S.W.; Hunter, M.A.; Levy-Bencheton, J.; Strauss, E. Intra-individual variability in cognitive performance in older adults: Comparison of adults with mild dementia, adults with arthritis, and healthy adults. *Neuropsychology* **2000**, *14*, 588–598. [CrossRef] [PubMed]

16. Anstey, K.J.; Christensen, H.; Butterworth, P.; Easteal, S.; Mackinnon, A.; Jacomb, T.; Maxwell, K.; Rodgers, B.; Windsor, T.; Cherbuin, N.; et al. Cohort profile: The PATH through life project. *Int. J. Epidemiol.* **2012**, *41*, 951–960. [CrossRef] [PubMed]

17. Bielak, A.A.M.; Cherbuin, N.; Bunce, D.; Anstey, K.J. Intra-individual variability is a fundamental phenomenon of aging: Evidence from an 8-year longitudinal study across young, middle, and older adulthood. *Dev. Psychol.* **2014**, *50*, 143–151. [CrossRef] [PubMed]

18. Der, G.; Deary, I.J. IQ, reaction time and the differentiation hypothesis. *Intelligence* **2003**, *31*, 491–503. [CrossRef]

19. Ghisletta, P.; Fagot, D.; Lecerf, T.; de Ribaupierre, A. Amplitude of Fluctuations and Temporal Dependency in Intra-individual Variability. *GeroPsych J. Gerontopsychol. Geriatr. Psychiatry* **2013**, *26*, 141–151. [CrossRef]

20. Ghisletta, P.; Renaud, O.; Fagot, D.; Lecerf, T.; de Ribaupierre, A. Age and sex differences in intra-individual variability in a simple reaction time task. *Int. J. Behav. Dev.* **2017**, 0165025417739179. [CrossRef]

21. Li, S.-C.; Huxhold, O.; Schmiedek, F. Aging and attenuated processing robustness. Evidence from cognitive and sensorimotor functioning. *Gerontology* **2004**, *50*, 28–34. [CrossRef] [PubMed]

22. Li, S.-C.; Lindenberger, U.; Hommel, B.; Aschersleben, G.; Prinz, W.; Baltes, P.B. Transformations in the couplings among intellectual abilities and constituent cognitive processes across the life span. *Psychol. Sci.* **2004**, *15*, 155–163. [CrossRef] [PubMed]

23. Lindenberger, U.; von Oertzen, T. Variability in cognitive aging: From taxonomy to theory. *Lifesp. Cognit. Mech. Chang.* **2006**, 297–314.

24. Lövdén, M.; Li, S.-C.; Shing, Y.L.; Lindenberger, U. Within-person trial-to-trial variability precedes and predicts cognitive decline in old and very old age: Longitudinal data from the Berlin Aging Study. *Neuropsychologia* **2007**, *45*, 2827–2838. [CrossRef] [PubMed]

25. MacDonald, S.W.S.; Hultsch, D.F.; Dixon, R.A. Performance variability is related to change in cognition: Evidence from the Victoria Longitudinal Study. *Psychol. Aging* **2003**, *18*, 510–523. [CrossRef] [PubMed]

26. Nelson, E.A.; Dannefer, D. Aged heterogeneity: Fact or fiction? The fate of diversity in gerontological research. *Gerontologist* **1992**, *32*, 17–23. [CrossRef] [PubMed]

27. Bielak, A.A.; Anstey, K.J. Intra-individual Variability in Attention across the Adult Life Span. In *Handbook of Intra-individual Variability across the Life Span*; Diehl, M., Hooker, K., Sliwinski, M., Eds.; Routledge: New York, NY, USA, 2015; pp. 160–175.

28. Fagot, D.; Mella, N. Evolution de la variabilité cognitive au cours de la vie. In *Différences et Variabilités en Psychologie*; Juhel, J., Rouxel, G., Eds.; Presses Universitaires de Rennes: Rennes, France, 2015; pp. 179–195. ISBN 978-2-7535-3622-7.

29. De Ribaupierre, A. Pourquoi faut-il étudier la variabilité intra-individuelle lorsqu'on s'intéresse au développement cognitif? In *Différences et Variabilités en Psychologie*; Juhel, J., Rouxel, G., Eds.; Presses Universitaires de Rennes: Rennes, France, 2015; pp. 159–178.

30. Williams, B.R.; Strauss, E.H.; Hultsch, D.F.; Hunter, M.A. Reaction Time Inconsistency in a Spatial Stroop Task: Age-Related Differences through Childhood and Adulthood. *Aging Neuropsychol. Cognit.* **2007**, *14*, 417–439. [CrossRef] [PubMed]

31. Robertson, S.; Myerson, J.; Hale, S. Are there age differences in intra-individual variability in working memory performance? *J. Gerontol. B Psychol. Sci. Soc. Sci.* **2006**, *61*, P18–P24. [CrossRef] [PubMed]

32. Salthouse, T.A. Implications of within-person variability in cognitive and neuropsychological functioning for the interpretation of change. *Neuropsychology* **2007**, *21*, 401–411. [CrossRef] [PubMed]

33. Kochan, N.A.; Bunce, D.; Pont, S.; Crawford, J.D.; Brodaty, H.; Sachdev, P.S. Is intra-individual reaction time variability an independent cognitive predictor of mortality in old age? Findings from the Sydney Memory and Ageing Study. *PLoS ONE* **2017**, *12*, e0181719. [CrossRef] [PubMed]

34. MacDonald, S.W.S.; Stawski, R.S. Intra-individual Variability—An Indicator of Vulnerability or Resilience in Adult Development and Aging? In *Handbook of Intra-Individual Variability across the Life Span*; Diehl, M., Hooker, K., Sliwinski, M., Eds.; Routledge: New York, NY, USA, 2015; pp. 231–257. ISBN 978-0-415-53486-4.

35. West, R.; Murphy, K.J.; Armilio, M.L.; Craik, F.I.M.; Stuss, D.T. Lapses of intention and performance variability reveal age-related increases in fluctuations of executive control. *Brain Cognit.* **2002**, *49*, 402–419. [CrossRef]

36. Schmiedek, F.; Lövdén, M.; Lindenberger, U. On the relation of mean reaction time and intra-individual reaction time variability. *Psychol. Aging* 2009, *24*, 841–857. [CrossRef] [PubMed]
37. Van Geert, P.; van Dijk, M. Focus on variability: New tools to study intra-individual variability in developmental data. *Infant Behav. Dev.* 2002, *25*, 340–374. [CrossRef]
38. Van Dijk, M.; van Geert, P. The nature and meaning of intra-individual variability in development in the early life span. In *Handbook of Intra-Individual Variability across the Life Span*; Routledge: Abingdon, UK, 2015; pp. 37–58.
39. Allaire, J.C.; Marsiske, M. Intra-individual Variability May Not Always Indicate Vulnerability in Elders' Cognitive Performance. *Psychol. Aging* 2005, *20*, 390–401. [CrossRef] [PubMed]
40. Stawski, R.S.; Smith, J.; MacDonald, S.W.S. Intra-individual Variability and Covariation across Domains in Adulthood and Aging. In *Handbook of Intra-Individual Variability across the Lifesapn*; Diehl, M., Hooker, K., Sliwinski, M.J., Eds.; Routledge Handbooks Online: New York, NY, USA, 2015; pp. 258–279. ISBN 978-0-415-53486-4.
41. De Ribaupierre, A. Working memory and attentional processes across the lifespan. In *Lifespan Development of Human Memory*; Graf, P., Otha, N., Eds.; MIT Press: Cambridge, MA, USA, 2001; pp. 59–80.
42. De Ribaupierre, A.; Poget, L.; Pons, F. The age variable in cognitive developmental psychology. In *Human Clocks. The Bio-Cultural Meanings of Age*; Population, Family, and Society; Sauvain-Dugerdil, C., Leridon, H., Mascie-Taylor, N., Eds.; Peter Lang: Bern, Switzerland, 2005; pp. 101–123. ISBN 978-3-03910-785-8.
43. Tamnes, C.K.; Fjell, A.M.; Westlye, L.T.; Ostby, Y.; Walhovd, K.B. Becoming Consistent: Developmental Reductions in Intra-individual Variability in Reaction Time Are Related to White Matter Integrity. *J. Neurosci.* 2012, *32*, 972–982. [CrossRef] [PubMed]
44. Papenberg, G.; Bäckman, L.; Chicherio, C.; Nagel, I.E.; Heekeren, H.R.; Lindenberger, U.; Li, S.-C. Higher intra-individual variability is associated with more forgetting and dedifferentiated memory functions in old age. *Neuropsychologia* 2011, *49*, 1879–1888. [CrossRef] [PubMed]
45. Fjell, A.M.; Westlye, L.T.; Amlien, I.K.; Walhovd, K.B. Reduced White Matter Integrity Is Related to Cognitive Instability. *J. Neurosci.* 2011, *31*, 18060–18072. [CrossRef] [PubMed]
46. Mella, N.; de Ribaupierre, S.; Eagleson, R.; de Ribaupierre, A. Cognitive Intra-individual Variability and White Matter Integrity in Aging. *Sci. World J.* 2013, *2013*, 1–16. [CrossRef] [PubMed]
47. Moy, G.; Millet, P.; Haller, S.; Baudois, S.; de Bilbao, F.; Weber, K.; Lövblad, K.; Lazeyras, F.; Giannakopoulos, P.; Delaloye, C. Magnetic resonance imaging determinants of intra-individual variability in the elderly: Combined analysis of grey and white matter. *Neuroscience* 2011, *186*, 88–93. [CrossRef] [PubMed]
48. Westlye, L.T.; Walhovd, K.B.; Dale, A.M.; Bjørnerud, A.; Due-Tønnessen, P.; Engvig, A.; Grydeland, H.; Tamnes, C.K.; Ostby, Y.; Fjell, A.M. Life-span changes of the human brain white matter: Diffusion tensor imaging (DTI) and volumetry. *Cereb. Cortex* 2010, *20*, 2055–2068. [CrossRef] [PubMed]
49. Grydeland, H.; Walhovd, K.B.; Tamnes, C.K.; Westlye, L.T.; Fjell, A.M. Intracortical myelin links with performance variability across the human lifespan: Results from T1- and T2-weighted MRI myelin mapping and diffusion tensor imaging. *J. Neurosci. Off. J. Soc. Neurosci.* 2013, *33*, 18618–18630. [CrossRef] [PubMed]
50. MacDonald, S.W.S.; Hultsch, D.F.; Dixon, R.A. Predicting impending death: Inconsistency in speed is a selective and early marker. *Psychol. Aging* 2008, *23*, 595–607. [CrossRef] [PubMed]
51. Bunce, D.; MacDonald, S.W.S.; Hultsch, D.F. Inconsistency in serial choice decision and motor reaction times dissociate in younger and older adults. *Brain Cognit.* 2004, *56*, 320–327. [CrossRef] [PubMed]
52. Hultsch, D.F.; MacDonald, S.W.S.; Dixon, R.A. Variability in reaction time performance of younger and older adults. *J. Gerontol. B Psychol. Sci. Soc. Sci.* 2002, *57*, P101–P115. [CrossRef] [PubMed]
53. Neuringer, A. Reinforced variability in animals and people: Implications for adaptive action. *Am. Psychol.* 2004, *59*, 891–906. [CrossRef] [PubMed]
54. Golay, P.; Lecerf, T.; Fagot, D. Against coefficient of variation for estimation of intra-individual variability with accuracy measures. *Tutor. Quant. Methods Psychol.* 2013, *9*, 6–14. [CrossRef]
55. De Ribaupierre, A.; Ghisletta, P.; Lecerf, T. *Inter- and Intra-Individual Variability across the Lifespan*; University of Geneva: Geneva, Switzerland, 2008.
56. Raven, J.C.; Court, J.H.; Raven, J. *Progressive Matrices Standard (PM38)*; Editions du Centre de Psychologie Appliquée: Paris, France, 1998.
57. Park, D.C.; Lautenschlager, G.; Hedden, T.; Davidson, N.S.; Smith, A.D.; Smith, P.K. Models of visuospatial and verbal memory across the adult life span. *Psychol. Aging* 2002, *17*, 299–320. [CrossRef] [PubMed]

58. Schneider, W.; Eschman, A.; Zuccolotto, A. *E-Prime User's Guide*; Psychology Software Tools, Inc.: Pittsburgh, PA, USA, 2002.

59. Delaloye, C.; Ludwig, C.; Borella, E.; Chicherio, C.; de Ribaupierre, A. L'Empan de lecture comme épreuve mesurant la capacité de mémoire de travail: Normes basées sur une population francophone de 775 adultes jeunes et âgés. *Rev. Eur. Psychol. Appl./Eur. Rev. Appl. Psychol.* **2008**, *58*, 89–103. [CrossRef]

60. Robert, C.; Borella, E.; Fagot, D.; Lecerf, T.; de Ribaupierre, A. Working memory and inhibitory control across the life span: Intrusion errors in the Reading Span Test. *Mem. Cognit.* **2009**, *37*, 336–345. [CrossRef] [PubMed]

61. Hofer, S.; Alwin, D. *Handbook of Cognitive Aging: Interdisciplinary Perspectives*; Sage: Thousand Oaks, CA, USA, 2008.

62. Mella, N.; Fagot, D.; Lecerf, T.; de Ribaupierre, A. Working memory and intra-individual variability in processing speed: A lifespan developmental and individual-differences study. *Mem. Cognit.* **2015**, *43*, 340–356. [CrossRef] [PubMed]

63. Craik, F.I.M.; Salthouse, T.A. *The Handbook of Aging and Cognition*; Psychology Press: New York, NY, USA, 1992; ISBN 978-0-8058-0713-4.

64. Salthouse, T.A. *Theoretical Perspectives on Cognitive Aging*; Erlbaum: Hillsdale, NJ, USA, 1991.

65. Jenkins, L.; Myerson, J.; Hale, S.; Fry, A.F. Individual and developmental differences in working memory across the life span. *Psychon. Bull. Rev.* **1999**, *6*, 28–40. [CrossRef] [PubMed]

66. Mella, N.; Fagot, D.; de Ribaupierre, A. Dispersion in cognitive functioning: Age differences over the lifespan. *J. Clin. Exp. Neuropsychol.* **2016**, *38*, 111–126. [CrossRef] [PubMed]

Journal of
Intelligence

MDPI

Article

Individual Differences in Developmental Change: Quantifying the Amplitude and Heterogeneity in Cognitive Change across Old Age

Nathalie Mella [1,*], Delphine Fagot [2], Olivier Renaud [3], Matthias Kliegel [1,2] and Anik de Ribaupierre [2,*]

[1]   Cognitive Aging Lab, University of Geneva, 1211 Geneva, Switzerland; Matthias.Kliegel@unige.ch
[2]   Center for the Interdisciplinary Study of Gerontology and Vulnerability (CIGEV), University of Geneva, 1211 Geneva, Switzerland; Delphine.Fagot@unige.ch
[3]   Methodology and Data Analysis, Section of psychology, University of Geneva, 1211 Geneva, Switzerland; Olivier.renaud@unige.ch
*   Correspondence: Nathalie.Mella-Barraco@unige.ch (N.M.); anik.deribaupierre@unige.ch (A.D.R.); Tel.: +41-22-379-90-53 (N.M.)

Received: 7 December 2017; Accepted: 12 February 2018; Published: 28 February 2018

Abstract: It is well known that cognitive decline in older adults is of smaller amplitude in longitudinal than in cross-sectional studies. Yet, the measure of interest rests generally with aggregated group data. A focus on individual developmental trajectories is rare, mainly because it is difficult to assess intraindividual change reliably. Individual differences in developmental trajectories may differ quantitatively (e.g., larger or smaller decline) or qualitatively (e.g., decline vs improvement), as well as in the degree of heterogeneity of change across different cognitive domains or different tasks. The present paper aims at exploring, within the Geneva Variability Study, individual change across several cognitive domains in 92 older adults (aged 59–89 years at baseline) over a maximum of seven years and a half. Two novel, complementary methods were used to explore change in cognitive performance while remaining entirely at the intra-individual level. A bootstrap based confidence interval was estimated, for each participant and for each experimental condition, making it possible to define three patterns: stability, increase or decrease in performance. Within-person ANOVAs were also conducted for each individual on all the tasks. Those two methods allowed quantifying the direction, the amplitude and the heterogeneity of change for each individual. Results show that trajectories differed widely among individuals and that decline is far from being the rule.

Keywords: individual differences; cognitive aging; cognitive heterogeneity; longitudinal method

---

1. Introduction

There is considerable evidence in the literature that the process of aging is associated with cognitive decline [1–4]. The main bulk of evidence comes from cross-sectional studies, despite the limitations inherent to this design [5–7]. In contrast, results from longitudinal studies suggest that cognitive decline is not as pronounced as reported by cross-sectional studies, and that most of cognitive abilities are preserved until the 60s' or even later [8–10]. The difference in results between cross-sectional and longitudinal designs is often attributed to cohort and historical effects or to sampling biases, but most of it is also simply due to interindividual differences in the rate or form of developmental change [11,12]. Only a longitudinal design allows addressing the crucial question of whether individuals differ in their developmental trajectories.

Studies investigating change in several cognitive domains report interindividual differences in both the rate of change and across domains heterogeneity in the rate of change [13–18]. Heterogeneity in change refers to variations in the patterns of change across a number of cognitive abilities. Although often explored by practitioners interested in assessing which competence is affected in a neuropsychological context, this notion has been scarcely explored in research setting. Results from these few studies suggest that change was not necessarily similar in different tasks, either for different individuals or within a given individual. Using latent growth modelling, Johnson et al [13] explored change in several cognitive domains over 36 months in 229 healthy older adults as well as in patients suffering from mild cognitive impairment (MCI). They observed significant change in memory tasks only, but not in processing speed, language, attention and visuo-spatial abilities. Similarly, Mungas et al. [16] reported more age-related change in verbal episodic abilities than in semantic memory or executive function. Go, An and Resnick [19] also explored longitudinal age effects in executive functions and memory in around 150 participants aged over 50 years. The authors report a longitudinal decline over a maximum of 14 years in several abilities, including inhibition, switching, memory, and visuo-spatial abilities, but also stability and/or improvement in abstraction, speed processing, vocabulary, discrimination and chunking. Thus, results from longitudinal studies suggest that aging is not a uniform process, at least in different tasks. We know still less as concerns the homogeneity or heterogeneity of change at the level of an individual.

By extension, very little is known about the degree of heterogeneity of change in the context of neuropsychological diseases. For example, homogeneous decline (i.e., similar across tasks) might reflect a general loss of attentional resources or of mental energy, which could in turn be the reflection of a weakened central nervous system. In contrast, strong heterogeneity in cognitive change might reflect alteration in a single cognitive ability or a subset of cognitive abilities but a good preservation of other cognitive abilities. The degree of heterogeneity in cognitive change may thus be important for diagnostic purposes. However, one needs first to have an overview of how heterogeneous are cognitive changes in healthy aging. All the studies cited above explored change in more or less diverse cognitive functions (executive functions, different forms of memory functions, speed processing, language, etc.) and therefore used different cognitive indexes, such as accuracy, ratios reflecting inhibition capacity or reaction times. Although interesting because of the diversity of cognitive functions that are covered, this may artificially reinforce the across tasks heterogeneity of change. In the present study, we focused on heterogeneity in change in the broad domain of processing speed only, assessed in reaction time tasks of varying complexity.

Most studies interested in age-related change in cognition have remained focused on group performance. Usual analyses allow summarizing general tendencies of a sample, but hides both inter and intraindividual differences that provide information about the diversity in cognitive aging. A number of authors have argued for the necessity to focus analyses on the individual. For instance, Nesselroade and Salthouse, suggest that "the prevailing emphasis on one of the seemingly most fundamental concepts in traditional differential psychology—stability of level of attributes across time—represents an oversimplification that can hinder the search for powerful and general lawful relationships" ([20], p. 49). Moreover, Molenaar has very elegantly demonstrated that a factorial structure applied to a group cannot apply to the individual of this group, thereby invalidating an "ergodicity" hypothesis, that is the relatively frequent hypothesis according to which interindividual variations are informative of intraindividual variations [21,22]. In the same vein, Nesselroade and Molenaar [23] recently suggested that similar results may reflect different meanings for different individuals. Based on a set of simulated data, they show that the presence of subject-specific factor loadings may be detected even though the correlations among the factors are invariant across subjects. In other words, a given psychological structure may differ from one individual to the other, and a same manifest variable may even have a different meaning for different subjects, whereas correlations among the factors are often wrongly taken to indicate that their meaning is the same for all the subjects. All these arguments underline the notion that analyses based on group statistics hinder large interindividual variations and mask the fact that a substantial proportion of individuals composing this group are not represented by these group statistics. Studying age-related change in cognition necessarily requires focusing on the individual if one aims at having a complete picture of cognitive aging, at predicting the diverse trajectories and their cognitive outcomes, or if one wants to ensure of the effectiveness of a given training or intervention. Focusing on the individual when assessing change is thus essential for both research and clinical considerations.

Modern statistical methods, such as latent growth curve modelling, have granted a larger place to individual differences. For instance, they make it possible to assess whether individual differences in change are significant. Yet, they still rely on the group, and do not provide estimates (or better inference) at the level of the individual other than, sometime, a quantitative estimate on how much this individual differs from the adopted model. Importantly, by letting the data of all individuals in the same model, the evaluation of a given individual is automatically influenced by the performance of the other individuals. The effect observed for a given individual might thus be different depending on the sample within which he/she is analyzed. Moreover, all current methods have distributional/parametric assumptions on the interindividual differences, because that is the only way to estimate the parameters of the model. For example, in mixed effect/hierarchical models, the random intercepts or random slopes are supposed to be normally distributed, which means that this model forces the individual differences to have this distributional form. Even if a sample fails to meet this assumption, the model is estimated but the individual effects are biased to match the model characteristics. Thus, the questions of whether change is significant for a given individual, whether it is heterogeneous or homogeneous, whether it goes in the same direction for all individuals remain. Defining the significance of change with aging at the level of an individual is important not only to refine our models of normal aging, to distinguish normal changes from pathological ones, but also for the development and testing of personalized interventions or training aiming at maintaining cognitive abilities in later life.

We are therefore still in need of methods to empirically define and investigate change at the level of the individual, independently of statistics provided by group variations, and remain as long as possible at this level before comparing individuals and groups. Interindividual differences in developmental trajectories have been mostly investigated in terms of correlations analyses (e.g., [24]), with a few exceptions [9,25]. For example, exploring cognitive change in a cohort of 1000 elderly catholic clergy members over 15 years, Hayden and collaborators [25] expressed the severity of decline as a function of the standard deviation (SD) proportion relatively to baseline level. They distinguished individuals showing moderate decline (-0.19 SD/year) from those showing severe decline (-0.57 SD/year). It is notable that the majority of participants (65%) were identified as non-declining elderly (-0.04 SD/year). Yet, standard deviation remained in this study a measure established on the group. Based on the Seattle longitudinal study, Schaie [14,15] reported descriptive statistics on individual trajectories in five abilities over 7 years, and showed that only a small percentage of individuals presented an overall significant decline—the significance being defined on the basis of a standard error of measurement—even though the change was significant at the group level. Decline varied across tasks and age groups and was rarely shown by more than a third of the individuals; even for the composite score (i.e., the score marking most decline), this percentage varied from 18% to about 50% (in the oldest group, who aged from 74 to 81 years). Moreover, when decline was observed, it was rarely on more than two tasks, even in the oldest age group. Finally, almost no individual declined over more than two consecutive 7-year intervals across a 28-year period. Schaie's report clearly contradicts the inference many readers would draw based on group curves. Yet, even in the case of the Seattle data, change is defined based on interindividual differences (standard error of measurement). It has also been proposed to evaluate the clinical significance of change using the reliable change index (RCI), which states the amount of change between two time measurements [26,27]. The RCI is expressed by a ratio of the difference between the time 1 and time 2 related to the standard error of the difference, itself derived from the normative sample. Although clearly focused on individual change, this index depends once again on the sample performance; if the sample size increases (or decreases) conclusion about change in a given individual will also change. It is useful for normative comparison, but does not provide any information concerning the meaningfulness of change relatively to one self's performance.

The objective of the present study was to analyze individual trajectories by relying solely on individual data. Two novel and complementary approaches are suggested here to advance this line of research, both of which aim at defining change based on within person data while assuring the reliability of change: (1) a bootstrap based confidence interval approach and (2) an individual analysis of variance approach (for details see below). We demonstrate their use in analyses exploring the magnitude and heterogeneity of individual change with aging across several cognitive measures, including simple reaction times, complex processing speed and inhibition, over a maximum of seven years and a half. Both analyses were made possible because each task contained a large number of trials (from 60 to 144 trials). The bootstrap based confidence interval approach allows defining, for each task and each participant, whether an individual showed a significant decline, stability or improvement over seven years. It thus provides an overview of each participant's decline/stability/improvement over each of the tasks. The second analysis quantified the degree of significance, for each individual, concerning both the amplitude and heterogeneity of change across all the tasks. This was achieved using individual analyses of variance conducted on the standardized scores by trial, so that performance in all tasks could be compared, for the first and last experimental waves. Results from the Time effect (change between the two time measurements) and for the Time by Task interactions for each individual were used to assess both the amplitude and the significance of heterogeneity of change.

2. Materials and Methods

2.1. Participants

Participants for the present analyses come from the Geneva Variability Study (GVS) that started in 2006 as a lifespan cross-sectional study including 557 participants aged 9–89 [28]. This initial wave was followed by a longitudinal follow up in the older adults only (n = 218), who were seen a total of four times at an interval of two and a half years between those four measurement occasions. The present analyses focus on change between the first and last wave of experimentation; this provides the largest interval (approximately seven and a half years), hence the highest chance to observe change. Older adults had been recruited either from the Senior University of Geneva or through newspaper and association advertisements for elderly. All participants were native French speakers or fluent in French and had normal or corrected to normal vision. The study was approved by the ethical committee of the Faculty of Psychology and Educational Sciences of the University of Geneva. All participants gave written informed consent and received a small amount of money as a compensation for their transportation costs.

The initial sample comprised 218 older adults (aged 59–89 years), whose characteristics are displayed in Table 1, and the fourth wave ended with 92 participants (aged 65–93 years). The wave-to-wave attrition rate was between 20% and 29%, which is close to what has been reported in other longitudinal studies of cognitive aging [29–31]. As in these studies, attrition was non-random: The older adults who participated in the fourth wave were initially younger and had better baseline levels (on average for the first wave: 67.53 years old; 38.70 Raven Progressive Matrices [32]; 38.49 at the Mill Hill Vocabulary Test [33]) in most cognitive tasks than those who dropped out at earlier steps (a description of the maximal sample for each experimental wave is provided in the Supplementary Material). The present analyses were conducted on the 92 individuals who completed the four waves.

Table 1. Participants' characteristics at baseline and at the last experimental waves (N = 92).

Time of Measurement	Age	Fluid Intelligence [1]	Vocabulary [2]
	M (SD)	M (SD)	M (SD)
Baseline	67.54 (5.51)	38.71 (8.02)	38.49 (4.27)
Last experimental wave	73.79 (5.59)	39.68 (8.37)	38.67 (4.16)

[1] Raven Progressive Matrices; [2] Mill Hill Vocabulary Test.

2.2. Experimental Setting

2.2.1. Overview

The GVS included several tasks assessing various cognitive domains, including working memory, simple reaction times, processing speed, interference, fluid and crystallized intelligence tasks as well as questionnaires on health-related issues and life-style [34–36]. The tasks were adapted from tasks already used in the cognitive aging literature and shown to present age differences; this is preferable when one adopts multivariate designs. The battery aimed not only at assessing a diverse range of aptitudes, from simple to more complex tasks, but also to make it possible to compare response times and accuracy responses (see Fagot et al., this issue). All experimental tasks were computerized, using a tactile computer screen and administered in a quiet room, in two sessions lasting around two hours each. For comparison purposes, the order of the tasks was kept constant across both participants and experimental waves. The present analyses focused on six reaction time tasks (9 experimental conditions) of different complexity levels: one simple detection task, two choice reaction times tasks, one inhibition task, and two processing speed tasks. All these tasks have the specificity of including a large number of trials; this is a condition for performing both individual bootstrap confidence intervals and individual analyses of variance.

2.2.2. Tasks

The simple detection task (SDT) consisted in pressing a button when a cross appeared on a screen (see [35,36] for a full description of all the tasks and data pre-processing). In two choice reaction times tasks, participants had to identify the location of the longest line between two (line comparison—LI) or the location of a cross (among six) changing into a square (cross-square—CS). These three tasks contained 120 trials distributed into five blocks.

Processing speed tasks consisted in a letter comparison task (LC) and a digit symbol (DI), both adapted from Salthouse [37] and computerized. In the LC tasks, participants had to determine whether two series of consonants (either 6—LC6 or 9—LC9) were similar or different. There were 60 trials distributed into three blocks for each condition. The DI tasks consisted in identifying whether a symbol-letter association was similar to an initial matrix of nine symbol-letter associations. This task comprised 144 trials distributed into five blocks.

Lastly a Stroop colour task with three conditions, neutral (colored symbols), congruent (e.g., the word blue written in blue) and incongruent (e.g., red written in blue) was given and included 144 trials by condition distributed into 18 blocks.

2.3. Analyses

We first investigated change in performance over seven years at the group level and then at the level of the individual. The analyses presented here were based on the mean level of performance (for correct trials only) at the first and fourth wave of testing, computed for each task/condition (some participants did not complete the entire protocol, mainly because of recording errors. It total, 92 participants completed the LI task at baseline and the last experimental wave, 91 the DI and the SDT tasks, 90 the CS task, 88 for the LC task, and 85 the Stroop task (colorblind participants were excluded for this task)) and each individual. Secondly, we investigated how demographic and cognitive measures at baseline were related to both amplitude of cognitive change, and heterogeneity in cognitive change.

2.3.1. Group Analyses

Paired *t*-test analyses were conducted on mean performance for each task/condition to explore the effect of age on cognitive change at a group level. A Bonferroni correction was applied to correct for multiple testing (9 comparisons).

2.3.2. Individual Bootstrap Confidence Intervals

To evaluate the change of the individual score distribution between wave 1 and wave 4, we computed confidence intervals (CI) on the difference in the mean score. These CIs were computed for each individual, separately for each task/condition. The choice of T1 for baseline was motivated by exploring change on the longest time-window. However, to ensure that there were not too much practice effects between T1 and T2, we also compared frequency of decline between T1-T2 and T2-T3, assessed with bootstrap confidence interval method (see the Section 2.3.2 for further details on the analyses). Results suggest that there were none-to-very little practice effects (5 conditions out of 9 show a difference of 5 to 10 points indicating more frequent decline for T1-T2, and 4 conditions out of 9 showed a reverse pattern: more frequent decline for T2-T3). A description of these results is given in the Supplementary Material.

CI for the change, measured as the difference in the mean score between wave 1 and 4, were computed for each individual, separately for each task/condition. If the CI contained the value zero, the individual for the given task was declared stable. If the CI was entirely above or below zero, we said there was a decline or an improvement, respectively.

Technically, to prevent the risky effect of possible non Gaussian distribution and serial correlation of the trials on the computation of CIs based on parametric and independence assumptions, we used a stratified block bootstrap method [38]. In the example of a task comprising 120 trials (e.g., LI, SDT, or CS), for each wave, it consisted in cutting the series of 120 trials in 12 pieces of 10 adjacent trials and in resampling with replacement 12 new pieces that formed the new bootstrap sample. This process was repeated 4999 times and the BCa (bias-corrected and accelerated) confidence interval was computed using the boot package from R software (version 3.4.2) [39]. Since we used these confidence intervals to classify changes as stable, declining or improving, and not to make formal significance tests, there was no reason to use the conventional 5% or 1% levels, nor to correct for the multiplicity of CIs/tests. Instead, as in Borella et al. [40], we opted for a 68% confidence interval, which in Gaussian settings would correspond to one standard deviation.

2.3.3. Individual Analyses of Variance

To make them comparable, for each task/condition and each individual, reaction times were first standardized across all trials of the first and the last experimental wave of testing. For example, in the SDT task, data were standardized across 240 trials for each individual, that is, the 120 trials of the first wave and the 120 trials of the fourth wave. Then, we conducted analyses of variance (ANOVAs) with two factors (Time: wave 1 vs. wave 4; Task: nine conditions) for each individual. Results from the main effect of Time addressed the question of a significant overall change in performance over seven years for a given individual, while results from the Time × Task interaction indicated whether an individual showed a similar trend of change in all tasks. Individual effect sizes (partial eta2) were used as a quantification of the degree of across-tasks homogeneity; the lower the eta2, the more homogeneous (similar) is the change across the nine conditions. As concerns the effect of Time, because effect sizes did not provide information concerning the direction of change (improvement or decline), individual regressions were conducted with the same variables and we used the Betas to indicate both the direction and amplitude of change, for each participant. Distributions of both indexes are provided in the Supplementary Material.

2.3.4. Relationships between Cognitive Change and Other Variables

In a subsequent step, we conducted a correlation analysis to explore relationships between, on the one hand, demographic or cognitive variables, and on the other hand, the amplitude and direction of change and the heterogeneity of change with aging. Demographic data included age and education. Cognitive measures included fluid intelligence, vocabulary, as well as both mean level of performance and intraindividual variability in performance, all at wave 1. Intraindividual variability, corrected for both practice effects and individual mean level of performance, was assessed for each task. Intraindividual variability was estimated for each participant by using the individual standard deviation computed on residual scores for each trial, after controlling for the participant's mean level and the order of trial (see Fagot et al., this issue). Lastly, to simplify the reading and to avoid too many multiple comparisons, both mean and intraindividual variability were pooled in three cognitive domains: simple reaction times (average of CS, LI, SDT), complex processing speed tasks (average of DI, LC6, LC9), interference (average of STn, STi, STc). These tasks were pooled based on a priori hypothesis of similar cognitive complexity, which was confirmed by subsequent factor analyses.

3. Results

3.1. Group Analyses

Results (Figure 1) from paired *t*-tests showed a significant slowing of performance over 7 years for the SDT task, t(90) = −3.07, *p* = 0.003, η^2 = 0.10, for the LI and the CS tasks, t(88) = −5.89, *p* < 0.001, η^2 = 0.29, t(89) = −5.75, *p* < 0.001, η^2 = 0.27, respectively, as well as for the neutral condition of the Stroop task, t(84) = −3.53, *p* < 0.001, η^2 = 0.13. No significant change was observed for the other conditions.

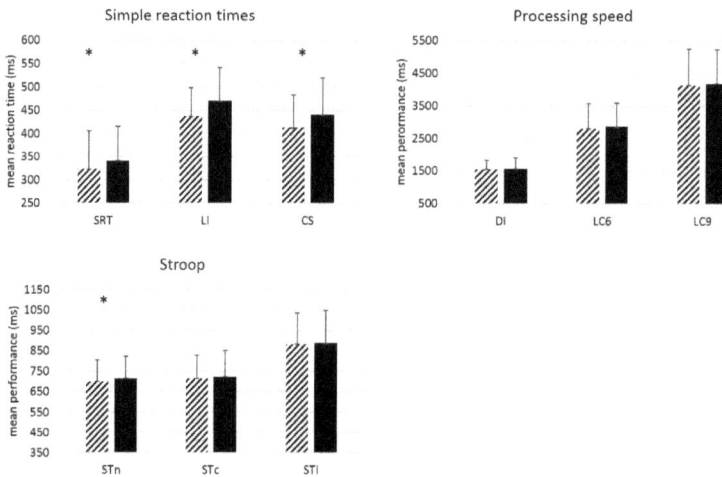

Figure 1. Mean performance (ms) by Task and Wave. Simple RT tasks (SDT, LI, CS), Processing speed tasks (DI, LC6, LC9) and Stroop task (STn =neutral condition, STc = congruent condition, STi = incongruent condition). Dashed bars: Wave 1. Plain black bars: Wave 4. Paired *t*-tests showed significant change in performance for simple tasks only. Error-bars represent standard deviations. * = *p* < 0.005 (Bonferroni correction).

3.2. Individual Analyses

Bootstrap Confidence Intervals

Inspecting individual trajectories underlying these group effects suggested, as predicted, enormous inter-individual variability and heterogeneity of changes (see Figure 2). Indeed, bootstrap confidence intervals showed that the three possible patterns of change—decline, improvement and stability—were present in all conditions. However, a larger proportion of individuals who declined was observed for simple reaction time tasks: More than half of the sample showed a slowing down in SDT (57%), LI (65%), CS (61%), and to a lesser degree STn (50%), the neutral condition of the Stroop task. These results join in with the group analyses, that showed a significant change at the group level in these tasks. For all other conditions, the three patterns were well represented (see Figure 3), with a substantial part of the sample showing improved performance after seven years (between 20% and 31% according to the condition).

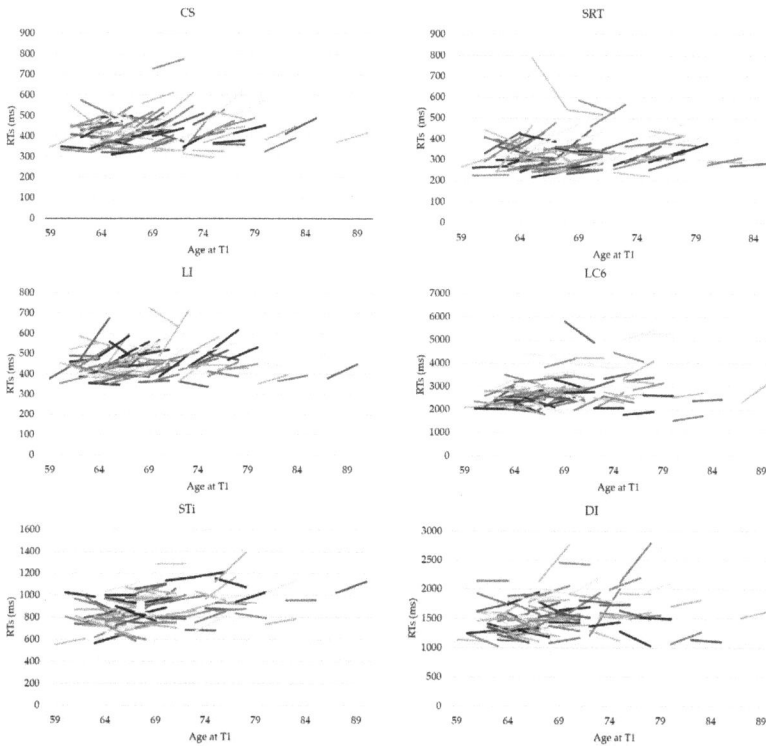

Figure 2. Intraindividual change by Age and Condition (six conditions out of nine). Each segment represents performance of a given individual at baseline and at the fourth experimental wave. Age is indicated at performance at baseline; each segment corresponds to approximately 7–8 years.

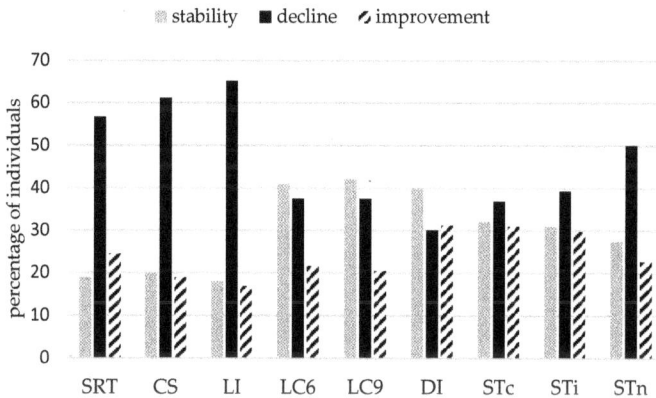

Figure 3. Bootstrap analyses: Percentage of individuals by task/condition and by pattern of change. Bars represent the percentage of individuals showing significant decline over seven years (black bars), significant improvement (dashed bars) and no significant change (grey bars).

We further analyzed homogeneity in the patterns of change, i.e., whether individuals showing a given pattern of change in one condition also showed the same pattern in the other conditions. Results showed quite heterogeneous patterns of change across conditions (see Figure 4). For example, there was no individual showing stability or improvement in all conditions, and very few individuals (less than 10%) improved significantly in more than three conditions; roughly 25% showed no significant improvement at all (Figure 3, improvement in 0 task). Stability was rarely observed in more than four tasks (less than 10% for more tasks). Decline was somewhat more homogeneous.

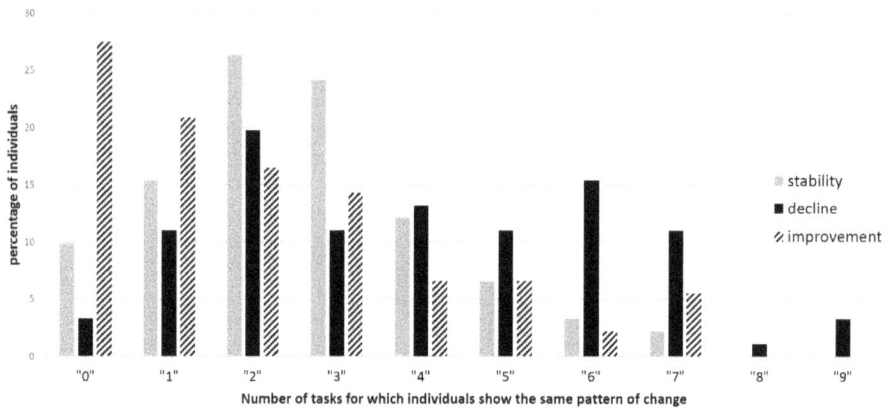

Figure 4. Heterogeneity in the pattern of change across all conditions: decline (black bars), improvement (dashed bars) and stability (grey bars). For example, 27% never presented a significant improvement, and 16% of individuals showed decline in six conditions.

3.3. Individual Analyses of Variance

Individual ANOVAs were conducted on 83 individuals only, as nine older adults did not complete all the trials in all the conditions at wave one and/or wave four and these analyses require a fully complete data set for each individual. Results showed a significant main effect of Time in 65 out of 83 older adults. Exploration of the direction of change revealed a global decline in 48 individuals and a global improvement in 17 individuals. A significant Time × Task interaction was observed in the quasi-totality of our sample ($ps < 0.05$), with the exception of four individuals who showed a homogenous trend of change across all the tasks. All the rest of the sample showed heterogeneous trends of change across the tasks.

3.4. Relationships between Change and Other Variables

Correlations were computed between the pattern of change (amplitude—beta; heterogeneity—partial eta2) and the cognitive variables administered at baseline.

Results showed a significant correlation between the heterogeneity in cognitive change and the initial level of intraindividual variability in complex processing speed tasks, $r = -0.38$, $p < 0.001$ (see Table 2, still significant after a Bonferroni correction). This negative correlation indicates that a lower level of variability at baseline was associated with a more heterogeneous subsequent change in performance. A negative correlation was also observed between age at baseline and amplitude of change, $r = -0.27$, $p = 0.016$, indicating that older participants at baseline were those showing a more pronounced subsequent decline. However, significance of this test did not stand the Bonferroni correction.

Table 2. Correlations between demographic and cognitive variables and amplitude and heterogeneity of cognitive change.

	Amplitude of Change (Beta)	Heterogeneity in Change (Partial eta2)
Age	−0.27	−0.17
Education [1]	0.22	−0.01
Simple RT_mean	0.15	0.10
Processing speed_mean	0.02	−0.21
Inhibition_mean	0.14	−0.13
Simple RT_IIV	0.09	−0.18
Processing speed_IIV	0.11	−0.38 *
Inhibition_IIV	0.04	−0.11
Raven PM	0.15	0.15
Mill Hill	0.20	0.14
Heterogeneity in change	−0.01	

Note: coefficients of correlation between, on the one hand, the amplitude of change and heterogeneity in cognitive change and, on the other hand, demographic and cognitive variables. [1] Number of education years. * $p < 0.002$; Bonferroni corrected for 21 comparisons.

4. Discussion

The present study aimed at examining individual change in a number of cognitive tasks of varying complexity, by defining change independently of the sample characteristics. We explored two statistical approaches allowing quantifying both amplitude/direction and heterogeneity in individual change. The use of those statistical tools was possible because our data set included tasks with a large number of trials in each condition. Results from bootstrap confidence intervals showed a large heterogeneity in the patterns of change—decline, stability or improvement—across both tasks and individuals; that is, most individuals did present a different pattern of change across tasks, and interindividual differences were also large. Individual analyses of variance revealed that this heterogeneity was significant for almost all participants. Lastly, correlational analyses showed that the degree of heterogeneity of change was negatively related to intraindividual variability at baseline in processing speed tasks.

The first notable result concerns the comparison between group-based and individual-based change analyses. Group-based analyses (*t*-tests) showed that, overall, our sample of older adults became significantly slower in simple reaction tasks—SDT, LI, CS and the neutral condition of the Stroop task—but not in more complex conditions. Looking at individual confidence interval results for these four tasks/condition, we also observed a larger proportion of individuals showing decline (between 50% and 65 %). These results are thus consistent with each other. Yet, the proportion of participants showing stability or improvement was large (between 35% and 50%). Significant decline at the group level was thus driven by individual decline in less than two thirds of the sample, suggesting that at least 35 % of individuals were not well represented by the group tendency. Exploration of the more complex cognitive tasks revealed that the three patterns of change were more equally represented, suggesting that more complex processing speed either is subject to more inter-individual variations or possibly declines later with aging. These results make echo to Schaie's observation that longitudinal change in aging is driven by change in only a small to moderate proportion of the sample [6,18]. They further suggest that most of aging studies, even those using a longitudinal design, tend to overestimate age-related cognitive changes. Hence the need to extend analyses beyond change at the group level.

An additional argument to explore change at the individual level is the observation of considerable intraindividual heterogeneity in the patterns of change. Intraindividual analyses of variance indeed suggest that the quasi-totality of our sample showed significant heterogeneous change across tasks, even though the tasks are all tapping processing speed. A closer examination of each task, based on the confidence intervals, shows that only a maximum of 16% of individuals demonstrated a similar pattern of change in more than four tasks/conditions out of nine. When an individual declines in a task, the probability of observing the same trend in another task is rather low. These results, together with those exploring group effects, strengthen previous observations that cognitive abilities do not have the same developmental trajectory across the lifespan [13,16,17,19,41]. They also demonstrate not only that differences in developmental trajectories vary across individuals but that such heterogeneity is actually the rule in normal aging. This argues in favor of dissociating factors that may differentially affect cognitive aging in individuals.

Questions remain concerning the meaningfulness of such heterogeneity: Is a more homogeneous change indicative of later pathological processes or, on the contrary, indicative of a better cognitive development than heterogeneous change? Correlational results indicated no relationships with the amplitude/direction of change, showing that a more homogeneous change does not necessarily go in the direction of cognitive decline. Interestingly, higher within-task intraindividual variability at baseline was significantly associated to a more homogeneous subsequent evolution of cognitive abilities; that is, individuals who presented a larger trial-to-trial within-task variability (averaged across tasks) were more uniform in their change. Within-task intraindividual variability in reaction times in aging has been related to negative subsequent outcomes, including change in cognitive status and attrition [42]. In Bielak et al. study, intraindividual standard deviation (iSDs) in complex tasks provided stronger prediction of change in cognitive status than iSDs in simple tasks, suggesting a greater age-related sensitivity for complex tasks. In the light of these results, one may hypothesize that changing in a more homogeneous way may constitute an early marker of later cognitive troubles. However, in Bielak et al. study, cognitive decline was measured with one task only; it is therefore not possible to extend their conclusion to the homogeneous or heterogeneous character of change. It is also interesting to note that we did not observe a significant relationship between either amplitude or heterogeneity of change, on the one hand, and demographic variables, such as age or education level, on the other hand, nor with the initial mean performance in the diverse cognitive abilities at baseline. Therefore, even though associated with inconsistency in complex processing speed tasks (iSD), reflecting a negative cognitive functioning, homogeneity in change did not depend upon the initial general level of cognitive performance. In order to have more indication on the relationships between heterogeneity and the direction of change, we conducted an ad-hoc exploration of how the patterns of change (decline, improvement, stability) were reparsed in individuals showing extreme homo/heterogeneity, using the first and last terciles. We observe no noticeable differences when looking at the number of "decline" (all tasks being considered): 125 in the group showing the more homogenous change against 113 in the group showing the more heterogeneous change. However, when looking at patterns of "improvement", data show a remarkable difference between the two groups: 26 in the group showing the more homogenous change against 78 in the group showing the more heterogeneous change. This observation suggests that more positive outcomes are associated to heterogeneous change in our sample. At the present stage, we can only speculate on possible mechanisms underlying homogeneity/heterogeneity in cognitive change. Our results suggest that a more heterogeneous change may have more favorable outcomes than homogeneous change. Futures studies focusing not only on quantitative but also qualitative individual differences in change, as well as on association with other variables, would help building stronger hypotheses.

The two methods presented here may offer potential tools for practitioners. Bootstrap confidence intervals at the level of the individual may notably be useful to assess the efficiency of cognitive training or remediation and constitutes an interesting alternative to the more frequently used RCI. Provided the number of trials is sufficient, they make it possible to assess individual change in performance, without the inconvenience of having to compare with change in a normative sample, subject to interindividual variability issues. Unlike the RCI, conclusions based on the bootstrap confidence interval would not vary if a given individual was studied or if participants were added or removed from the sample. Our method offers a reliable tool to draw conclusions solely based on individual performance. The index of heterogeneity/homogeneity of change in diverse cognitive abilities may also be a meaningful tool for practitioners. The design of the present study does not allow exploring the becoming of individuals showing a more or less homogeneous decline across tasks and further experiments are necessary to refine our understanding of interindividual differences in cognitive change in both normal and pathological aging. Our results open interesting directions of research concerning heterogeneity in cognitive change. A question concerns the meaning of heterogeneity as a function of the cognitive domains. We conducted analyses within the broad domain of speed processing, but we might observe different results in another cognitive domain (e.g., memory). Future studies should provide further data to have a more complete view of how heterogeneous cognitive change is in normal aging.

This study presents a number of limitations that have to be underlined. First, the sample is composed of older adults coming on their own at university to undergo a battery of tests. Our participants were then cognitively well preserved and reflect only part of the population of healthy older adults. Note that this is the case of a large number of cognitive aging studies. Second, the sample is rather small, particularly when the focus is placed on individual differences. Future studies should be conducted at larger scales. Third, the proposed analyses, being based on merely two time measures can only assess change in the cognitive abilities and cannot educate on the trajectories of change. It is however highly probable that not all individuals experience cognitive decline in the same manner. As mentioned, results from confidence-based analyses of change for intermediate experimental waves suggest a huge interindividual variability in the pattern of change over time, as well as across-tasks intraindividual variability in the pattern of change (change may be linear for a given task but not for another one). Further analyses of interindividual differences in the patterns of change were beyond the scope of the present study, but would undoubtedly be needed to fully understand individual developmental trajectories in healthy aging and the characteristics of trajectories that might be related to unhealthy aging.

5. Conclusions

To conclude, this study constitutes, to our knowledge, a first attempt to explore a reliable change (amplitude and heterogeneity) at the level of the individual, with no influence of the sample size or of the composition of the group. Although still essentially descriptive, it provides a general picture of the large heterogeneity of cognitive change across and within individuals, which is much larger than what could be expected based on the extant literature. Reciprocally, it points to the necessity to analyze change at the level of the individual. One can also wonder whether a more homogeneous change under the form of a cognitive decline should call for more attention on the clinicians' part. The methodology proposed here brings a novel way of investigating within individual changes and offers new considerations on this increasingly crucial research question.

Supplementary Materials: The following are available online at http://www.mdpi.com/2079-3200/6/1/10/s1, Figure S1: Bootstrap analyses: Percentage of individuals by task/condition and by pattern of change, Table S1: Participants' characteristics at baseline and at each experimental wave

Acknowledgments: This grant was supported by the Swiss National Foundation for Science (grants numbers 100011-107764, 100014-135410, 100014-120510, and PMPDP1_158319). The authors would like to thank their colleagues in the group of Developmental and Differential Psychology at the University of Geneva for their help with data collection and for fruitful discussions, and the participants for their patience and willingness to sit for several hours through a rather heavy experimental protocol.

Author Contributions: Anik de Ribaupierre conceived and designed the experiments; Nathalie Mella and Delphine Fagot performed the experiments; Nathalie Mella, Olivier Renaud and Delphine Fagot analyzed the data; Olivier Renaud contributed analysis tools; Nathalie Mella, Anik de Ribaupierre, Olivier Renaud and Matthias Kliegel wrote the paper.

Conflicts of Interest: The authors declare no conflict of interest.

References

1. Salthouse, T.A.; Atkinson, T.M.; Berish, D.E. Executive functioning as a potential mediator of age-related cognitive decline in normal adults. *J. Exp. Psychol. Gen.* **2003**, *132*, 566–594. [CrossRef] [PubMed]
2. Salthouse, T.A. When does age-related cognitive decline begin? *Neurobiol. Aging* **2009**, *30*, 507–514. [CrossRef] [PubMed]

3. Park, H.L.; O'Connell, J.E.; Thomson, R.G. A systematic review of cognitive decline in the general elderly population. *Int. J. Geriatr. Psychiatry* **2003**, *18*, 1121–1134. [CrossRef] [PubMed]

4. Salthouse, T.A. *Theoretical Perspectives on Cognitive Aging*; Erlbaum: Hillsdale, NJ, USA, 1991.

5. Schaie, K.W. The Seattle longitudinal study: A 21-year exploration of psychometric intelligence in adulthood. In *Longitudinal Studies of Adult Psychological Development*; Schaie, K.W., Ed.; The Guilford Press: New York, NY, USA, 1983; pp. 64–135.

6. Schaie, K.W. The Seattle longitudinal studies of adult intelligence. *Curr. Dir. Psychol. Sci.* **1993**, *2*, 171–175. [CrossRef]

7. Hofer, S.M.; Rast, P.; Piccinin, A.M. Methodological issues in research on adult development and aging. In *The Wiley-Blackwell Handbook of Adulthood and Aging*; Whitbourne, S.K., Sliwinski, M., Eds.; Wiley-Blackwell: Malden, MA, USA, 2012; pp. 72–93.

8. Rönnlund, M.; Nyberg, L.; Bäckman, L.; Nilsson, L.G. Stability, growth, and decline in adult life span development of declarative memory: Cross-sectional and longitudinal data from a population-based study. *Psychol. Aging* **2005**, *20*, 3–18. [CrossRef] [PubMed]

9. Schaie, K.W. *Intellectual Development in Adulthood: The Seattle Longitudinal Study*; Cambridge University Press: Cambridge, UK, 1996.

10. Schaie, K.W. What can we learn from the longitudinal study of adult psychological development. In *Longitudinal Studies of Adult Psychological Development*; Schaie, K.W., Ed.; The Guilford Press: New York, NY, USA, 1983; pp. 64–135.

11. de Ribaupierre, A. On the use of longitudinal research in developmental psychology. In *Transition Mechanisms in Child Development: The Longitudinal Perspective*; de Ribaupierre, A., Ed.; Cambridge University Press: Cambridge, UK, 1989; pp. 297–317.

12. McCall, R.B.; Appelbaum, M.I.; Hogarty, P.S. Developmental Changes in Mental Performance. *Monogr. Soc. Res. Child Dev.* **1973**, *38*, 1–84. [CrossRef] [PubMed]

13. Johnson, J.K.; Gross, A.L.; Pa, J.; McLaren, D.G.; Park, L.Q.; Manly, J.J.; Alzheimer's Disease Neuroimaging Initiative. Longitudinal change in neuropsychological performance using latent growth models: A study of mild cognitive impairment. *Brain Imaging Behav.* **2012**, *6*, 540–550. [CrossRef] [PubMed]

14. Schaie, K.W. Intellectual development in adulthood. In *Handbook of the Psychology of Aging*; Birren, J.E., Schaie, K.W., Eds.; Academic Press: San Diego, CA, USA, 1990; pp. 291–309.

15. Schaie, K.W. The optimization of cognitive functioning in old age: Predictions based on cohort-sequential and longitudinal data. In *Successful Aging: Perspectives from the Behavioral Sciences*; Baltes, P.B., Baltes, M.M., Eds.; Cambridge University Press: Cambridge, UK, 1990; pp. 94–117.

16. Mungas, D.; Beckett, L.; Harvey, D.; Farias, S.T.; Reed, B.; Carmichael, O.; Olichney, J.; Miller, J.; DeCarli, C. Heterogeneity of cognitive trajectories in diverse older persons. *Psychol. Aging* **2010**, *25*, 606–619. [CrossRef] [PubMed]

17. Christensen, H.; Mackinnon, A.J.; Korten, A.E.; Jorm, A.F.; Henderson, A.S.; Jacomb, P.; Rodgers, B. An analysis of diversity in the cognitive performance of elderly community dwellers: Individual differences in change scores as a function of age. *Psychol. Aging* **1999**, *14*, 365–379. [CrossRef] [PubMed]

18. Schaie, K.W.; Willis, S.L.; Caskie, G.I.L. The Seattle longitudinal study: Relationship between personality and cognition. *Aging Neuropsychol. Cognit.* **2004**, *11*, 304–324. [CrossRef] [PubMed]

19. Goh, J.O.; An, Y.; Resnick, S.M. Differential trajectories of age-related changes in components of executive and memory processes. *Psychol. Aging* **2012**, *27*, 707–719. [CrossRef] [PubMed]

20. Nesselroade, J.R.; Salthouse, T.A. Methodological and Theoretical Implications of Intraindividual Variability in Perceptual-Motor Performance. *J. Gerontol. Psychol. Sci.* **2004**, *59*, 49–55. [CrossRef]

21. Molenaar, P.C.M. A Manifesto on Psychology as Idiographic Science: Bringing the Person Back Into Scientific Psychology, This Time Forever. *Meas. Interdiscip. Res. Perspect.* **2004**, *2*, 201–218. [CrossRef]

22. Molenaar, P.C.M. The future of analysis of intraindividual variation. In *Handbook of Intraindividual Variability across the Lifespan*; Diehl, M., Hooker, K., Sliwinski, M.J., Eds.; Routledge: New York, NY, USA, 2015; pp. 343–356.

23. Nesselroade, J.R.; Molenaar, P.C.M. Some Behaviorial Science Measurement Concerns and Proposals. *Multivar. Behav. Res.* **2016**, *51*, 396–412. [CrossRef] [PubMed]

24. Wilson, R.S.; Beckett, L.A.; Barnes, L.L.; Schneider, J.A.; Bach, J.; Evans, D.A.; Bennett, D.A. Individual differences in rates of change in cognitive abilities of older persons. *Psychol. Aging* **2002**, *17*, 179–193. [CrossRef] [PubMed]

25. Hayden, K.M.; Reed, B.R.; Manly, J.J.; Tommet, D.; Pietrzak, R.H.; Chelune, G.J.; Yang, F.M.; Revell, A.J.; Bennett, D.A.; Jones, R.N. Cognitive decline in the elderly: An analysis of population heterogeneity. *Age Ageing* **2011**, *40*, 684–689. [CrossRef] [PubMed]

26. Jacobson, N.S.; Truax, P. Clinical significance: A statistical approach to defining meaningful change in psychotherapy research. *J. Consult. Clin. Psychol.* **1991**, *59*, 1–19. [CrossRef]

27. Farrell, M.; Khan, A.; Rothman, B.; Karantzoulis, S. Using Reliable Change Index (RCI) and clinical change to predict Alzheimer desease. *Alzheimer's Dement. J. Alzheimer's Assoc.* **2014**, *10*, P918–P919. [CrossRef]

28. Fagot, D.; Mella, N.; Borella, E.; Ghisletta, P.; Lecerf, T.; de Ribaupierre, A. Intraindividual variability from a lifespan perspective: A comparison of latency and accuracy measures. *J. Intell.* **2018**, in press.

29. Zahodne, L.B.; Glymour, M.M.; Sparks, C.; Bontempo, D.; Dixon, R.A.; MacDonald, S.W.; Manly, J.J. Education does not slow cognitive decline with aging: 12-year evidence from the Victoria Longitudinal Study. *J. Int. Neuropsychol. Soc.* **2011**, *17*, 1039–1046. [CrossRef] [PubMed]

30. Van Beijsterveldt, C.; van Boxtel, M.P.; Bosma, H.; Houx, P.J.; Buntinx, F.; Jolles, J. Predictors of attrition in a longitudinal cognitive aging study:: The Maastricht Aging Study (MAAS). *J. Clin. Epidemiol.* **2002**, *55*, 216–223. [CrossRef]

31. Schaie, K.W. *Developmental Influences on Adult Intelligence. The Seattle Longitudinal Study*, 2nd ed.; Oxford University Press: New York, NY, USA, 2013; p. 587.

32. Raven, J.C.; Court, J.H.; Raven, J. *Progressive Matrices Standard (PM38)*; Editions du Centre de Psychologie Appliquée: Paris, France, 1998.

33. Deltour, J.J. *Echelle de Vocabulaire de Mill Hill de J. C. Raven: Adaptation Française et Normes Comparées du Mill Hill et du Standard Progressive Matrices*; Editions l'Application des Techniques Modernes: Braine-le-Château, Belgique, 1993.

34. De Ribaupierre, A.; Ghisletta, P.; Lecerf, T. *Etude de la Variabilité Inter-et Intra-Individuelle au Cours du Cycle de vie*; Presses Universitaire: Rennes, France, 2006.

35. Mella, N.; Fagot, D.; Lecerf, T.; de Ribaupierre, A. Working memory and intraindividual variability in processing speed: A lifespan developmental and individual-differences study. *Mem. Cognit.* **2015**, *43*, 340–356. [CrossRef] [PubMed]

36. Mella, N.; Fagot, D.; de Ribaupierre, A. Dispersion in cognitive functioning: Age differences over the lifespan. *J. Clin. Exp. Neuropsychol.* **2016**, *38*, 111–126. [CrossRef] [PubMed]

37. Salthouse, T.A. Influence of processing speed on adult age differences in working memory. *Acta Psychol.* **1992**, *79*, 155–170. [CrossRef]

38. Davison, A.C.; Hinkley, D.V. *Bootstrap Methods and Their Application*; Cambridge University Press: Cambridge, UK, 1997; Volume 1.

39. Team, R.C. *R: A Language and Environment for Statistical Computing*; R Foundation for Statistical Computing: Vienna, Austria, 2014.

40. Borella, E.; Delaloye, C.; Lecerf, T.; Renaud, O.; Ribaupierre, A. Do age differences between young and older adults in inhibitory tasks depend on the degree of activation of information? *Eur. J. Cognit. Psychol.* **2009**, *21*, 445–472. [CrossRef]

41. Hartshorne, J.K.; Germine, L.T. When does cognitive functioning peak? The asynchronous rise and fall of different cognitive abilities across the life span. *Psychol. Sci.* **2015**, *26*, 433–443. [CrossRef] [PubMed]

42. Bielak, A.A.; Hultsch, D.F.; Strauss, E.; MacDonald, S.W.; Hunter, M.A. Intraindividual variability in reaction time predicts cognitive outcomes 5 years later. *Neuropsychology* **2010**, *24*, 731. [CrossRef] [PubMed]

MDPI
St. Alban-Anlage 66
4052 Basel
Switzerland
Tel. +41 61 683 77 34
Fax +41 61 302 89 18
www.mdpi.com

Journal of Intelligence Editorial Office
E-mail: jintelligence@mdpi.com
www.mdpi.com/journal/jintelligence

www.ingramcontent.com/pod-product-compliance
Lightning Source LLC
Chambersburg PA
CBHW051315020426
42333CB00028B/3348